THE TWAIN SHALL MEET

SUSAN MADELINE BAILEY

AND

DEBORAH LYNN GOSSELIN

First Printing, 2014

ISBN-13: 978-1499799491
ISBN-10: 1499799497

Cover Photograph Courtesy of The Mark Twain
House & Museum, Hartford, CT

Cover and Interior Design by Graphikitchen, LLC
(www.graphikitchen.com)

This book is dedicated to
Henrietta Gosselin
and Elwood Bailey,
parents extraordinaire,
gone but never forgotten.

CONTENTS

PROLOGUE

APRIL 21, 1910

THE DEATH OF MARK TWAIN

"Of my fair fleet all my ships have gone down but you."
SAMUEL LANGHORNE CLEMENS (MARK TWAIN) TO DAUGHTER CLARA,
FEBRUARY 21, 1910

I
T WAS THE DAMNEDEST THING. For a man who had paid his way through life with the coin of humor, Samuel Langhorne Clemens had suffered more than his fair share of losses and sorrow. Now, as he lay dying, all that was left to him of his once large family was thirty-five-year-old daughter Clara.

The body-blows had come with regularity throughout his life.

When Sam was just shy of four years old, his nine-year-old sister Margaret succumbed to "bilious fever." Just three years later, brother Benjamin died at the age of ten.

In 1847, the Clemens family's foundation was shattered when Sam's father, John Marshall Clemens, died of pneumonia. A mercurial man possessed of less than stellar financial sense, "The Judge" had nonetheless held the family together. Twelve-year-old Sam left school the next year, going to work as a printer's apprentice.

At twenty-two, Sam earned a riverboat pilot's cub apprentice license and, in 1859, earned his full pilot's license. Enamored of the lifestyle, he spun tales of the river to younger brother Henry and eventually found Henry a spot as "mud clerk" on the steamboat *Pennsylvania*. After Sam reputedly got into a fight with another of the *Pennsylvania*'s pilots, he left the boat on June 5, 1858. Just eight days later, a horrific explosion ripped through the *Pennsylvania*. After seven agonizing days, Henry Clemens died in

Memphis, Tennessee, of injuries sustained in the explosion. The *Memphis Eagle and Enquirer* of June 16, 1858, reported:

> *We witnessed one of the most affecting scenes at the Exchange yesterday that has ever been seen. The brother of Mr. Henry Clemens, second clerk of the Pennsylvania, who now lies dangerously ill from the injuries received by the explosion of that boat, arrived in the city yesterday afternoon, on the steamer A. T. Lacy. He hurried to the Exchange to see his brother, and on approaching the bedside of the wounded man, his feelings so much overcame him, at the scalded and emaciated form before him, that he sunk to the floor overpowered.*

Sam blamed himself for the loss of brother Henry, and with that death, Sam's family had been reduced to his mother Jane, sister Pamela, and brother Orion.

On February 2, 1870, Sam married the great love of his life, Olivia Langdon. Nine months later they rejoiced in the birth of son Langdon in Buffalo, New York. From the beginning, Langdon, like Sam himself, was a sickly child. During a carriage ride with his father in early April of 1872, a blanket reputedly slipped off Langdon, turning the child's lips blue before Sam noticed. A month later, little Langdon died of diphtheria, but Sam never shook the erroneous notion that what he saw as his neglect on that April carriage ride had led to the child's death.

The next eight years witnessed the births of daughters Olivia Susan ("Susy"), Clara Langdon, and Jane ("Jean") Lampton Clemens. There ensued one of the longest periods of Sam's life to be uninterrupted by tragedy. Marred only by the death on October 27, 1890, of his eighty-seven-year-old mother, Jane Lampton Clemens, Sam enjoyed a twenty-four year respite from the familial losses that had dogged his life.

Then, in August of 1896, while Sam was in England at the conclusion of his Equator speaking tour, his beloved eldest daughter Susy contracted spinal meningitis. Sam, Olivia, and Clara took ship for home, but did not arrive in time to bid farewell. Shattered by the loss, the family left their home in Hartford, Connecticut, unable to return to the place where Susy had been raised.

A year later, Sam's brother Orion died, leaving Sam and sister Pamela as the only survivors of an original family of seven siblings.

After a decline of many years, on June 5, 1904, death took Sam's beloved wife Olivia. He would later write in a letter to a Father Fitzsimmons: "Marriage—yes, it is the supreme felicity of life. I concede it. And it is also the supreme tragedy of life. The deeper the love, the surer the tragedy. And the more disconsolating when it comes." Marrying a woman ten years his junior had meant no guarantee that Sam would have his soul mate at his side when his time came.

Just two months after the death of Olivia, Sam's sister Pamela passed away. Surely it must have seemed to the great humorist that his personal losses had come to an end, but fate had one more heartache in store. On December 24, 1909, his daughter Jean, an epileptic, drowned in the bathtub during a seizure at "Stormfield," Twain's Redding, Connecticut, home.

Sam Clemens's large family had been reduced to one. In his lifetime, humorist Mark Twain had lost father and mother, five siblings, a wife, a son, and two daughters.

Only daughter Clara Langdon Clemens Gabrilowitsch was left to bear witness to Sam's passing. Just six months before, Sam had welcomed to the family Clara's new husband, Ossip Gabrilowitsch. A Russian-born pianist of towering talent, Gabrilowitsch had shared a tempestuous ten-year relationship with Clara before the couple tied the knot on October 5, 1909.

As petite Clara stood by the bedside of her father, beneath her heart she carried a secret. She was five months pregnant with Sam's only grandchild. If the veracity of a news article published in The *San Diego Reader* on May 8, 2003, can be trusted, Clara never shared with her father the news of the child she carried:

> *After Jean died, Clemens was prostrate with depression. A pregnant Clara arrived, hoping he'd be well enough to hear about a grandchild. But Clemens, listening as Clara sang several Scottish airs he loved, never knew she was pregnant—she may have withheld the news from spite or from fear of over-exciting him.*

And so it was that on April 21, 1910, when America's beloved author and humorist Mark Twain died in Redding, Connecticut, he did so without the knowledge that he had left behind what was to be his only grandchild. Nina Clemens Gabrilowitsch was born on August 18, 1910, in Redding, Connecticut, less than four months after the great author's death.

Clara, exhausted from the years of caring for her ailing family, felt a guilty sense of relief:

> At last if nothing happens to my husband I have really landed in a beautiful harbor & soon enough [can] worship every ripple in the delicious blue sunflecked water. Even father's & Jean's deaths can not take from me this longed for happiness which is actually mine.

But life with Nina was to be far from clear sailing for anyone whose life she touched.

Introduction

Deb

2014

A Tall Tale With Long Legs

At the age of 20, I found physical proof that Drucilla Bailey
was not my biological mother. Since that time I have been searching
for the woman who is.

Susan Madeline Bailey, June 4, 2007

I T ALL BEGAN WITH A LIE. Told by my great-great grandfather, Ira Clemens Lucia, that lie, echoing down through four generations and more than one hundred and fifty years, led me to Susan Bailey.

It also, the two of us came to believe, indirectly led to the continuation of Mark Twain's bloodline.

I grew up craving words the way a lover of sweets craves chocolate, so learning that Mark Twain was a relative was the granddaddy of all fudge sundae moments.

I began inhaling books at the age of four. By the time I was in junior-high, I had worked my way through the family's dog-eared twenty-four volume set of *The Complete Works of Mark Twain*.

It never occurred to me to wonder why so many Mark Twain books lined our shelves. Then one day, when I was thirteen and nose-deep in a Twain book, my mother casually announced, "We're related to him you know." I looked at her in confusion until she said, "Mark Twain. We're related to Mark Twain."

To a book junkie of a kid, that was pretty big news. When I asked her how we were related to Twain, she retrieved a faded, much-folded scrap of paper. I opened it, found a hand-drawn family tree, and read a note next to my great-great grandfather Ira's name:

Ira's parents died when he was very young. Ira's mother was Cynthia Clemens, a sister to Mark Twain's father, John Marshall Clemens.

That meant that my great-great grandfather, Ira Lucia, was a first cousin to Mark Twain. For the next several years, I carried around as a secret source of pride, the knowledge that I was a distant cousin to America's most famous author.

It wasn't until the genealogy bug bit me during my junior year at college that I thought to check out the veracity of that claim. After concerted digging, I was utterly dismayed to find not a shred of evidence that Mark Twain had an aunt named Cynthia.

Not wanting to give up on the Twain connection, I considered that the story might simply have been twisted somehow. Over the years, I spent innumerable hours poring over old books and microfilms, trying to prove any tie at all between Ira Clemens Lucia and Samuel Langhorne Clemens. I began to reluctantly suspect that orphaned Ira had spun a tall tale to create a sense of family. Who better to claim as cousin than a famous author?

In 2005, I decided to take a new approach to the problem. Ira Lucia had fathered a brood of eight children and, over time, his descendants had scattered throughout the country. I wondered if the tale of a Twain connection had been handed down in lines other than mine. I set out to find the answer.

Whenever I located another of Ira's descendants, each confirmed that he or she had been told of a connection to Mark Twain, but none possessed any explicit information. One distant cousin provided me a letter written in April of 1927 by Ira's daughter Emma (my great-grandmother). She had been asked to explain the Lucia family's connection to Mark Twain and answered as follows:

My father Ira was a first-cousin of Samuel L. Clemens, "Mark Twain" and they looked enough alike to be twin brothers. Another musical branch of the family is Clara Clemens Gabriolowitch [sic]

of Detroit. She is Mark Twain's daughter and is known all over the
country as a contralto and the wife of the famous pianist.

Reading this, there was no doubt that Ira Lucia had convinced his daughter Emma, and presumably all of his children, of the tie to Mark Twain. That, sadly, did not constitute proof of his assertion. It did, however, explain why the story had been handed down so faithfully.

While trying to track Ira's descendants, the line that most eluded me was that of his grandson, Charlie Lucia.

Charlie, a musician, had moved from Detroit, Michigan to Tampa, Florida around 1920 leaving behind his mother and bachelor brothers Ira (namesake of the older Ira) and Marcus (perhaps named after Twain). There, he married a woman with the unusual first name of Bruce and more prosaic last name of Bailey. Charlie and Bruce Lucia's only surviving child was a daughter named Eileen.

I found a record of Eileen's marriage to a man named Russell Gooley; however, I was unable to determine if she had left any offspring. In an effort to find out, in January of 2007, I posted messages on a number of genealogical message boards.

On June 4, 2007, nearly six months after posting the messages, I received an e-mail that read in part:

I saw your post online. I am Eileen Lucia's daughter.

It was signed Susan Bailey.

I immediately sent an email back to Susan explaining that Eileen Lucia, the woman she indicated was her mother, was my relative. I briefly described my quest to prove that the Lucia family was related to the Clemens family of Mark Twain fame via a long ago connection and wondered if she had grown up with this same story. She replied:

I do know some information about the Clemens story and I some-
times had a bizarre childhood because of it. I had a great uncle who

lived in Detroit and he was very much in touch with some members
of the Clemens family. I have to dig up some records and notes
before I write more to you about the Clemens connection. I learned
of this when I was 9 years old and have been sorting through fact
and fiction ever since I grew up.

I read that email over and over, wondering what Susan meant when she indicated that her great-uncle had been "in touch with" members of Twain's family, what members of the Clemens family she was referring to, and why this branch of my family was the only one to have direct contact with someone in Twain's family.

Since Susan had included her phone number, I promptly placed a call. A charming woman with a subtle Southern drawl answered. After countless contacts with other distant family members over the preceding two years, I expected to hear yet another general recounting of the story of how old Ira Clemens Lucia was Mark Twain's first cousin. Susan had, indeed, also been told she was somehow related to Mark Twain. Her next comment, however, was of a far different nature:

I'm sure we are related to Mark Twain because I knew Clara Clemens
when I was a child. I visited with her a few times in Detroit.

All of my genealogical research on Mark Twain had focused on determining how or if the Clemens and Lucia families might have overlapped near the time of Twain's childhood in the 1830s. I had spent little time attempting to trace Twain's line forward in time, thinking that the lives of his children had no bearing on the long-standing mystery.

I knew that Twain's sole child to survive to adulthood and marry was his daughter, Clara. I had, based on the letter from my great grandmother Emma, only the barest knowledge that Clara had ties to Detroit, Michigan.

Now, Susan Bailey, a woman with Lucia family connections, was expressing a personal acquaintance with that very woman. In a wholly unexpected turn of events, the paths of a descendant of Ira Lucia and of his 'cousin' Samuel Langhorne Clemens, had just crossed.

I could suddenly picture brothers Ira, Charlie and Marcus Lucia, firm in their belief in the veracity of their grandfather Ira's tale of being a first cousin to Mark Twain, boldly introducing themselves to Twain's daughter Clara upon her arrival in Detroit.

Clara, almost completely devoid of relatives on her famous father's Clemens side, probably had no way of knowing whether or not that kinship claim was true.

However, none of that explained how Susan herself came to know Clara. During that first conversation, she alternately mentioned Charlie Lucia's daughter Eileen as her 'mother' and a couple named Elwood and Drucilla Bailey as her 'parents.' When gently pressed for an explanation, Susan replied:

> *I really do not know who my mother was. The Baileys raised me when I was young. Both their names are on my birth certificate but I was sent to live with Daddy's niece Eileen when I was seven and she was the mother of my heart.*

Those words touched me profoundly. Having been blessed with two wonderful parents who gave my eight siblings and me unconditional love, and who instilled in me the importance of family, I could not conceive of going through life never knowing where or to whom I belonged.

With Susan's words, the nature of my search, and of hers, irrevocably changed. We had been two women, strangers, raised in different parts of the country, each on an independent quest for proof of a distant kinship to Mark Twain. Susan, however, had also been struggling alone to solve the much greater mystery of her parentage. But in that instant a bond formed, and we became a team of two, determined to solve both riddles.

From the beginning, my instincts, honed by over thirty-five years of genealogical research, told me that the answer to the Clemens-Lucia connection and the key to determining the identities of Susan's mother and father were somehow intertwined.

Over the next seven years we would follow a convoluted and tantalizing trail of evidence that involved our families, Twain's daughter Clara, her husband Ossip, and, most especially, their daughter Nina.

In the hunt, we came to know and love the latter, Mark Twain's troubled only grandchild, Nina Clemens Gabrilowitsch. We also came to understand that old Ira's lie had placed not only Charlie Lucia but also his brother-in-law and best friend, Elwood Bailey, solidly in Nina's path.

All of the puzzle pieces had been there from the beginning, but it took the chance meeting of two determined women to begin to assemble those pieces into what eventually fit together as a startling conclusion.

Our journey down that twisted path began with the tale of certain pivotal events in her childhood that Susan related during that first conversation.

CHAPTER 1

SUSAN

1944

A VISIT FROM A STRANGER

THE DAY THE LADY TOOK ME OUT OF SCHOOL, I had no idea that Drucilla Bailey, the woman I called *Mama*, was not my real mother. A lifetime would pass before I would come to know who the lady was, but her determination to see me that day changed my life forever and the events of that day haunt me still.

It was hot and sticky that fall in Tampa, Florida and, in spite of the wall of windows that ran the entire length of the second grade classroom at Henderson Elementary, there was no breeze at all. The old fan, mounted up in a corner near the ceiling, sent a feeble breeze to the first couple rows of desks, but I was sitting in the back row so didn't get the benefit of even that little bit of air. The day had a heavy feel to it, still and hazy. I was not concentrating on the teacher but thinking about the air raid warning from the night before.

Tampa is a port city and we lived right by the Hillsborough River just before it flowed into Tampa Bay. German submarines had been spotted off the coast. The sirens woke me up and I had huddled with my parents and little brother Bobby in the dark, black-out curtains drawn, until the all clear sounded.

But then I couldn't go back to sleep so just lay there tossing and turning for what seemed like hours. Had I known then that I had only one more night to sleep in that little bed, I probably would not have slept at all.

The teacher, Mrs. Youngblood, was starting on subtraction that day and I was falling asleep at my desk. She had already scolded me once for putting my head down on the desk and, besides, I very much wanted to stay awake because my Daddy, an accountant, had already taught me to add and subtract. I thought that if the teacher would just call me to the blackboard, I could show off what I knew and the kids would like me.

So I was ticking my arm lightly with my fingernails to try and keep myself awake when someone came to the door and said I was wanted in the principal's office. This was the first time I had ever been called there but since I had never gotten in trouble at school, I wasn't nervous, just curious.

When I got to the office, I saw a small, well-dressed lady standing with the principal. He said, "Susie, your aunt has come to get you." I didn't think I had ever seen this aunt before, but I had a large extended family. I just thought she was one of them. She held out her hand for me and said, "Are you ready to go?" and I took her hand. We left the school and got into a waiting yellow cab.

She took me to an ice cream parlor that was decorated in purples, yellows, and greens and had high tables and chairs. It was quite beautiful and I was now fully awake. She ordered each of us vanilla ice cream sodas.

While we were waiting for the sodas, I was beginning to get a little nervous because I really didn't know who this aunt was. I was also afraid that I would get in trouble with my mother for being out of school in the middle of the day. This had never happened before.

She noticed this nervousness and told me, "You don't have to worry about being with me. I know *you*. I even know your middle name!" I asked her what it was and she said, "It's Madeline, and you're a little French girl."

As she said this, she gave me a little poke on the tip of my nose. I asked her how she knew my name and she said, "Because I named you!"

That was a small shock to me, but since my middle name was indeed Madeline, I relaxed a little. I didn't know what to make of the "little French girl" or the "I named you" parts. It gave me a very odd feeling though because I had dreamt in French for as long as I could remember and I wondered if what she said was somehow connected to my dreams.

While we were sipping our delicious sodas, the lady asked me questions about my family. She knew their names so I relaxed even further and just enjoyed the time with her. The air conditioned soda shop was certainly better than being in that hot sticky school and this beautiful woman was fascinating and obviously so interested in me!

She asked about the lessons my father was giving me and told me she heard I was a smart girl. She wanted to know about my cousin Eileen, and if she was still in Tampa. I told her Eileen had gotten married and moved to Chicago. She asked about my mother and if she was good to me.

I told her my mother sometimes spanked me when I was bad. This seemed to upset her and she then asked about my four-year-old little brother, Bobby, and wanted to know if he got spanked too. I admitted to her that Bobby never got spanked, only me. She then said, "That's probably why you spend so much time with your father in his office."

I had never thought about this before but the truth was I didn't spend much time alone with my mother. Daddy picked me up after school almost every day and took me straight to his office. Even on my vacation days he brought me there. His office, like our home, was in a city park by the river. There were no children anywhere close to us for me to play with, so Daddy simply took me to work with him.

He kept snacks for me there and I had my own little table and chair where I did my homework. We sometimes played chess because he thought it was a great way for me to learn to think ahead.

Since the office was located in a city park, there was lots for me to do. Daddy had built me a swing, and there were many secret places to explore and things to climb on. The only rules were that I was not allowed on the dock or on the bridge near the water. I obeyed those rules as they seemed very important to my father.

When we finished our sodas, the lady asked me if I wanted to see a movie and, of course, I did. Since she knew my family members and was so nice to me, I was totally relaxed with this new aunt now.

The theater was just across the street from the ice cream parlor so we walked over and she purchased our tickets. There were very few people in the theater watching the show which was a musical and had something to do with a fair. She was holding my hand and I was enjoying the movie and the coolness.

Suddenly the picture stopped and the theater lights came on. I was so engrossed in the movie that I didn't know what was happening at first. Then three policemen came down the aisle, stopped at our row, and told us to stand up.

One of them asked me my name. When I responded, "Susie Bailey," they put handcuffs on the lady without ever asking her name. I started crying because I was scared that I was in big trouble. She never said a word.

They put both of us in the back seat of a police car, me on the left, she on the right. Her handcuffed hands were in her lap, beautiful patent leather purse thrown on the floor at her feet.

By this time I was crying uncontrollably because I had never been in a police car before and didn't know what was going to happen. I knew I would probably get a spanking when I got home.

The lady looked at me with tears in her eyes and said just two words: "I'm sorry."

The police car soon pulled up to my house and my daddy and mommy were standing on the sidewalk, both looking very grim. The minute the car stopped, Daddy came around to my side and lifted me out of the car.

I put my arms around his neck and was crying, "Please don't let Mama spank me." He said, "No one's going to spank you, and you don't ever have to worry about that lady. Forget about her! She's an alcoholic."

Daddy was so angry when he said this that he was shaking. I knew what an alcoholic was because my Daddy's sister, my Aunt Bruce Lucia, drank too much and I had witnessed a few bad scenes with her. It was hard to believe that this lady who was so nice to me, and who I had spent such a wonderful day with, was also an alcoholic.

My father handed me over to Mama and told her take me inside and call Bob Joughin, my uncle who was the former sheriff of Hillsborough County. As Mama was taking me into the house, I looked back and saw him open the door on the side where the lady was and lean into the car. I didn't know who she was, but it seemed like my Daddy did.

My Uncle Bob and Aunt Bruce came over and they had a family conference from which I was excluded. This went on for a long time. They had left their car keys on a table in the entrance hall and I took them and hid them as I was still afraid that when they left I would get a spanking from my mama for going with the lady. Daddy never spanked me, but I always seemed to do bad things that made Mama punish me.

I was told by Daddy to play in my room and not go outside. So, while the adults were in their meeting I busied myself the best way I could, reading my books, playing with my dolls, and making up stories about their lives.

What I didn't do was play with my little brother, Bobby. He wasn't there and I didn't know where he was. When Uncle Bob and Aunt Bruce were ready to leave, there was much searching for the car keys until I 'found' them where I had hidden them in the pantry. Instead of getting a spanking, I was a big hero.

My Daddy told me I hadn't done anything bad, but the next day I was put on a train with my Aunt Bruce and sent to Chicago to live with her daughter, my cousin Eileen.

I never saw the lady again. Throughout my life though, I thought from time to time of that day and wondered why it had happened and who she really was.

It was more than six decades before a series of events led me to the conclusion that the nice lady who took me out of school and spent one memorable afternoon with me was Mark Twain's only grandchild, Nina Clemens Gabrilowitsch.

Susan at around age seven
Tampa, Florida
Photo from personal collection of Susan Bailey

CHAPTER 2

SUSAN

1944–1946

CHICAGO BOUND

THE DAY AFTER THE NICE LADY TOOK ME OUT OF SCHOOL, Daddy put me on a train with his sister and we headed for Chicago. Part of me was excited at the new adventure, but part of me felt as if I was being sent away for some reason. I had no idea when I would see him again.

The last thing he had said to Aunt Bruce at the train station was, "Tell Eileen to buy her some warm clothes. I don't want her catching pneumonia up there." This made me feel like he wasn't planning for me to come back soon.

After Daddy took me out of that police car, time just seem to speed up. It would be years before I realized that the lady who took me out of school was exactly the *reason* I was sent away the next day.

But now I was on a train! As children do, I quickly put everything else out of my mind to explore my new surroundings. We had the luxury of our own little compartment and bathroom. There were two beds stacked one above the other, and I remember the thrill of getting to sleep in the top bunk.

I was fascinated with the room, but I didn't stay there long because I was a curious child and wanted to explore the rest of the cars. Since Aunt Bruce didn't pay much attention to me, and mostly ate (and drank) in our room, I had complete run of the train. I ate in the dining car, where the porter would always put me at a table with an older couple who were very kind to me. This compelled me to use my very best manners.

Because I was a small child, I had to use all my strength to open the heavy doors between cars and go out on the open platforms, but I was determined to do it. It was very noisy, windy and cold out there but I was so amazed by the scenery flying past me that I barely noticed.

In retrospect, I can't imagine an adult allowing a seven-year-old child to engage in such dangerous activity, but then my aunt spent most of that trip drunk as usual, and all but passed out in our little room. Watching me was the last thing on her mind. It must have been extremely important to my father to get me out of Tampa quickly for him to allow his sister to take me on a train. Perhaps he had hopes that, for once, she would stay sober and responsible for the few days it took to travel between Tampa and Chicago. He was mistaken.

As the train rumbled along, I saw the beauty of mountains for the first time and also sad little shacks by the side of the railroad tracks that were made of flattened tin cans.

Standing right beside them were children my age, or even younger, who were waving to the people on the train. Most had on tattered clothing and no coats. I stared, wide-eyed, because I had never seen children who looked that ragged. Compared to those shacks, my own home in Tampa seemed like a palace, and, although my clothes were mostly hand-me-downs from an older cousin, they weren't old or torn.

I believe at the age of seven I had my first real lesson in how unfair life can sometimes be. I have thought of those children standing by the railroad tracks in their old dirty clothes and tin can houses all of my life.

By the time we arrived in Chicago a few days later, the novelty of the train had worn off. As we pulled into the station, I was thrilled to see Aunt Bruce's daughter, Eileen, waiting for us. Even though Eileen was fourteen years older than I, she had been a big part of my life in Tampa. I had been sad when, the year before, she had married a soldier named Russell and moved to Chicago to live with his family. With World War II in full swing, he was stationed in Germany, so she was alone on the platform.

As soon as we retrieved our luggage, we got into a yellow cab. After my experience a few days before with the lady who *called* herself my aunt, it was comforting to be getting into a cab with my *real* family.

The cab took us to a part of downtown Chicago that Eileen called "The Loop." There, at the corner of State and Monroe, stood the tallest and grandest hotel I had ever seen. "The Palmer House," read a sign over the entrance. We pulled up to the front entrance and a bellman took our luggage and saw us to the front desk.

When we first walked inside, it looked like something out of a movie. The lobby had marble columns and thick carpets. Elaborate scenes were painted on the ceiling. I couldn't believe we were going to stay in this fancy place. The only place I had seen that was even remotely as ornate as this was the Tampa Theater in downtown Tampa. I was entranced.

After we checked in, the bellman took us to our room on the second floor and it was beautiful. It had two large windows overlooking the street below and it was the first time I had ever seen a radiator and steam heat. The radiator was under one of the windows but I could climb up on the window seat of the other one and look down at the street below. There were two beds in the room, one for Aunt Bruce and one for Eileen and me. We had our own bathroom and it was the first time I had ever seen a bathtub with a shower. So many firsts!

While we were getting unpacked, Eileen told me an unbelievable story about stairs you didn't have to climb. She said they moved all by themselves and were called escalators. She also told me about a museum that had huge dinosaurs and real mummies from Egypt. I imagined Chicago to be like a giant amusement park and couldn't wait to get started seeing all the sights. But the first thing I saw was the most amazing of all. I saw snow!

Growing up in Tampa with my parents, our travels had been limited to occasional excursions to the beach or to visit my fathers' relatives in Georgia. I had never experienced anything as enchanting as those first snowflakes gently falling on my face as Eileen and I walked through the streets of downtown Chicago.

Little Southern girl that I was, I had no clothing appropriate for this wintry Northern climate, so Eileen took us on our first adventure—a trip to the Carson Pierie Scott department store.

Sure enough, there were the "moving stairs" that she had described. As I rode an escalator for the very first time, I thought, "If this part is true, then there probably are real dinosaurs and mummies in this magical city."

There, she bought me a snowsuit with matching mittens and lots of other warm clothes. The snowsuit was brown, which had never been my favorite color. But this one was soft with colorful embroidery on the jacket so I loved it. All the boots were black and she just said they wouldn't do. I needed brown boots to match my new snowsuit! Used to hand-me-downs, being suddenly gifted with all those brand new clothes felt like my birthday and Christmas rolled into one.

After our marathon shopping trip, we took a cab to the home of Russell's brother where I met my new Chicago "cousins," Gail and Bobby Gooley. They were a little younger than me but Gail and I became immediate friends. She had an extra pair of boots I could squeeze into so Eileen took the three of us out in the yard to make a snowman and snow angels. She got right down in the snow with us and played like a child.

I was racking up "firsts" at a dizzying rate. Prior to this trip, I had never had any friends in Tampa, never remembered being on a train, never seen snow, and never had such fun as riding on moving stairs. The shopping trip where I got all new clothes and making a snowman and throwing snowballs with Eileen and my new cousins, kept me constantly thinking, "What wonderful thing is going to happen next?"

Although I missed my father very much, I was happy those first few days in Chicago. I didn't know then just how long it would be before I would be going back to Tampa to see him again.

Eileen had not enrolled me in school. She told me that she didn't know where we would be living yet and that I was way ahead in my schoolwork because of the constant tutoring from Elwood since I was three. She also had a theory that travel was much more educational than sitting at a school desk so this gave me endless time to explore and play.

Aunt Bruce returned to Tampa just days after we checked in, but Eileen and I stayed at the Palmer House for the next few months. Today, I wonder at our stay at this historic jewel.

From its inception, the Palmer House regularly had as guests dignitaries including United States presidents, famous actors and musicians, as well as wealthy businessmen and socialites. In 1879, at a huge banquet held in honor of the return of former President Ulysses S. Grant from a world tour, his good friend, author Mark Twain, acted as master of ceremonies. He reportedly jumped on a table at 2 a.m. to give a rousing speech to a crowd of five hundred dignitaries.

I have a lot of wonderful memories of the time Eileen and I lived at the Palmer House but one of the best was at Christmas time when it was decorated so beautifully for the holiday. The hotel had huge wide stairs and I would run down them daily to look at the wonderful Christmas trees and lights in the lobby. Eileen would let me go by myself and I always came back when she told me to.

The staff knew me by then and were always kind to me. It was from one of these staff members that I heard for the first time a question that troubled me. He asked me if I had been, "naughty or nice," the past year. He told me Santa Claus only brought presents to nice children.

I'm sure he was just teasing me, or perhaps trying to slow me down as I sometimes tore through the lobby. But this did give me some concern. I thought back to opening all those doors on the train platforms and thought that was probably naughty.

But mostly I thought of going with the lady who said she was my aunt and causing my family to be so frightened that someone had taken me that day. I sometimes convinced myself that Santa Claus would surely forget about me that year.

I remember sitting on the windowsill of our room on Christmas Eve and watching carolers sing on the street below. I could barely hear them, but I loved the faint sounds of their voices drifting up on the cold air. That winter, I perched on that sill many times just watching the snow falling.

Eileen and I spent wonderful hours Christmas shopping, and visiting with Eileen's in-laws and my new cousins. We bought presents for everybody, including ourselves. We bought presents for our family that we had left back in Tampa and we had fun wrapping them and taking them to the post office for shipment. We bought toys for my brother, Bobby, and my only regret was that I wouldn't be with him Christmas morning to see him open them.

The highlight of Christmas Eve though was that I got to call my daddy in Tampa. It was the first time I had ever spoken to anyone long distance and the connection wasn't as clear as it is today. But I did manage to relate to him stories about all the new and wonderful things I was experiencing.

When I asked him when I would see him again, his only answer was, "Soon, honey, soon. Meanwhile you be a good girl for Eileen. She is taking good care of you."

Because he had asked me to, I was determined to be an especially good girl from now on. He also spoke with Eileen and she assured him that she had bought me warm clothing suitable for the Chicago winters.

The next day was Christmas and we spent it with the Gooley relatives. It was a magical day for my cousins and me. Their tree was stacked almost to the ceiling with presents and I got as many and Gail and Bobby. This was the best Christmas I had ever had and I thought I must have been a pretty good girl that year after all!

In the early months of our hotel stay, we also set off by train for Detroit, Michigan, on the first of what were to be many visits to Eileen's uncle, Ira Clemens Lucia.

I remember signs at the railway station saying, "Is This Trip Necessary?" Eileen would always make a joke out of this and say, "Yes, this trip is definitely necessary!"

Her father, Charlie Lucia, had died before I was born, and Eileen explained to me that Uncle Ira was her father's only surviving brother. From her own childhood visits to Detroit, Eileen had come to know and love this somewhat dour uncle and, after her own father had died when she was just thirteen years old, he had become more like a father to her. I had no notion then that this man would become one of the most important links in the chain that eventually led me to my real mother.

Sometime in 1945, we checked out of the Palmer House and Eileen and I took a train back to Tampa. This time the trip was entirely different as Eileen was with me constantly, supervising my every move. She wouldn't allow me to go out the heavy doors between the railroad cars and play on the platforms as I had done with Aunt Bruce. While this was a disappointment to me, it also made me feel safe with Eileen, made me feel as if she really cared about me.

After months away, I was delighted to see my father again. Although it was wonderful to be with him, I realized for the first time that he was sick. He had recently had two surgeries and was recovering in the front bedroom in our house. I could go in and talk to him—but not for long.

As a child I didn't realize the gravity of the situation and was just relieved to know that I would not be moving back into the household with my mother but staying at Aunt Bruce's house with Eileen.

I remember being at my aunt's house when we heard the news that World War II had ended. We were actually out in the back yard hanging up clothes when one of the neighbors came screaming into the yard announcing that the war was over.

Soon the entire neighborhood was out on the street laughing and crying in sheer joy. Eileen was particularly jubilant because it meant her husband Russell would be coming home.

Almost immediately we returned to Chicago to await his return. This time we stayed with Russell's brother's family and, as soon as he got back from Germany, he and Eileen started looking for a house to purchase.

Not long after, we got a phone call that my daddy was very sick and wasn't expected to live much longer. In retrospect, I realize that his cancer diagnosis had been made years before, but to me, it was shattering news that was new and terrifying.

Despite having been physically separated from him a great deal of the time for the previous year, I still loved my father with all my heart. I could not imagine life without him.

Eileen and Russ drove me back to Tampa in the summer of 1946 and left me with her mother. They went back to Chicago because they were in the middle of buying their first home.

Over the summer Daddy's condition worsened. I wasn't allowed in the hospital, but Aunt Bruce went to see him regularly and sometimes took me with her. I had to wait in the lobby while she went up to see him.

A few days before he died they did allow me in his room to say goodbye to him. Even as a child I could see he was in pain and we didn't stay long.

I wish I could remember his last words to me but by this time he couldn't even talk but just looked at me and held my hand while I willed myself not to cry.

On August 17, 1946, my father died, taking from my life one of the few stable adults to shape my early childhood. Now I had only Eileen—and thank God I had her!

After my father's funeral, Eileen and Russ returned to Tampa and immediately took me back to Chicago. By this time, they had purchased a house on Cullom Avenue in the Portage Park area of Chicago. The rest of my childhood was spent in that beautiful home.

CHAPTER 3

SUSAN

1946

FIRST POSITION ~ BARRE

"The first time I ever saw our house in Portage Park was late at night when we arrived back in Chicago after Daddy died. We were tired and hungry and Eileen made us tomato soup and Ovaltine. I never tasted anything so good in my life."

SUSAN MADELINE BAILEY, AUGUST 21, 1946

I WAS NINE YEARS OLD before I ever felt like I had a home of my own. But now, living in Chicago with Eileen and Russ, in a real home with my own beautiful bedroom, I thought I was in heaven.

I was also enrolled in school and found myself in the fourth grade. I don't remember what happened to the third grade but I got along just fine and was able to keep up with my new classmates and new neighborhood friends.

The first time I saw my room there, I thought it had been designed for a fairy princess! In Tampa, my room had been spartan, furnished with just a single bed that was covered with a sheet in summer and a blanket in the winter. There was no bedspread, no rugs, and no closet. When I stayed over at my Aunt Bruce's, I slept in Eileen's old bedroom. At my Aunt Belva's (my father's other sister), a scratchy horsehair sofa was my bed.

I had even spent a lot of nights in a scary part of town at the house of my Uncle Bob Joughin's maid who lived in a shotgun house in Ybor City, Florida. There I piled into a big double bed in the living room with all four of her children.

Now this beautiful room was to be all mine! It had light blue walls and a blue rug on the floor. The furniture was white French provincial except for the double bed, which had a white leather tufted headboard. On the bed was a thick blue silk comforter and blue and white pillows to match.

In the corner was a soft white chair. There were blue silk drapes on the windows and a closet with a real door. On the back of the door was a full-length mirror. There was also a bookcase in this room with lots of children's books, including stories by Mark Twain and others on Greek mythology.

Snuggled up in bed with my latest choice from the shelves, I conceived a passion for reading that had begun in my father's office down by the Hillsborough River and that lasted me a lifetime.

Eileen did all she could to make me feel at home there. I remember one Saturday afternoon she remarked to Russell that I was the only child in the neighborhood who did not have a bicycle. So off the three of us went to the bike store to get one. But when we got there I couldn't make up my mind what color I wanted so they bought four!

Eileen reasoned it this way: "Well, she needs one bike to ride and can't decide on the red or blue. We need bikes to go riding with her in the park. And then what if we want to take Gail with us who has no bike at our house? She needs a bike."

So we came home with four English bikes in red, blue, green, and yellow. These were thin-tire racing bikes and I was the envy of the neighborhood to have such cool looking bikes.

Gail was very much in my life. We went to different schools but our houses weren't too far apart and Eileen made an effort to have her over as much as possible. Perhaps she was remembering when her own father died when she was thirteen. There was probably no one to comfort or distract her. Those first few months in Chicago, Eileen did everything possible to make me feel that I now had a real home and that I was wanted.

One night Gail was spending the night with me and we were sleeping in the same bed. In the middle of the night I woke up very sick and burning up with a fever. I made my way into Eileen and Russell's room and woke her up.

My fever was so high that we were soon racing to the hospital, Russ driving with Gail in pajamas in the front seat and me in pajamas with my head on Eileen's lap in the back seat.

I had polio! I was in the children's ward at a Chicago hospital for months. The memories I have of that time are dark and unpleasant but I was far luckier than many of the children around me in that ward. The polio just affected my legs.

I remember the treatments in the hospital, the packs they put on my legs each day, the children in iron lungs that were breathing for them, the water treatments each week.

Finally I was released from the hospital but my legs were very weak. I couldn't go to school and had to have a tutor come in each day to try and catch me up. Portage Park where we lived had an indoor heated swimming pool and Eileen would take me there daily for swimming lessons.

Little by little my legs started getting stronger. Then Eileen decided that ballet would make them even stronger so she enrolled me in classes. These two activities, swimming and dancing, along with the drama I soon discovered on the stage, were to become lifelong activities.

Soon I was able to go back to school and became just one of the neighborhood kids again. I loved my life in Portage Park and slowly the years of living in Tampa with an abusive mother began to fade from memory.

As I grew older, strangers began to simply assume that Eileen was my mother and to comment on how much we looked alike. We were first cousins, and I knew that could explain our resemblance.

But the niggling doubt that had sprouted in my mind as to whether Drucilla Bailey was my biological mother, gave rise to a new speculation. I began to wonder if perhaps Eileen was, in fact, my *real* mother.

She certainly treated me as if she were. On the few occasions when I worked up the courage to voice my thoughts, she denied being my mother, but by the time I was a teenager, I was convinced that was indeed the case.

I am still in touch with my cousin Gail. A few years ago I called her and asked, "When I first just showed up in Chicago with Eileen, who did your family think I was?"

She said, "My parents just told us you were Eileen's daughter from a previous marriage."

So Russell's family thought I was Eileen's daughter too! But she was only fourteen years old when I was born so there couldn't have been a previous marriage.

Still, since there were no other likely candidates in my family, and since Eileen had been a constant presence in my life since I was three years old, I just stopped asking questions and assumed that somehow she was my mother.

This was all I had to go on concerning my parentage until years later when I would stumble across some photographs that changed everything!

CHAPTER 4

SUSAN

CIRCA 1945–1946

MEETING CLARA

GROWING UP IN CHICAGO IN THOSE YEARS, I was a voracious reader, and Eileen and Russ provided me with a variety of books. One afternoon when I was about eight or nine years old, I had plopped down onto the living room floor to read *Tom Sawyer*. Eileen casually said, "We're related to him, you know."

I was startled and asked, "We're related to Tom Sawyer?" She said, "No, we're related to Mark Twain, and his real name is Samuel Clemens."

I'm sorry to say that this made no impression on me at all. I would have been far more thrilled had we been related to Tom Sawyer. Being a relative of Mark Twain meant nothing to me at that time.

Several times each year we made road trips to Detroit to visit Eileen's bachelor uncle, Ira Clemens Lucia. The thing I remember most vividly about those visits is how incredibly boring I found them. Tall, grey-haired Ira was in his mid-fifties, an ancient age in my young eyes. I never understood why Eileen enjoyed the visits so much, as she and Russ did most of the talking while Ira quietly listened.

I realize now that a younger Ira had been part of the happy summers Eileen spent in Detroit as a child, and that he was her last real link to her deceased father, Charlie. I always took a book with me so I would have something to do while the adults were talking about old times.

As we were preparing for one of our Detroit trips, I perked up when Eileen told me that we were going to meet some new relatives whom she referred to as "Aunt Clara" and "Uncle Jack."

Surely, I thought, they could not be more boring than Uncle Ira! I had no idea that "Aunt Clara" was Mark Twain's daughter or that "Uncle Jack" was her second husband, Jacques Samossoud, let alone that she wasn't really my aunt.

On that trip, when I met Clara for the very first time, Eileen, her husband Russ, and I motored there from Chicago and then picked up Uncle Ira. He lived in a second-floor walk-up apartment that consisted of a living room, kitchen, bathroom, and a single bedroom. It was nothing fancy, but neat and clean.

I had expected to meet my new relatives there, but we headed instead to a very nice hotel. We rode up in an elevator and knocked on the door of a room. We were greeted by a trim, dark-haired woman in a nice dress and heels. She looked a lot older than Eileen to me but was still very attractive.

Eileen and Russ had told me in advance that we were going out to dinner with Aunt Clara and Uncle Jack. I was very surprised when Clara looked right at Eileen and announced that we couldn't go out because it was too cold and Eileen hadn't brought a proper coat for me!

When we had gotten ready in Chicago, Eileen and I had decided that the brown snowsuit coat that she had bought me looked all wrong with the nice dress I put on, so I was wearing a lightweight grey coat with a red collar from my days in Tampa. That meant Clara was right about it not being very warm, but I could see that Eileen was still annoyed by Clara's comment.

Clara turned to me with a smile and asked me what my favorite color was, and I said "blue." She very matter-of-factly took my hand and said, "Then we'll just have to find you a blue coat."

Eileen gathered up her purse to go with us, but Aunt Clara very firmly told her, "It will just be us this time."

Off we went down the elevator and into one of the shops off the lobby of the hotel. The minute we entered the store, I saw a small mannequin sitting on a table and wearing a beautiful white rabbit fur coat. My face must have lit up because Aunt Clara smiled and took the coat off the mannequin.

She helped me put my arms into the sleeves, settled the coat around me, and it fit perfectly! The coat also had a matching muff. I was intrigued because I'd never seen such a thing.

I would have been happy to stop shopping right then and take this treasure home, but Aunt Clara insisted that we look for a blue coat too, since I had told her that color was my favorite. Clearly, she didn't just want me to have a coat to keep me warm: she wanted me to really love the gift she was giving me.

We went through the racks of winter garments and I tried on both a blue and a red coat as well. Then Aunt Clara told me I could have whichever one I wanted. There was no question. I wanted the rabbit fur coat with that fancy muff!

She asked the saleslady to remove the tags so I could wear it immediately. We went back upstairs to join the others, and I twirled around so everyone could admire my wonderful new fur coat.

Then I noticed that a man who must be Uncle Jack was there. I had not seen him before but he was obviously joining us. He had a pronounced accent and, although he didn't have much to say, I could hardly understand the words he did speak. Like Uncle Ira, he really didn't talk very much.

Everyone put on their coats and I noticed that Aunt Clara's had a fur collar, which made me feel even more pleased with my choice of coat.

We then all piled into a taxi which took us to a nearby restaurant. It was pretty fancy—fancier than the restaurants Eileen and Russ and I went to in Chicago. There were beautiful dark wood sideboards, a chandelier and fireplace, and lots of shiny brass. The tables were covered in snowy white cloths with matching linen napkins, pretty china, and the waiters wore fancy uniforms that looked like tuxedos. The trip was just getting better and better.

The waiter brought us menus and I looked at all the choices. I saw that they had my very favorite food—spaghetti. It was marked *for children only*, which made me feel very special.

When Eileen asked me what I wanted, I pointed to my choice. She frowned and said, "Oh, that's so messy. I'm afraid you'll get it all over your dress."

Clara turned to Eileen and said, "Let the girl have spaghetti if she wants it," so Eileen gave in. I was really beginning to like Aunt Clara.

During dinner, I was very careful with my spaghetti, but I dropped my fork on the floor. When I started to pick it up, Clara said, "No dear, let the servant pick it up."

Eileen said, "Don't you mean the waiter?" We all laughed at this.

It was at this meal that I got my first lesson from Clara in proper etiquette. I learned about "twirling" spaghetti with a big spoon instead of just chopping it up as I had done previously.

Eileen and Clara did most of the talking. What Russ, Ira, and Jacques talked about, I have no idea. It seemed to me that they barely talked at all. At some point, Jacques got up and left the table, and Clara said he was just going out for a smoke. Russ was sitting right there smoking so, as young as I was, I thought this was odd.

I did notice that everyone referred to him as "Jacques." I had been told to call him Uncle Jack. This confused me so I decided not to address him at all.

I was sitting between Eileen and Clara when, right over the top of my head, Clara began to pepper Eileen with questions. She asked how I was doing in school, if I had enough school clothes, if I had made any friends in the neighborhood yet, and if she had found a good doctor for me.

Eileen answered all these questions in a matter-of-fact way, but I could see that she was beginning to feel defensive. When Clara told me that I had to follow good habits every day to grow up strong, something seemed to snap in Eileen.

She looked Aunt Clara right in the eye and asked, "And how is Nina?"

Aunt Clara ignored this question, but immediately stopped grilling Eileen about me. I had no idea then that the woman named Nina was Clara's daughter and that she was already deeply troubled with the issues that were to bedevil her for the remainder of her life.

Even as a child though, I understood that Eileen had uttered the one question guaranteed to stop Clara's pointed inquiries about how I was being raised.

After dinner, we dropped Clara and Jacques off at their hotel, got into our car, took Ira back to his apartment, and traveled back to Chicago.

The last thing Clara said to me before we left was, "The next time you're here, we'll have to introduce you to the symphony." When I asked Eileen what this was, she said it was like a large band that Clara's first husband had directed before he died. Her father Charlie, she said, had also sometimes been a musician in this band.

Wow! That was really something to look forward to, and I certainly hoped I would see Aunt Clara again.

CHAPTER 5

DEB

2007

AN INKLING OF SOMETHING IMPORTANT

AFTER THIRTY YEARS OF GENEALOGICAL RESEARCH, both personal and professional, I had learned to trust my instincts when something seemed important or out of place. Susan's visit with Clara pinged on my radar screen on both counts.

My original reason for contacting Susan had been to see if she could shed additional light on the old family legend of the Lucia family being related to the Clemens family of Mark Twain fame. She had responded to my online message for the same reason.

Now, in the story of Eileen Lucia and young Susan visiting with Clara Clemens in Detroit (with our mutual relative Ira Clemens Lucia as host), I had proof of a connection between the two families. But proof of what?

My great-grandmother's letter had mentioned Clara Clemens, but gave absolutely no indication that she actually knew her. None of the other Lucia family branches, other than the one of which Eileen, her uncle Ira, and father Charlie were immediate members, actually lived in Detroit, but some did live elsewhere in Michigan.

I wondered what was unique about Eileen's branch that they, and only they, had ever met Clara.

For no reason I could put my finger on, my instinct told me that the answer had something to do with Eileen or with Susan herself. The circumstances of Susan's childhood seemed the stuff of soap operas.

By this time, I was as intrigued with the question of Susan's parentage as I was with whether or not *my* family was related to Mark Twain. It never occurred to either of us then that the answer to both questions might be related.

Susan said she had a "knowingness" growing up that there was something mysterious about her birth. She felt as if she belonged to the Bailey family and yet, in some way she couldn't define, she also felt as if she did not.

While most children retain very few conscious memories of their earliest years, Susan is that rarity: an adult who retains isolated specific memories of her very early childhood. Up until about age five, Susan told me, she dreamed in French, and had vague memories of living as a toddler in a place where French was the spoken language.

Those early memories bothered Susan enough to repeatedly quiz her relatives about her origins. However, at no point did Elwood or Drucilla Bailey ever tell Susan that she was "adopted."

Drucilla, in fact, regularly and firmly denied it. In a family with names like Belva, Bruce, Elwood, and Drucilla, the relative sophistication of her first name, and the very French flavor of her middle name of Madeline, niggled at Susan. She could not, she said, get out of her head the memory of the assertion made by the lady who took her out of school that she was a little French girl.

When she pestered the adults in her life about what the lady had meant, they either evaded answering or invented stories, no two of which matched.

Her aunt Belva told her that her French middle name was in honor of a woman that her father Elwood had met and fallen in love with while serving in France during World War I.

Drucilla Bailey told her that Eileen had named her and just thought the name was pretty.

Then there was the mysterious lady who had kidnapped Susan and claimed that *she* had named her.

Drucilla was verbally and often physically abusive to Susan, and at times, seemed to actually hate her. Susan simply could not understand how a "real" mother could possibly treat her child as Drucilla treated her.

When Susan's younger brother Bobby was born, Drucilla treated him with nothing but love and kindness, as she did other children in general. In fact, Susan said, people regularly told her how lucky she was to have such a wonderful mother.

None of them knew the abuses that Drucilla heaped upon Susan. She once told little Susan that there were snakes in a closet and then locked her inside it. She also shut Susan out of the house in bad weather, leaving her to crawl through a small doggie door in the garage just to get out of the rain.

When beautiful little Susan, wanting feedback from her mother as all little girls do, asked, "Am I pretty?" Drucilla laconically answered, "You'll do."

In her twenties, Susan discovered physical proof that Drucilla Bailey was not her biological mother.

After having her blood drawn one day at a routine doctor's appointment, Susan casually posed a question to the doctor: "My mother's blood type is AB and she is RH negative. I know that because her blood type is supposed to be rare and she sometimes gets called upon to give blood for emergencies in other parts of the county. My own blood type is O positive though, so does that mean that my father must have been O positive?"

The doctor frowned and excused himself for a moment, returning with Drucilla's medical file in his hands. Flipping through, he located confirmation of Drucilla Bailey's blood type.

As gently as possible, he explained to Susan that she must have been adopted because, regardless of her father's blood type, it was impossible for a woman with AB and RH negative blood to give birth to a child with O positive blood.

Susan said, "When he told me this, I started crying and the doctor tried to comfort me. He probably assumed that I was devastated by the news, but my tears were tears of relief. What I had suspected my whole life was true—Drucilla Bailey, the woman who never seemed to really love me, had not given birth to me."

Besides considering Eileen as her possible mother, Susan and I also spent time sorting through other possibilities about her parentage. Since she knew definitively that Drucilla Bailey was not her biological mother, Susan reluctantly entertained the idea that her beloved daddy, Elwood Bailey, was not her biological father.

She explored the idea that the other strong adult male from her childhood, her "uncle" Bob Joughin, was actually her father, but testing her DNA against that of Bob's daughter Lula ruled out that possibility.

Since the mystery lady who had taken her from school told Susan that she was "a little French girl," I searched fruitlessly in the family trees of the Baileys, the Joughins, and the Smiths (Drucilla's family) for any woman with French roots or with the name Madeline.

The closest I came was a female in-law of Bob Joughin: she spoke French and hailed from New Orleans. I knew there were no candidates to fit the description in the Lucia family tree.

We considered the unknown woman who had kidnapped her. Susan could describe her but did not recall the woman's name. She said she had taken to heart her father's instructions to "just forget about her."

Despite having only limited belief in alternative medicine, I nevertheless knew from my education and work experience in psychology, that hypnotherapy could be a powerful tool in aiding recall. Susan and I discussed the notion of her undergoing hypnosis to see if she could recall anything further about the woman who took her out of school, but we decided to shelve the idea at that time.

Since Susan's instinct told her that Eileen could be her biological mother, I asked her to tell me more about the woman who raised her for so many years.

I hoped, of course, that Eileen's story would also provide some clue how it was that Susan came to know Clara Clemens.

CHAPTER 6

SUSAN

EILEEN HARRIET LUCIA

M Y COUSIN EILEEN WAS A VERY IMPORTANT PERSON in my young life. In many ways, she was my salvation.
Eileen was born in Tampa, Florida, on September 23, 1923, to my dad's sister Bruce and her husband, Charles ("Charlie") Lucia.

Eileen grew up in a tumultuous household. Her father Charlie was a musician who had lived in Detroit, Michigan, before moving to Tampa around 1920. Sadly for Eileen, both Charlie and Bruce were alcoholics.

Bob Joughin, sheriff of Hillsborough County, gave her father a job when he was unemployed, but also "took care of" her mother when Charlie was out of town. Bob was, in fact, in love with Bruce.

However, Eileen had several stabilizing influences in her young life. The first was our maternal grandmother, Juliet Hurst Bailey ("Big Mama") who lived with her daughter Bruce during all the years Eileen was growing up. Big Mama came from a family of some wealth. I remember visiting with her relatives in Georgia and being impressed with their large plantation style houses.

Big Mama was actually a tiny, loving woman who provided a buffer between Eileen and her alcoholic parents and also between me and Drucilla Bailey on some of the occasions that Drucilla let her temper get away with her in front of family members. I recall one time Big Mama grabbed me away during one of Drucilla's tirades, locked us in her room, and said, "No one's going to hurt *my* baby!"

The second positive influence in Eileen's life was her paternal grandmother, Harriet Churchill Lucia, who lived in Detroit and with whom Eileen spent most of her childhood summers. Eileen often recounted stories of how much she loved this grandmother who taught her manners and allowed her to be a normal little girl, something she was sadly lacking at home in Tampa.

It was also in Detroit that Eileen came to know her father's brothers, Ira Clemens Lucia, (named after his grandfather), and Marcus Lucia, said to be named after Mark Twain.

I believe that Eileen also came under the influence of Clara Clemens Gabrilowitsch during those childhood summers in Detroit. During the time I spent as a child with Eileen and Clara together, it always seemed to me that they knew each other well and had a history. Whether or not the Clemens and Lucia families were actually related by blood as Eileen's great-grand-father Ira Lucia claimed, it certainly appears that Clara and Eileen *believed* their families to be relatives.

Even with Big Mama's influence, growing up in Tampa with Charlie and Bruce was no picnic for a bright, sensitive little girl like Eileen. Her father was away a lot, sometimes traveling for musical gigs, and sometimes traveling with Bob Joughin and my father just to get out of Tampa.

Bob, Charlie, and my dad were the three "bad boys" who took off on these jaunts, leaving family obligations behind. Bob bankrolled these frequent trips to Detroit and also to New York. That left Eileen with her drunken mother, my Aunt Bruce. An alley cat would have been a better mother for her.

Eileen was a talented child who took piano, dance, voice, and gymnastic lessons and excelled in all of them. Big Mama and Drucilla managed to get her to these lessons or she caught rides with the mothers of her friends, all of whom felt sorry for her because of her home situation.

When Eileen was thirteen years old, tragedy struck. Her father Charlie and Uncle Bob took another trip to Detroit, supposedly heading to a gig for Charlie. To everyone's shock, Bob returned from this trip alone, saying that Charlie had fallen into the Detroit River and drowned. This happened before I was born, but when Eileen told me many years later, it was clear that she was still devastated by the loss of her unreliable, mercurial, but charming and talented father.

Due to Charlie's alcoholism, the story Bob told about his demise was never doubted. Eileen, Bruce, and my dad could well imagine Charlie tumbling into a river in a state of drunken clumsiness. Strangely though, Big Mama was the only one who questioned this story about her son-in-law's death. Several times I heard her say, "He was *pushed* into that river!"

When Deb checked out the story in 2008, no mention of Charlie's death was located in Detroit records. Did he really drown or did he just take off? For the next five years, both Deb and I dug for any signs of Charlie and would joke that if one of us found him we could call the other with the news even if it was 3:00 a.m.!

Then in November 2013, seventy-six years after Charlie disappearance, I was perusing ancestry.com and they sent me a "hint" about one of my relatives. It was Charlie!

There it all was in black and white. A death certificate showed that Charlie did indeed drown in the Detroit River but his body washed up across the river in Ontario, Canada, where all legalities were handled. His body wasn't found for almost a month. All the information to identify him was given by his brother, Ira.

He died in 1937 and we found out these bare facts in 2013. Despite Ira identifying Charlie's body, to the best of my knowledge, my Aunt Bruce, Charlie's wife, was never notified. I am absolutely sure that Eileen never knew what happened to her daddy. Although his immediate family members are long dead and gone, I'm proud that I finally found my Uncle Charlie!

Charlie's death left Bob Joughin complete access to Bruce, and from that time on, they all but lived together. From my earliest memories, he was introduced to me as "Uncle Bob." I never knew until I was much older that he was not actually married to my Aunt Bruce and, therefore, not my real uncle. I truly thought he was Eileen's father until she later told me the stories about Charlie.

Bob was definitely enamored of Bruce despite her drinking problems. However, with Charlie gone, Bob quickly found that the path to Bruce was far from clear. Due to strained financial circumstances, Bruce's household had grown to include not only Eileen and Big Mama, but also Elwood and Drucilla Bailey.

It was the Depression and, while Bob owned a large company and was well to do, most people didn't have two nickels to rub together. At least when Charlie was alive he was bringing in *some* money. His death left Bruce and her family destitute and more dependent on Bob's financial resources than ever.

Bob quickly set about "cleaning up" this household. He used his political connections to get my dad a job with the City of Tampa. This job came with a house in a city park along the Hillsborough River, thus reducing the household by two adults. It was in that house that I was later to live until being moved to Chicago.

When Eileen was just seventeen years old, Bob bought a house for her on Haya Street, across the street from Bruce's. That way they could keep an eye on her, but she and her friends were out of Bruce's house. Eileen was still in high school but had her own house! This was probably the first time in her young life that she could take a deep breath away from the drunken antics of her mother.

A title search conducted in 2010 showed that both Haya Street houses were solely in the name of Bruce Bailey. So even before Charlie died, his name was not on the title to the house where he resided with his wife, and Bob had generously given Bruce another house, although Eileen lived there.

That house of Eileen's came to play a part in some of the few happy memories from my early childhood. At home, I lived in fear of my mother Drucilla, never knowing when something I did would bring down her wrath. When I was at Eileen's house, those were the good times! Eileen took me to her high school parties and let me sit on her lap in the back seat of her friend's car.

I also remember sleepovers at the house with Eileen and her best friend, Billy June. For a little girl, this was pretty heady stuff. Looking back, I can't imagine how teenage Eileen felt, being made a surrogate mother to her little cousin, but I only remember being welcomed and taken along on her adventures.

Eileen lived in that house for three years until she met and married the love of her life, Russell Gooley, in 1943. Russell was in the Army and she met him at a USO club in Tampa when he was stationed there.

But World War II was in full swing, and soon after their marriage, Russ was sent to Germany for the duration of the war. Eileen saw her ticket out of Tampa and the constant upheaval of her family life, and shortly thereafter moved to Chicago to stay with her husband's family and wait out the war.

I can't imagine how Eileen felt when her brief time as an unencumbered young bride came to an abrupt end a year later when, after being taken from school, I was sent to live with her.

Once again, she took on the role of mother figure for me. Apparently she did not feel comfortable bringing me into the household of her husband's relatives, which explains our stay of many months at the Palmer House.

I adored Eileen but, as an adult, wondered why it was that Eileen was chosen as the one to raise me after my father felt that it was not safe for me to stay in Tampa anymore. Perhaps the move was originally meant to be temporary.

But then my father found out he had cancer. How did he feel as he lay dying? Did he wrestle with how I was to be provided for? Was he worried about keeping me away from the lady who told me I was a little French girl, or was he worried about shielding me from Drucilla's abuse?

Those were questions that plagued me throughout my life. Recently, my daughter Jennifer sent me some things she had found when cleaning out one of our old garages. These things had actually belonged to my father.

There in an old box was a letter that he had written to Drucilla as he lay in the hospital, clearly knowing that his time was drawing to an end:

Cilla, I am sending Susie to Chicago to live with Eileen permanently. Please see to it that she has some warm clothes before she leaves as it is cold up there and I don't want her to get pneumonia. Elwood.

I had my answer at last. My father had loved me and felt that the best way to protect me was to send me to his niece Eileen permanently. There was just no one else in the family that he trusted to raise me more than he trusted her.

Susan and Eileen, Chicago 1945

From Personal Collection of Susan Bailey

CHAPTER 7

SUSAN

1947–1948

MORE VISITS WITH AUNT CLARA

I LOVED EILEEN WITH ALL MY HEART, but the trips we made to Detroit to visit the woman I knew as Aunt Clara were the highlights of my young life.

Living with the Baileys in Tampa, I had learned to make myself as small and invisible as possible to avoid bringing down the wrath of the woman I knew as my mother. When Eileen and Russ took me to Chicago to live with them, I felt like a welcome addition to the bustle and chaos of their life.

But only with Aunt Clara did I feel that I was the *total focus* of an adult's attention, and, for the first time in my life, I felt important. I feel lucky that this reserved, lovely woman chose to indulge me in ways I had never experienced and to introduce me to the world of music and culture.

Thinking back to our first trip to Detroit when Clara had taken me on a shopping trip and bought me the rabbit fur coat, I realized that every time I saw Clara, she made me feel like a princess. So when Eileen, Russ, and I took another road trip to Detroit not too long after that first meeting with Clara, I was very excited because Eileen said she had a big surprise for me.

I was wearing a new pair of boots and, of course, the rabbit fur coat, so I hoped it was something really nice, maybe a visit to another wonderful restaurant. For a nine-year-old girl who had grown up poor in Tampa, life had certainly taken a dramatic turn for the better. Now, motoring to Detroit to see Clara, I was on top of the world.

Once again, we first went to Uncle Ira Lucia's apartment to pick him up, and then on to the same hotel as before to meet Aunt Clara and Uncle Jacques. Remembering the fun of our first meeting (an adult who didn't care if I made a mess with my spaghetti), I was all smiles at seeing her again.

She looked happy to see me as well, but she only exchanged hugs with Eileen. She complimented me on how cute I looked in my coat and told Eileen she was glad to see that she had finally gotten me some new boots for the snow.

She had brown hair and dark eyes that sparkled as she told me we were going to the symphony to hear some music. I loved music and couldn't think of anything more fun to do. Eileen had told me that Clara's first husband, Ossip, had been the director of the Detroit Symphony, so this made me even more anxious to get to the performance.

The six of us piled into a cab, and we pulled up in front of a beautiful building called Symphony Hall. I realized this must be the surprise that Eileen had promised me. When we got out of the cab, I was shocked when people surrounded Clara; she was treated like a movie star.

It was not until I was a teenager that I was told that Clara was Mark Twain's daughter. Later, I looked back on my meetings with her in awe, but at the time I had no notion that this was the source of much of the crowd's interest. Decades passed before I realized that this adoration stemmed nearly as much from her being the widow of Detroit's beloved Ossip Gabrilowitsch, who had been a rock star in his own right, as it did from her being the daughter of Mark Twain.

Once we got inside, I looked around in delight at the soaring ceilings and velvet curtains. Someone asked Clara if she would be sitting in her box and she said, "No, we are sitting on the floor this evening." I thought, "Oh great, like a picnic." I pictured us sitting right on the floor.

When I expressed this thought, Clara seemed to find it enormously amusing. For some reason, it seemed to annoy Eileen that Clara delighted in my sense of wonder and smiled at my innocent gaffes. Later in her life, Clara developed a reputation for being somewhat staid, even dour. I feel blessed that my acquaintance with her came at a time when she still exhibited traces of the curious, light-hearted young woman about whom her friend and poet Richard Watson Gilder wrote in a delightful little doggerel:

A Gentle Ode On Dark-Eyed Clara:
A terrible Earthquake shook the land,

Inquisitive Clara was quickly at hand;
The experts prepared to measure the spasm—
But Clara's nose was first in the chasm.

When we took our seats on the first row to the right of the stage, Clara asked me if I had ever been to a symphony, and I told her "yes," because Russell owned a nightclub with his brother, and there was a band there. I thought it was the same thing. When the music started, I realized I was very wrong. I was mesmerized.

The music surrounded me and seemed to go right through me. I had never experienced such a consuming fascination as I did the first time I heard that orchestra. It was an enchantment and love that would last a lifetime. I was impressed that Clara's first husband had actually been the director of this amazing group and that Eileen's daddy used to play there sometimes. I wished I could have known them, but they both died before I was born. I was caught up in the magic of the music.

In those moments, I had no thought about the importance of being with Aunt Clara. Years later, by the time I understood what it meant, Clara was lost to me.

During intermission, we weren't able to leave our seats because Clara was again mobbed, and people were taking her photo. Russ was a photographer, and I had gone to weddings with him since I was seven, so I was used to flash bulbs and by now was taking this in stride.

Someone asked her who I was (she was holding my hand) and she said, "This is my little friend, Susie, from Chicago." I was so proud that my "aunt" called me her friend.

Several people asked her how Nina was, and once, she said, "Oh, I believe my darling girl is in New York at the moment." I didn't remember ever meeting this Nina, but I understood from that exchange and hushed conversations between Clara and Eileen—and between Eileen and Russ—that Nina was Clara's daughter.

I remember wondering why she was never around and why everything was such a secret concerning Nina.

We left a few minutes before the concert was over, sneaking down the side aisle because Clara wanted to avoid the frenzy that had occurred during intermission.

We headed next to a small bistro, and we all crowded into a large booth near the front. I don't remember what I had to eat, but this time, there was no spaghetti dispute. Even at the restaurant, several people came over and said *hello* to Clara and interrupted our meal.

Eileen asked Clara if this happened all the time, and she said, "Yes, and that's why we don't go out very often." This statement made me feel dejected. I had just had the most wonderful evening, and now I thought we would never go to the symphony again. I wished everyone would just leave Aunt Clara alone.

I remember something else very clearly from this little dinner—I got an etiquette lesson from Clara on the proper way to butter bread. I had taken a piece and was spreading butter on the whole thing when Clara tapped me on the arm and showed me how to tear off just one little piece at a time and cover that from the butter on my plate.

Now I could twirl spaghetti and butter bread. I felt positively grown-up! What marvelous skills for a little girl who, until age seven, had been living in a home with a dirt yard and an abusive mother. It seemed sometimes that magical thinking had produced this change in my life, and I was often frightened that it was a beautiful dream that might be taken away from me.

I absorbed the manners that Clara taught me like a sponge. To this day, I still twirl my spaghetti and butter my bread the way Clara taught me so many years ago. Maybe I'm still afraid that the magic will go away.

When we dropped Aunt Clara and Uncle Jacques off at their hotel, she asked me if I had enjoyed the symphony. I told her how much I loved it and that it was the best night of my life. She said, "Well then, we'll have to do it again," so I was once more elated.

Then, on the way back to Uncle Ira's apartment, Eileen said, "Well, I'll never do *that* again!" My mood sank to the bottom of the barrel. I had fallen in love with Clara, but I loved Eileen too, and knew that she could be temperamental. I was so afraid I would never see Aunt Clara again.

At the time, I thought little of the tension between them. After doing research on Eileen's childhood, I now realize that her acquaintance with Clara probably stretched that far back. I suspect that when Eileen came from Tampa to Detroit for summer visits to her grandmother, Harriet Lucia, she probably came under Clara's tutelage then, as I did twenty years later. Clara was forty-nine years older than Eileen, old enough to be her grandmother. Their relationship was affectionate, but contentious at times.

However, I doubt that the tension started as far back as Eileen's childhood. Perhaps it began when Eileen realized Clara was usurping some of her parental authority with me. Eileen didn't want her parenting skills questioned, but Clara was not afraid to give her opinion as evidenced by an exchange that took place between the two at dinner that evening.

Clara had asked me if I was taking piano lessons, and I told her I was. She asked me what I had learned, and I proudly told her I could play "Ole' Black Joe." She looked directly at Eileen and said, "She needs another piano teacher!" I was not sure who would win in a battle of wills between these two powerful women that I adored.

We got back to Uncle Ira's, said goodnight to him, and headed for home. We never stayed in Detroit, no matter how late it was, probably because his bachelor apartment was too small to accommodate us. We always drove back to Chicago, and I'm sure I slept all the way. In fact, Eileen and Russ were famous for staying out half the night and always kept a pillow and blanket in the back seat for me.

On another visit to Detroit, Eileen and I drove to the city without Russ, and went straight to Uncle Ira's apartment. During the war years we always took a train as Eileen couldn't drive. But by our post-war visits, Russ had taught her and bought her a car so we were pretty independent.

I was dreading the inevitable boredom of our visit with the elderly Ira, but I had my ever-present book with me. Boredom was not in the cards though, because Aunt Clara was there, this time without her husband, Jacques. As usual, she was wearing a dress and heels.

Looking back, I realize that Clara was in her seventies at the time, but she appeared far more youthful with her brown hair and elegant mode of dressing. The first thing she did was bend down and give me a hug, the first one I had ever gotten from her! Unlike the perfunctory hugs she gave Eileen, this was a nice, strong embrace, and I was thrilled.

After the initial greeting, we sat down and Uncle Ira offered us Cokes that he had in the refrigerator. Before long he asked me if I liked horses and if I wanted to see some. I loved horses, so whatever he had in mind, I was ready to go. He took my hand, and we walked down the stairs to a park-like area near his apartment and soon came the horses.

There were policemen on horseback, two of them, and they came right up to us and let me pet the animals' noses. The only policemen I had ever seen were on foot or in cars, so I was amazed by the sight of these men on horses. What a wonderful place Detroit was with Aunt Clara, rabbit fur coats, spaghetti in posh restaurants, the symphony, and now policemen on horseback. I was a lucky little girl with not one, but two magical cities to explore.

Soon the policemen were on their way, and Uncle Ira and I went back upstairs to his apartment. Eager to see Aunt Clara, I bounded into the room, but saw only Eileen. My heart dropped when I realized that Clara was gone. I had been excited wondering what adventure she would take us on that day, and now I was devastated that she left without even saying good-bye to me.

I felt a kind of emptiness that I hadn't experienced before. I had only seen Aunt Clara a few times, but I felt very connected to her. Even though I loved Eileen, I had a bond with Clara that I was too young to understand at the time. I never got over that sense of connection. Eileen and I left for Chicago shortly thereafter. That trip to Detroit was the quickest one we had ever made.

Although it was twenty years later, the day I found out Clara had died I was in a state of shock and grief. It would be a lifetime before I understood why I had never seen her again.

Clara Clemens Gabrilowitsch, 1933

Photo from Nina's personal effects
Courtesy of The Mark Twain House & Museum
Hartford, CT

CHAPTER 8

SUSAN

2007

AN EXTRAORDINARY CLUE

S OON AFTER DEB AND I MET, we realized that we had both been doing almost identical research for years (searching for our familial relationship to Mark Twain). We decided to combine the information we already had and to join forces on further research in order to try and establish the connection to our famous ancestor. This turned out to be a momentous decision.

We started searching the Internet for photos of all known Clemens descendants. One day I opened an email from Deb to find an attachment that was an image of Nina Clemens Gabrilowitsch, Mark Twain's only grandchild.

I was astounded by the picture before me. I couldn't stop looking at the shape of her eyebrows, her smile, her distinctive chin. For a moment I questioned what I was seeing. Hadn't I seen this face before?

My stomach was churning as I forwarded this image to my daughter, Karen. She was at work so I didn't expect to hear from her until evening but she called me within five minutes and said, "Just who is this person with my son's face?"

When I told her that it was Mark Twain's granddaughter, Nina, she said, "So the story you told us all those years ago about being related to Mark Twain is actually true. We *are* related to him!"

That was exactly my reaction. Nina looked like a female version of my grandson, Kyle, who was fifteen years old at the time. The shape of their faces was almost identical but even more telling, the right eyebrow on both is a rounded arch while the left eyebrow is straight. Their mouths and smiles looked like twins.

My immediate thought was that this proved what Deb and I (and eight other branches of the Lucia family) had each been told as children—that we were related to Mark Twain.

I took this remarkable resemblance as proof that our 150-year-old connection had skipped several generations. It looked as if Nina's DNA had landed squarely on the face of my grandson, Kyle, as if it had never intended to evade our notice.

For a few weeks I was happy that we had discovered this picture and were at least on the right track.

But the Internet is vast and had many more secrets to give up. With the next family image we found, my level of astonishment went through the roof. I was about to derail my own train of thought about who I believed I really was!

CHAPTER 9

SUSAN

2007

ENTER OSSIP GABRILOWITSCH

A FTER THE STARTLING DISCOVERY that Mark Twain's granddaughter, Nina Gabrilowitsch, looked so much like my grandson, Kyle, my next step was to enthusiastically scour the Internet for more Twain family photos. Because of my childhood relationship with Twain's daughter, Clara, I knew a fair amount about Nina's mother and remembered quite well what she looked like. My knowledge of her father Ossip Gabrilowitsch, who died before I was born, was practically nil.

A Google search brought me to a Wikipedia article. A quick scan of the article revealed that Ossip Gabrilowitsch had been born in Saint Petersburg, Russia, and studied piano and composition at the Saint Petersburg Conservatory. After graduation from the conservatory, he then spent time in Vienna studying under a world-renowned piano tutor named Theodor Leschetizky.

This dovetailed with a vague recollection that Clara had studied piano in Vienna as well and it seemed possible that was where the two met. Further research revealed that their romance had indeed been sparked while under the mutual tutelage of Leschetizky.

After a protracted courtship, Ossip and Clara were married on October 6, 1909. He then went on to be the conductor of the Munich Philharmonic for several years. He was actually imprisoned in Munich in 1917 and, according to Wikipedia, was rescued by the intervention of an archbishop who later became Pope Pius XII.

After a narrow escape from Germany, the family moved back to the United States. Ossip accepted a position as Director of the Detroit Symphony Orchestra in 1918, with the understanding that the City would build a new symphony hall. He held this post until his death from stomach cancer in 1936.

Those were the bare bones facts of the life of Nina's father, and they dovetailed with my vague recollections. However, what I had never seen before was a picture of him.

And there, staring at me from the Wikipedia sidebar, was Ossip Gabrilowitsch as he looked in his twenties. What a handsome man he was with his intense eyes, European features, full, sensuous mouth, and shock of dark hair falling down his forehead.

I had been blindsided when I first saw the image of Nina and noted her marked resemblance to my grandson, Kyle. However, I had been able to explain away that resemblance on the grounds that it simply provided evidence that the long ago Lucia family connection to Mark Twain, as told to both Deb and myself when we were children, might actually be true.

I assumed that the resemblance between Nina and Kyle simply reflected some features handed down in the related Lucia and Clemens lines. It had also strengthened my conviction that Eileen must indeed be my mother. If I was not a Lucia by blood, I thought, the resemblance would not be there.

But, oh my god, how did I now explain that this picture of Ossip Gabrilowitsch? Looking out at me from the web page was a man who could have been a twin to my son Greg at the same age! Ossip was Mark Twain's son-in-law, not a blood relation. He had simply married into the Clemens family and fathered Nina. There was absolutely no way to explain *this* resemblance based on the old Lucia family legend of a relationship to Mark Twain.

My heart was pounding as I stared at the picture. My son Greg was now in his forties. Was this resemblance just a fluke or would it hold up as more photos of Ossip came to light?

A deeper search was launched, with a particular interest in seeing how Ossip looked at an age close to Greg's. Since Ossip had been a world-class pianist, as well as Director of the Detroit Symphony Orchestra, photographs of him proved far easier to find than for his little-known daughter, Nina.

The next picture located was of Ossip circa age thirty. Unearthing a picture of Greg at around the same age, and placing the images side by side, they still looked like two peas in a pod. My palms were beginning to sweat.

Further digging eventually turned up photos of Ossip Gabrilowitsch in his forties. Although these photos were taken seventy-five years apart, the two were aging the same way. Still handsome, both showed receding hairlines with look-alike widow's peaks and a tendency for the appearance of their noses to look more pronounced as their faces thinned with age.

Their full mouths were identical and if you covered up the rest of their faces you could not discern one from the other. At first I couldn't process what it meant that the two were the spitting image of each other, but I instinctively knew that, whatever the explanation, it was nothing I had ever anticipated.

During the search, I had a picture of Ossip on my desktop when Greg, visiting over the Christmas holiday, walked behind me and said, "Mom, where did you get that picture of me?"

I felt a chill come over me. It was one thing for me to think the resemblance was strong, but for Greg to actually believe he was looking at a picture of himself? There could be no more doubt that the resemblance was uncanny and not a figment of my imagination.

I had to tell him with tears running down my cheeks, "It isn't you honey, but someone whom there's a good chance you're closely related to."

So what did this mean about my parentage? I knew Drucilla Bailey, my father's wife and the woman whose name is on my birth certificate, was not my biological mother. I had always thought that left my cousin Eileen Lucia as the only logical candidate to be my mother. She had, after all, raised me all those years in Chicago, and had shown me a mother's love.

For years, my focus had been on finding proof that Eileen was my mother, but she had died in Oregon in 2000 and, right up until the end, would never discuss any details of my birth with me.

On the final occasion when I sent a letter asking yet again for her to explain who my mother was, she responded that her entire earlier life was "too painful to remember." So I had given up on proving it and had just accepted that this was more than likely the case.

The photographs of Ossip Gabrilowitsch turned my life upside down. I was so shaken up that I could barely even think about what it could mean. I tried to calm down and think rationally, but the thought that I couldn't escape seemed too fantastic to be true—the logical explanation for my son

Greg looking like Ossip Gabrilowitsch was that Nina Clemens Gabrilowitsch, only grandchild of Mark Twain, had given birth to me.

Kyle and Nina

Susan and Clara

Ossip and Greg

*Susan, her grandson Kyle, and son Greg displaying startling
resemblances to Nina, Clara, and Ossip*

*Photo of Nina courtesy of The Hannibal Free Public Library
(see Acknowledgments for full photo credits for this image)*

CHAPTER 10

DEB

2007–2008

THE SEARCH FOR NINA BEGINS

THE JURY WAS STILL OUT on whether or not Ira Clemens Lucia had told the truth or simply spun a tall tale when he claimed to be related to Mark Twain, but one thing was certain: his tale set in motion a series of events whose consequences were turning out to be astonishing.

I tried to wrap my mind around it. Thanks to my great-great grandfather Ira Lucia's long-ago story, I had spent decades trying to determine whether I was distantly related to Mark Twain.

Susan, on the other hand, had been taking some sort of relationship to Mark Twain for granted because of a childhood acquaintance with her "aunt" Clara Clemens. Susan's driving passion was simply to determine her parentage.

Now, those two quests, driven by different purposes, had led to an incredible and unforeseen possibility. If Nina Clemens Gabrilowitsch were Susan's mother, then Susan was Mark Twain's great-granddaughter!

All of the sad commentaries that the bloodline of Samuel Langhorne Clemens had died out would be untrue. In my years as a genealogist, I had turned up many an interesting tale, but nothing to rival this.

The side-by-side pictures of Ossip Gabrilowitsch and Susan's son Greg, and of Nina and Susan's grandson Kyle, fairly screamed, "It's true!" But, would research on the life of Nina support this?

Questions tumbled through my mind. Where did Nina live at various times in her life? If Nina was Susan's mother, who was her father? How did they meet? How could we find evidence to prove or disprove that Nina was Susan's mother?

As the child of famous parents and an even more famous grandparent, it seemed reasonable that a plethora of information about Nina would be available.

I couldn't have been more wrong. The paucity of data was astonishing. A quick search yielded only the bare bones facts that Nina had been born in Redding, Connecticut, on August 18, 1910, that she graduated from Barnard College in 1934, that she christened the Mark Twain Zephyr train in April of 1935 in Hannibal, Missouri, and that she died of an overdose of drugs in a Hollywood hotel on January 16, 1966, at the age of fifty-five.

More concerted initial digging yielded a charming watercolor portrait by Eulabee Dix housed at the National Museum of Women in the Arts, rumors of a possible marriage to artist Carl Roters, and a passport photo of a gawky, bespectacled ten-year-old Nina.

Locating and reading copies of *Mark Twain's Clara* by author Caroline Harnsberger and *My Husband Gabrilowitsch*, written by Clara Clemens herself, yielded a few more clues, mostly about Nina's childhood and her final declining years. The data-stream trickled to a halt, but a rough chronology of Nina's life could be constructed.

Nina had been raised in Europe from shortly after her birth until 1914 when the family returned to the United States. For the next several years, the family continued to travel extensively on her father's concert piano tours. When her father Ossip accepted the position as conductor of the Detroit Symphony Orchestra, that Michigan city continued to be the family's home base until Ossip's death in 1936.

That did put Nina in the same city where Charlie Lucia lived until 1920 and where his brother Ira and mother Harriet continued to live throughout the time Ossip was alive. It was also where Charlie Lucia and daughter Eileen, Susan's father Elwood Bailey—and his friend Bob Joughin—made those frequent trips up until about 1937.

Since Clara believed the Lucias to be relatives, this meant that Nina could certainly have known any of those three men.

Nina attended Barnard College from 1929 to 1934 and then stayed on in New York for the next couple of years. When mother Clara moved to California, Nina opted to move with her and spent the remainder of her life there until her death by overdose in 1966.

None of that gave us any real sense of Nina as a human being. Besides Carl Roters, who were the men in her life? Did she have a sense of humor? What did she look like other than in the limited number of photos we had seen? Did she have a lot of friends? Would it be possible to find any specific additional evidence to support or refute our evolving theory that she was Susan's mother?

During this search period, Susan decided to act upon my earlier suggestion of undergoing hypnosis to try to remember more about the lady who had taken her out of school as a child.

Having by this time seen photos of Nina, who was a petite dark-haired woman, we both had a strong suspicion that the lady in question had been Nina. It would explain so much about the swift action taken to spirit Susan away if Nina were violating some "rules" about keeping her distance.

Susan searched and evaluated the credentials of several professionals before settling on the services of Dianne Greyerbiehl, Ph.D. Four advanced degrees (including an interdisciplinary Ph.D. in neuro-cognitive psychology and speech pathology, and a master's degree in counseling) and over thirty years of experience, made Greyerbiehl's credentials impressive.

When Susan got out of the session, she called me immediately, voice shaking with emotion, and said:

> *Most of what came out of the session was just what I already told you, but with one major new memory. When I first walked into the principal's office, he didn't just say, 'Your aunt is here.' He said, "Your Aunt Nina is here!' Then the lady turned to him and said, "It's Nina [with a long "e" sound], not Nina [with a long "i" sound].*

Despite having half-expected this answer, we were both astounded. The ties between Susan and Nina were strengthening. As time went on, and we interviewed people who knew her, we found that she had indeed pronounced her name as "Neena."

The data search continued for months. Then, in March of 2008, there it was—a 1986 article from The *San Francisco Chronicle* entitled "Tragedy of

Mark Twain's Daughter" indicating that a treasure trove of Nina's photos and possessions had been donated to The Mark Twain House & Museum in Hartford, Connecticut.

Firing off an email led to a response from Jeffrey Mainville, then Curatorial Assistant at The House.

We couldn't have been more fortunate when we found Jeff. Passionate about his work, and intrigued by our story, he engaged in concerted digging until he located the mysterious box of Nina's things.

He delved through the box and copied a few photos that he thought seemed to be from the key period of roughly 1936 to 1950 and selected any that included babies or images of Nina with a man.

Among the photos were two with a baby perhaps a few months old and then several more of a toddler. There was one of Nina all dressed up and gazing adoringly at a man in a fedora. I forwarded all the photos to Susan. Just as for the first times she saw photos of Nina and Ossip, her reaction was instantaneous:

That's my father in that photo with Nina, and I swear that baby could be me.

Nina with Elwood Bailey

Photo from Nina's personal effects
Courtesy of The Mark Twain House & Museum
Hartford, CT

Chapter 11

Susan

July 2008

A Trip to Hartford

I HADN'T SEEN MY FATHER, Elwood Bailey, since the day before he died on August 17, 1946. Now, there in my email as a forward from the Mark Twain House & Museum, was a picture of him with Nina Gabrilowitsch staring up at him adoringly! My heart was pounding at seeing this image, but the attachment contained more.

There was a picture of Nina and what looked like a newborn baby, and then one of a toddler out on a porch with other adults. These toddler pictures looked like the first baby picture I had of me, but they were fuzzy so I couldn't be sure although the hairline and the curl over the forehead was identical.

How was it possible that the Mark Twain House had pictures of my father and a baby that looked like me? Deb and I decided immediately that we needed to go to Connecticut to see what was in that donated box of Nina's possessions. We could not have imagined how much material there would be.

July 2008 found us meeting Curatorial Assistant Jeff Mainville at The Mark Twain House & Museum in Hartford where we were welcomed as long-lost members of the family. Standing in the ultra-modern museum portion of the site, and looking out the windows at the beautiful Victorian house fronting on Farmington Avenue, I realized that I was visiting the home that had been most dear to Mark Twain's heart, where he had raised his children and where he had done much of his writing.

I did not know it until later, but out of my earshot, Jeff immediately said to Deb, "It is astonishing how much Susan looks like Clara Clemens."

Jeff first took us on a private tour of the Mark Twain House itself, a beautiful Victorian "painted lady" and showed us parts that the general public never gets to see. One room that was off the dining room and that greatly impressed me was the butler's pantry. It was full of china, crystal, and even the original silverware that the Clemens family had actually used.

When Jeff took us to the children's bedroom where the three girls slept and played, for some reason chills ran up and down my spine. He showed us the bed where Susy Clemens, who I was possibly named after, had slept.

That's when it struck me—if Nina were really my mother, then this was where *my grandmother* Clara had spent much of her childhood. She had slept in that bed and played in this room with her sisters.

When Jeff allowed us a very brief foray into Mark Twain's personal study, I was even more overwhelmed at the thought that this was where *my great-grandfather* had written some of his most famous works. I felt such a connection to this family.

On the outside porches there were American flags draped on each balcony. It was a windy day and Jeff took me out on the balcony where he ask me to straighten the flags and took some quick pictures. He also wanted pictures of me on the octagonal shaped porch where the most famous picture of Samuel and Olivia Clemens and their daughters had been taken.

This was a humbling experience for me and I felt tears running down my cheeks. They were not sad tears but rather tears of joy that I was in this place where I had never been and yet felt so much a part of.

Jeff then took us to the archival area upstairs where I soon learned about museum "white gloves." They are thin cotton gloves, apparently not well made, as I went through about six pairs of them over the next few days. You have to wear them when touching articles and artifacts in museum archives so oil won't be transferred from your skin onto the priceless documents.

Genealogist Deb seemed perfectly at home with this process but it was all new to me. It's impossible to explain how I felt in that room handling letters and postcards actually touched by Nina and Clara. I wanted to take off those gloves and touch them myself but knew that wasn't allowed.

Watching materials come out of that box was like opening Christmas presents. Prior to this visit, we had only seen a handful of pictures of Nina, and now here were a veritable feast of photos. There were Nina, and Clara, and Ossip, and a variety of men and women we assumed were friends. Jeff had me hold up a picture of Nina and Clara on each side of my face and then he took pictures of the three of us!

Deb seemed most thrilled with the handful of postcards and letters to and from Nina. That's when the researcher in her went on point. She was practically vibrating with excitement.

Going through the collection, the view that I previously held of Nina changed drastically. Before going to the museum, I had very little information about her that was not known to the general public, and that mostly negative.

Here, emerging like a phoenix from that box, was a delightful, intelligent, funny human being who worshipped her father, had problems with her mother and stepfather, had loving and loyal lifetime friends, and who had her share of trouble with the men in her life. I could relate to all of that.

To the world, she was "Mark Twain's last heir," an alcoholic who committed suicide and died alone in a hotel room. To me, Nina was becoming a real person, someone who was perhaps done in by the circumstances of her life but kept trying to make something of it and to find meaning in it right up until the end.

I thought back to the one day I had with her when I was seven years old, to her telling me she had named me Madeline and that I was a little French girl, to her buying me the first ice cream soda I had ever tasted, to her holding my hand in the movie theater. That was the Nina I remembered and was rediscovering as I sifted through her things in my thin white gloves. I fell in love with Nina in that little room in the house where her mother had grown up.

Jeff graciously made copies of the letters and postcards and some of the key photographs that we wanted so that our research could continue after we left Hartford. Now, here we were with a fat stack of information on Nina and Clara that probably few people in the world even knew existed.

While I was out of the room, Jeff told Deb: "You have no idea how many people contact me every year claiming to be related to Mark Twain. This is the first time I have ever believed it could be true. I don't know if you will ever be able to find the concrete proof that you are seeking, but I sincerely hope that you do."

Deb said that she couldn't wait to get home, delve into the papers, and "let Nina out of the box for all the world to see."

As he was walking us to our car on the last day, Jeff said to me, "Susan, I hope you found what you were looking for here."

I told him that I had found a certain peace there and finally, a certainty in my own mind of who the family was that I had been searching for my entire life. Now I thirsted for more knowledge of the specifics of my mother's life and how our lives—lived separately except for one memorable day—compared.

Susan with Nina and Clara

Taken by Jeffrey Mainville, Assistant Curator
The Mark Twain House & Museum
Hartford, CT

CHAPTER 12

DEB

INTERNATIONAL MONKEY: NINA (1910-1928)

"Nina is wide awake and her mind is one great camera."
THE TIMES, LONDON, JULY 31, 1921

IN AN AUGUST 9, 1907, letter to young Dorothy Quick, Mark Twain wrote: "What is a home without a child?" Sadly, Twain did not live to see the birth of his first and only grandchild.

Just shy of four months after the death of her famous grandfather, Nina Gabrilowitsch entered the world on August 18, 1910, in Redding, Connecticut. Unlike Susan, who had been far from welcomed by Drucilla Bailey, the addition of Nina to the Gabrilowitsch household was a source of great joy to her mother Clara.

The love affair between her parents had been tempestuous. Clara Clemens, a carefree young woman studying piano in Vienna under noted Polish music professor Theodor Leschetizky, first set eyes on her future husband circa 1898 at a dinner party hosted by her famous parent.

Leschetizky had accepted Twain's invitation to dinner with the stipulation that he be allowed to bring two former pupils. One of those pupils was rising Russian-born piano star Ossip Gabrilowitsch. Clara later related that Ossip "shone like a lamp in a cave."

They would not, however, marry for nearly a decade. Letters between the two show a couple conflicted by their own fears of commitment and buffeted by their rigorous schedules. Ossip had also been concerned that Clara would not be accepting of his Jewish heritage, but that fear was clearly laid to rest.

Ossip's star was on the rise, and his concert schedule took him all over the world. Clara continued traveling with her parents. Despite carrying on an extended long-distance flirtation punctuated by infrequent meetings, both Clara and Ossip expressed aversion to marriage, even jokingly referring to each other as "Padre" and "Nun."

As her mother Olivia's health declined, Clara became more and more caught up in the role of nursemaid. A brief engagement with Ossip was soon broken. Olivia's death in 1904 further strained the relationship between Clara and Ossip.

It was not until after Ossip suffered a nearly fatal bout of mastoiditis, and Clara had nursed him back to health at the Clemens family home at Stormfield, that the couple finally wed in Redding, Connecticut, on October 6, 1909. Six months later, Clara's beloved father, Mark Twain, was gone.

In October of 1910, with Nina just six weeks old, the Gabrilowitsch family sailed for Europe, accompanied by German nursemaid Marie Koehn. This sojourn in Europe was to last until 1914.

Nina's first several months of life were spent at the Palast Hotel in Munich where Ossip's brother George and sister Pauline were frequent guests. In the spring of 1911, the family settled into a home at Aiblinger-Strasse 4 in Nymphenburg, a German community located approximately five miles from Munich. Summers were spent in the tiny town of Kreuth.

Clara and Ossip had found a lifestyle that eminently suited them. Both thrived on the cultural richness of Europe and the musical sub-culture around them. The couple formed friendships that were to last a lifetime with musical giant Bruno Walter and his wife Elsa and with conductor Leopold Stokowski.

And what of Nina in this time? In a fashion typical of wealthy households of the day, much of Nina's childrearing was undertaken by nursemaids, much as Clara's own had been. The heavy involvement of her parents in the world of music and the general social whirl certainly limited the time that Nina spent with them.

But, by all indications, Nina's early childhood, unlike Susan's, was a stable and happy one.

The family's idyllic days came to a sudden and frightening end in the summer of 1914 with the advent of World War I. With Germany and Russia at war, Ossip's Russian citizenship suddenly drew the attention of the government.

While young Nina slept, German officials entered the Gabrilowitsch home in Kreuth and arrested Ossip, leaving a frightened Clara to fend for herself in a home where officials had cut the phone lines and were guarding the house. Knowing that Russian "spies" were often summarily executed, the next several hours were terrifying.

While his fame as a concert pianist did not exempt him from arrest, the family's connections extricated Ossip from the situation. Clara managed to steal out of the house through a back garden and call friend Bruno Walter, then Music Director at the Munich Royal Opera.

Walter in turn prevailed upon Herr von Treutler, Prussian Ambassador to Bavaria and a casual acquaintance of the Gabrilowitsch family, to intervene. Von Treutler's efforts resulted in Ossip's release. The family quickly left Germany for Switzerland and thence to Italy.

Eager to leave Europe amid the escalating threats, Ossip and Clara nonetheless lingered long enough to untangle the paperwork needed to permit Nina's German-born nursemaid to accompany them home.

The ship's log shows that the family embarked on October 11, 1914, from Naples, Italy, and arrived in New York on October 28, 1914. For the first time, Nina had returned to her native soil. She was four years old.

At home, Clara and Ossip, dedicated lovers of the German culture, were surprised to find that their belief that Russia had started the war was a sentiment that led to social ostracism by many of their friends.

Clara, to whom social acceptance was so important, particularly suffered from this temporary change in social status.

Growing up, she seems to have felt that her father's love rested far more easily on her sister Susy than it did on her. As a result, she displayed a lifelong predilection for "doing the right thing" socially and was very uncomfortable when public censure of any sort was directed her way.

This same fear of having the Twain legend tarnished in any way eventually led her to suppress some of Twain's more controversial works such as his *Letters From The Earth*.

For the next four seasons, the family moved about, spending time in

New York, Ardmore and Byrn Mawr, Pennsylvania, St. Albans, Vermont, and Seal Harbor, Maine. Ossip and Clara surrounded themselves with a primarily expatriate community of musicians and artists.

For Nina, this temporary respite in her parents' social life must have been a delight. In *My Husband Gabrilowitsch*, Clara describes how the rotating cast of characters decamping to and from the Gabrilowitsch home formed a "very special kind of school, for Nina's benefit" with everyone taking turns at being instructor.

World famous conductor Leopold Stokowski apparently delighted in playing "lion" for little Nina. How she must have basked in all the attention! Her exposure to this moveable feast of international culture surely helped earn her the charming family nickname of "International Monkey."

Even in such happy circumstances, it is apparent that the time Clara spent focused on husband Ossip far outweighed time she spent with Nina. While not inconsistent with the typical manner in which most children of wealthy parents were then raised, it still created a certain distance between mother and child.

In one small, telling comment, Clara herself unwittingly articulated this gap. In describing a photography session in which Ossip had requested that she be photographed having breakfast in bed, she commented on the various poses she held and remarked on one with "Nina in my arms, something she had never done for breakfast before."

In an effort to build greater financial security and stability, Ossip began supplementing his highly successful concert piano tours with stints as a guest conductor. In 1918, he began to cast about for a permanent spot as a symphony conductor in a city whose performance schedule was light enough to permit him to continue his regular tours as a concert pianist.

As we had already learned, when the city of Detroit, Michigan, made an offer for him to conduct their fledgling symphony orchestra, he snapped it up with the stipulation that Detroit build a new symphony hall. It was to be the same hall where Clara would eventually bring Susan to hear her very first symphony when she was about eight years old.

For eight-year-old Nina, this meant that the remainder of her childhood and young adulthood would be spent in Detroit.

The family rented a home at 1068 Cass Avenue, moved to another at 5456 Cass and then, by 1924, settled into ownership of a home at 611 Boston Boulevard in the swank Boston-Edison neighborhood.

"Settled in" is perhaps a misnomer as the travel-loving family continued to crisscross the country and the world. Ships' logs show Clara, Ossip, and young Nina on European trips in 1921, 1922, 1923, and 1924.

Clearly those trips were considered educational for young Nina, as three of the four occurred during the school year, indicating that Nina was pulled out of school to accompany her parents.

Ironically, Susan was also pulled out of school regularly as a child to accompany her cousin Eileen and her husband Russ on trips.

On one such trip, an article headline in the July 31, 1921, edition of London's *Times* trumpeted: "Mark Twain's Grandchild Makes Big Hit in London." Ten-year-old Nina, it seems, had won the hearts of Londoners and vice versa.

Writer Emilie Frances Bauer, laboring under the mistaken impression that this was Nina's first trip abroad wrote:

> *Only the pen of the illustrious Mark Twain could have done justice to the sayings, the doings and the enjoyment of the first travels abroad of little Nina Gabrilowitsch, and that pen is stilled... How interested he would have been to note the impressions of his only grandchild whom he never knew.*

> *The more the pity, for the mere remembrance of him would have been her greatest treasure through the years that are to come to her and which promise to bring her a great heritage from the master humorist and analyst. Those who knew Mark Twain, the man, can see in her outspoken frankness, her well-nigh singular grasp of things as they are related to the sense of humor and her fearlessness of expression.*

Bauer was charmed by Nina's "gentlest and most musical American accent. Her smiles . . . brightened one up wonderfully. I wished the two little drummer boys who beat in . . . a pageant band could have heard Nina say of them: "Oh, Look! Ain't they Puffickly cute!"

Nina's happy, privileged childhood continued with summers spent in Maine, at camp, and on Michigan's Mackinac Island.

Nina's childhood drew to a close with her graduation in 1928 from Detroit's prestigious Liggett School. Gabrilowitsch family home movies in the possession of The Mark Twain House & Museum show a cap and gown clad Nina clowning for the camera, filming fellow students, and generally grinning from ear to ear. It continues with images of her graduation party at the family home in Detroit.

There, among the party guests, were a couple that Susan recognized as her Aunt Bruce Lucia and a man she presumed to be her Uncle Charlie Lucia. There could be no more doubt that well prior to Susan's birth, Clara and Nina had known and socialized with members of the Lucia family.

Nina and her nurse, probably Marie Koehn

Photo from Nina's personal effects
Courtesy of The Mark Twain House & Museum

CHAPTER 13

DEB

YOUNG ADULTHOOD: NINA (1929-1935)

NINA SHOOK THE DUST OFF Detroit in 1929, heading off to New York City and Barnard College. For the first time in her life, she was out from under the watchful eye of nursemaids and parents and able to make her own choices.

At Barnard, Nina met the first great love of her life, Carl George Roters. When Carl passed away in 1989, his obituary indicated that he first became involved with Nina in 1934; however her letters home began to mention him from the time she left the residence hall system and moved into her own apartment during her junior year in 1931. While the exact date is uncertain, the general time frame indicates that Nina met Carl around the time of a major upheaval in his life—his divorce.

How attractive Carl must have been to Nina, a cosmopolitan young woman who grew up surrounded by art and music, and who happily spent the first four years of her life in Germany.

Carl, born in December 1898 to German-born Charles Roters and his first-generation American wife Helen, was nearly twelve years Nina's senior, a pattern she was to repeat many times in her life. While father Charles, involved in the grocery business, was solidly blue collar, Carl showed a passion and flair for art from a very young age.

Per his 1918 World War I draft registration card, twenty-year-old Carl was already making his living as an artist. By the time of the 1920 United States Federal Census, he was listed as an artist with his own studio.

On December 8, 1923, the *New York Times* reported the marriage of Carl Roters to first wife Kathleen Feehan, the daughter of an Irish immigrant father who served as coachman for a private family.

In an interview with Carl's daughter Carlene (from his second marriage to a woman named Ramona Morgan), she disclosed that the couple were believed to have married in secret many years prior to that date, but no record of an earlier marriage was located in New York City records.

The 1930 United States Federal Census showed Carl and Kathleen still married, but the marriage had been disintegrating for years. Carlene indicated that after Kathleen took a solo trip to Europe (in 1926), the relationship never recovered.

Ships' logs show Carl himself returning alone to the United States from a trip to St. Johns, Newfoundland, in October 1930 and again from Hamilton, Bermuda, (a place beloved by Mark Twain) in October 1931.

The end of Carl's first marriage came shortly thereafter. The December 15, 1931, *Nevada State Journal* reported the divorce of Kathleen from Carl Roters on the grounds of "extreme cruelty."

While there is no evidence to suggest that Nina contributed in any way to the break-up of Carl's marriage, the timing of their meeting certainly suggests that Nina was Carl's "rebound" relationship.

Photos of Carl held by The Mark Twain House & Museum show a handsome, debonair, smiling man with a young, happy Nina. Their relationship was to last for several years, and their friendship for a lifetime.

Mother Clara, however, was less than pleased with Nina's choice of beau. Clearly viewing Carl as a Good-Time-Charlie who was introducing Nina to hard drinking and a fast lifestyle, she wrote:

> *You greatly underrate your intelligence and intellectual capacity, but you do not make the best of them because you lack the self-control in certain directions that you could easily have!...I find no pleasure in seeing you deliberately throw away good Health, which means throwing away cart-loads of will-power at the same time; for it is very difficult to keep a strong spirit with a weak body.*

The first cracks in the mother-daughter relationship had begun to show. While Clara blamed Carl Roters for Nina's introduction to drinking, this time of experimentation with making adult choices seems ordinary behavior for a young college woman.

Carl, on the heels of a messy divorce, quite likely released stress with social drinking. However, there is no evidence that his drinking was in any way out of control, and he continued to pursue his career as an artist. By the time of the 1939 New York World's Fair, he had begun to achieve repute as a mural painter.

Later in life, Nina claimed to have been briefly married to Carl, but no record of such marriage has ever been located. Paradoxically, daughter Carlene indicated that while her father had loved Nina, he had never married her *because* her drinking was getting out of control, and he simply could not see himself married to a woman he believed was on the road to alcoholism.

Nina, on what today is referred to tongue in cheek as "the five-year plan," graduated from Barnard in 1934, achieving a feat her parents had not. Father Ossip Gabrilowitsch, a brilliant, multilingual man who came from a highly educated family, had never earned a college degree due to his musical studies and touring. Clara, also possessed of a bright inquisitive mind, was a product of the late Victorian era when pursuit of university studies was a rarity for a woman.

During college, and shortly after graduation, Nina began to appear in theatre productions and to dabble in sports and charity events. She also began to take on the mantle of representative of the Twain family.

News articles from the time period mention her waiting tables at a charity event in Los Angeles, playing in Greek games and other sporting events with fellow co-eds, as a guest of honor at Carnegie Hall for a production of her famous grandfather's *Tom Sawyer,* and attending a dinner at the Waldorf Astoria in honor of the centennial of Twain's birth.

Clara, ceding her usual role at such events to Nina, allowed her the honors at the christening of The *Mark Twain Zephyr* train in Hannibal, Missouri in October 1935. It was one of the photos taken at that event that, viewed over seventy years later, sent a shockwave through Susan Bailey.

Nina did not know it at the time, but the halcyon days of her youth and young adulthood were drawing to an end.

Nina and Ossip

Photo from Nina's personal effects
Courtesy of The Mark Twain House & Museum
Hartford, CT

CHAPTER 14

DEB

THE PIVOTAL YEARS: NINA (1935-1937)

"It is wonderful to be able to remember such love as you had in your life...If I could find a Love like that, I would gladly give up anything and everything."

NINA GABRILOWITSCH TO MOTHER CLARA, ORIGINAL LETTER, MARCH 3, 1938

B Y 1935, TROUBLE WAS BREWING both for the Gabrilowitsch family in Detroit and the Bailey and Lucia families in Tampa and Detroit. In Tampa, the affair between Susan's Aunt Bruce and former County Sheriff Bob Joughin was roaring and the long-standing friendship between Bob, Bruce's husband Charlie, and Susan's dad Elwood Bailey, was severely strained.

For Nina, fresh from graduation in 1934, the next few months in New York had been a time of great pleasure as she acted in theatre and enjoyed her freedom.

Then, on March 22, 1935, the foundations of her world were shaken when her beloved "Vati" (Father) suffered a stomach hemorrhage while preparing for a concert performance in New York.

Displaying his usual indomitable will, Ossip soldiered on, and over Clara's violent objections, proceeded with his planned performance the next evening. The family could not know it at the time, but Ossip had just given his last public performance.

Returning to Detroit, Ossip checked into the Henry Ford Hospital for what was anticipated to be a brief stay. Thinking his prognosis to be good, on April 25, 1935, Nina and Clara even made the trip to Hannibal, Missouri, for the dedication of The *Mark Twain Zephyr*.

Just a few days later, Ossip was scheduled for surgery. Clara, in *My Husband Gabrilowitsch,* stated that she was worried at this news, "but neither of us had the least foreboding of a mortal illness. I believe we thought nothing so cruel could happen while we were still young in heart."

Mother and daughter waited together on May 3, 1935, hoping for good news. It did not come. Returning from surgery, the doctor delivered the verdict: Ossip Gabrilowitsch had cancer and was expected to live only a few months. Clara made the decision not to share the devastating diagnosis with Ossip:

> *the patient must not suspect the nature of his illness, nor doubt that perfect health would return. An unseen power supports us in these tragic lies and packs us in mental armor.*

It was the same decision that Drucilla Bailey initially made a decade later when her husband Elwood was also diagnosed with terminal cancer. Up until his final year, he thought he was suffering from stomach ulcers.

Clara devoted herself from that point on to her husband's care while Nina attempted to get on with her life, continuing acting lessons at the Dekohanava School of Acting in New York.

Caught in the fiction created by her mother, Nina could not communicate with her father in an honest and open fashion about their impending permanent separation, but was forced to maintain a light-hearted communication with her beloved father whom she affectionately addressed as "Brown Bear."

That she did indeed go along with Clara's decision to keep the truth from Ossip is evidenced in letters such as one of April 7, 1935, in which she wrote: "I am tickled to hear that you are getting much better and being a very good Bear."

After a second surgery in July of 1935, Ossip went home and experienced a brief remission. Nina, Clara, and Ossip were able to share a final Christmas together that year.

By early 1936, Ossip's health took a decided turn for the worse and, per author Caroline Harnsberger's interviews with Clara, Nina made frequent trips home.

A February 23, 1936, news article mentions her playing an angel in an amateur production by the Detroit Theatre Arts group and another April article mentions her as a member of the same group.

Whether it was this troupe or another touring theatre company is unclear, but in a postcard to her father that was mailed from Charlevoix, Michigan, Nina shared news of her performances:

> *Our play is getting along well but the audiences are pretty sparse— due to the fact that tickets cost 75 cents;...be a good little Bear and don't forget me! Loads of love—Monkey.*

Harnsberger also makes reference to letters written by Nina to Clara from Ironton in Michigan's Upper Peninsula, but the date of such letters is unspecified.

On April 3, 1936, Ossip Gabrilowitsch executed a Last Will and Testament requesting, among other things, that simple funeral services be held at Orchestra Hall with the Detroit Symphony Orchestra providing the music. The terms of his will specified that his personal property and effects (excluding stocks and bonds), be split equally between Clara and Nina.

Substantial bequests were made to his brother George and sister Pauline (listed as living in Zurich, Switzerland) and smaller bequests to his secretary Phyllis Harrington and to chauffer Edward Glanzer. All of the real estate, stocks and bonds, and the residue of his estate went to wife Clara.

The terms of Ossip's will regarding contingent beneficiaries provide a window into his assessment of daughter's Nina's maturity. In the event that Clara predeceased him, Ossip specified that the estate was to go to his executors in trust to be managed on Nina's behalf with the income therefrom doled out to her in the form of quarterly allowances.

Despite the fact that Nina was twenty-six years old and a college graduate, her father did not trust her to manage her own money.

Susan and I speculated that Clara was likely behind these terms as it reflected a money management methodology that she later utilized to care for Nina, the daughter she deemed incompetent to handle her own affairs.

The will also provided that in the event both Clara and Nina predeceased him (highly unlikely in light of his terminal condition), the principal and income of the trust were to be turned over "to her [Nina's] issue if such there be."

Ironically, since the stocks and bonds constituted the bulk of Ossip's personal effects, after payment of estate taxes, a widow's allowance to Clara during probate, and other expenses, Nina effectively received nothing from her father's will, a situation he probably never anticipated. By this time he was probably not in a position to be thinking clearly and trusted his wife and attorney to do the best thing for all.

As early 1936 saw Ossip's decline, so too was Harriet Lucia, mother of Charlie Lucia and beloved grandmother of Eileen, failing.

While the distance in terms of social status was great between the posh Gabrilowitsch home on Boston Boulevard and the blue-collar Lucia abode on West Philadelphia Street, the two families actually lived just over a mile from each other in Detroit.

We know that Charlie made visits to his ailing mother with brother-in-law Elwood in tow, just as Nina made visits to her dying father. Since the home movies of Nina's Liggett School graduation show that the Gabrilowitsch family knew their Lucia "cousins," it is certainly conceivable that visits took place between the two sickrooms.

It seems more than plausible that the simultaneous illnesses of Ossip and Harriet threw a grieving Nina together with Elwood Bailey that spring.

The last specific mention of Nina in a performance that year seems to be the July 6 postcard to her father although her work with the touring company may have continued beyond that date. On August 28, 1936, Clara sent Nina a letter describing Ossip's state:

How I have absorbed and assimilated all your darling expressions of affection! They warmed up my poor frozen heart—frozen with anguish these days, because Vati is so utterly and unspeakably wretched. I am ready to pray for his release...I am looking forward to our telephone call on Sunday.

In light of the incredible closeness between father and daughter, it seems astounding that Nina would have stayed away from her father's bedside in what were so clearly his dying days unless there was a very good reason for her absence.

On September 14, 1936, cancer claimed the life of Ossip Gabrilowitsch. Clara and Nina, two sensitive women, for whom loving, responsible, gregarious Ossip had been the anchor, were set adrift.

By newspaper accounts, and Clara's own report, neither wife nor daughter attended Ossip's funeral at Orchestra Hall in Detroit.

For Clara, who had thrived on the social attention of being the wife of the symphony's conductor, and who was highly conscious of maintaining a proper social image, this absence seems nearly inconceivable.

But if Nina was indeed Susan's mother, and Susan was born sometime in late 1936 or early 1937, a very rational reason existed for the absence of Clara and Nina at Ossip's Detroit funeral—Nina was pregnant and showing.

Other than condolence telegrams and letters and Clara's responses, little is known about the movements of Clara and Nina in the three months following Ossip's death. Clara's cousin Jervis Langdon made a trip to Detroit and accompanied Ossip's body back to Elmira where a second funeral was held.

Because the funeral was closed to all but family, it is unknown whether Nina attended. What is certain is that Clara and Nina set sail for Europe sometime that fall, arriving in Rome prior to Christmas.

On January 10, 1937, Nina addressed a letter to friend Dorothy Glenz (copy held by Dorothy's daughter, Miggie Warms). Writing from a hotel in Bordighera, Italy, Nina described traveling for some time without mother Clara. Her movements as described to Dorothy place her in Rome shortly before Christmas: "On Dec 22 I moved from the Parisien to the Grand Hotel.

She was clearly taking no pains to hide at that point as she wrote:

Xmas day there was a beautiful tree in the dining room, mistletoe, & lovely table decorations. Graham Erskine came to the hotel and had lunch with me.

Erskine, in Rome working on a doctoral degree in architecture, seems to have been someone known to both Dorothy and Nina.

The letter also describes other post-Christmas meetings with Americans and even relays an incident that took place on a train from Rome to Florence:

> *An old duffer of about 50 came into my compartment and started to chat with me. You should have heard my painful efforts to speak Italian for two hours! He was very nice, and all was fine, till suddenly he tried to get fresh—& that ended our acquaintanceship. He was married with a little girl. Really, something ought to be done for men that age—their wives never seem to suffice.*

Clara and Nina reunited sometime shortly after this letter was written, for passenger lists show that the two set sail for home on January 27, 1937, departing from Villefranche, France, on the ship *Rex*. The voyage was to be a rough one, reported in a *New York Times* article, as one of the worst storms in the captain's experience:

> *Mrs. Clara Gabrilowitsch, daughter of Mark Twain, left the ship with her arm in a sling and a bandage on her head. The injuries, not serious, were suffered when she was thrown against the side of her cabin in the storm. She was accompanied by her daughter, Nina.*

No baby accompanied Nina home. Her long grieving had begun.

CHAPTER 15

SUSAN

1936–1944

POOR LITTLE FRENCH GIRL

MY CHILDHOOD WAS SO DIFFERENT from Nina's who always knew who her parents were and her place in the world.

I was a little girl at home in my bed down by the Hillsborough River, but I woke up having *that* dream again. It came to me over and over with new details each time, but the setting was always the same.

I was living with three people in a small house that was cozy but dark, and in retrospect, looked like a cottage to me because the ceilings were low. It was the only house I knew then, and I felt safe there.

An older man and woman lived in the house with me. There was also a younger woman named Gladys, who walked with a slight limp. She handled most of my care, watching over me at play, feeding me, and giving me my bath. She slept on a cot in the same room as me. I was in a crib so I must have been very young in these dreams.

I loved Gladys and liked the man a lot but the older woman never paid any attention to me and I never felt like she liked me.

My own little room in this house was right off the kitchen. The kitchen's back door led to a little porch and a small park. Across a small sidewalk were more houses like ours whose kitchen doors also opened up onto the park.

In the dream, the older couple always spoke French to me, a language that I dreamt in for the first five or so years of my life. Gladys sometimes spoke French, but usually spoke English to me. I understood both languages.

The three adults almost always spoke French to each other but another language that I didn't understand was sometimes spoken.

In the kitchen, a single light bulb hung down from the ceiling. One of my greatest delights was to beg for the man to hold me up so I could pull this string repeatedly and turn the light on and off, on and off. When he held me up like that I could see that he had a round bald spot on the top of his head.

I also loved to go out the kitchen door into the park area in back of the house and play with two little girls who lived in the house directly behind ours. I could not understand the language they spoke but it didn't interfere with our play.

The oldest girl seemed to be about my size and her name was Synopia. Her sister was smaller but, if I ever heard her name, I don't remember it. The man was the one who always took me outside to play. I think it was because that's where all the neighborhood men gathered, smoking and talking. They always had a lot to talk about.

One very clear memory I have about this time concerned my baby bottle, which I always called my "bottle of monk." This was always so clear that I didn't think it was a dream but a true memory.

The three adults were trying to wean me off the bottle. They would put a baby bottle and a glass of milk side by side on a chair and ask me to choose the glass of milk. I would always take the bottle of monk. There was no punishment involved, and I didn't care that I wasn't the "big girl" they wanted me to be. The bottle was a comfort to me.

After several times they gave up on this method of training and just let me have my bottle. As an adult I wondered why I called it a "bottle of monk." I thought perhaps "monk" might be milk in another language. I couldn't find it on the Internet.

But what I *did* find was that in the 1930s in Germany they sold rum in bottles with a monk carved on the bottle. They were called, "bottles of Monk," or Monk bottles. I can just see my caregivers as a joke saying to each other, "Oh, go ahead and give her a bottle of Monk!"

Now, as an adult, exploring the nearly overwhelming idea that Nina Clemens Gabrilowitsch could be my mother, those childhood memories and dreams suddenly took on a new significance.

Clues were tumbling one over the other. I dreamt in French as a child and Nina was known to have sailed back from France in late January of 1937, around the time I believe I was born. Nina had told me I was "a little French girl," and that she had named me Madeline. Per Ossip's will, his brother George and sister Pauline, both unmarried and middle-aged, were living in Zurich in 1936. Both spoke fluent French.

It seemed important that I try to retrieve as much detail as possible about the people in those childhood dreams that I now fully believed to be actual memories. Deciding to again put my trust in therapist Dianne Greyerbiehl, PhD, I returned for another hypnotherapy session, fervently hoping that I might recall the name of the place where the little house had been or the names of the older couple.

I was to be disappointed in those hopes, but the session took me right back to my time as a toddler. Several startling additional memories emerged that explained how I came to live in the United States.

Since my little bedroom was right off the kitchen, and the kitchen was where the family generally congregated in the evening, I sometimes overheard things that certainly weren't meant for my little ears.

On one occasion, I recalled the older couple talking about what they were going to do with me, and the woman said, "There is no other way. Her father will have to come and get her." I was scared because I knew they were talking about me and I didn't know who this "father" was and where I would be going. Theirs was the only home I knew.

My next very strong memory was of being on a ship with Gladys and feeling very, very sick. Dr. Greyerbiehl said that my memories of that seasickness were so vivid that she feared I would be literally ill.

We had arranged in advance that if anything in the session upset me too much, she would direct me to a "safe" place of my choosing. I chose my wonderful little bedroom that I loved very much in the years I had lived with Eileen. It was necessary to "send" me there at this point.

The next memory that surfaced was of arriving in a city, being handed over to a man and an older woman and being told that he was my daddy and she my grandmother.

I had just met my father, Elwood Bailey, and his mother, "Big Mama," for the first time.

Then I realized Gladys was leaving me and I started crying and trying to get out of Elwood's arms and get her to take me back. She told me she would be back in a few minutes and turned and walked away. That's the last time I ever saw her.

I didn't remember the actual train ride, but the memory that surfaced was of arriving at the train station in Tampa, Florida, and meeting the man I later came to know as Uncle Bob Joughin and my aunt, Bruce Lucia. We then went to Bob and Bruce's house where I met Eileen and Drucilla for the very first time.

That first night in Florida was frightening to me. After supper, where I had to drink my milk from a glass, I was put to bed in the front bedroom. It was a big double bed and I had only slept in a small crib before. After my daddy kissed me goodnight, he turned off the light and closed the door. I didn't remember ever sleeping without Gladys in my room or without a little night light.

I started crying but it was only a few minutes until Eileen opened the door and came in. She had a small lamp with her which she placed on the dresser and turned on. Then she got into bed with me and hugged me until I fell asleep. For the rest of the time we lived with Aunt Bruce, Eileen slept with me every night and left the little lamp light on.

Although I called Drucilla "Mother," I spent a lot of my time with Eileen when she wasn't in school. I don't know why a teenage girl would welcome a toddler into her life and take such good care of her, but she did. I had been so attached to Gladys but I transferred this attachment to Eileen and slowly I forgot about Gladys or that I had ever had another life in another country.

When we moved into our own house by the Hillsborough River they again got me a crib to sleep in. Since we were no longer living with Eileen's family, it was a comfort not to be in a big bed by myself.

One day when I was about three, Drucilla told me she was going to get me a baby brother. I asked her if I could go with her and she said, "Go brush your teeth and I'll wait for you."

I ran to brush my teeth, but, to my disappointment, when I came outside, she was gone. Sometime later, she came back with my new baby brother, Bobby. She put him in the crib I had slept in the night before.

The day Drucilla brought him home, there were a lot of her family members visiting, including her father. I wasn't sure whether I liked this new baby, and I climbed into the crib to get a better look at him.

He started crying, so I bit him on the arm. Then he started wailing. The next thing I knew, Drucilla's father yanked me out of the crib by one arm and gave me a really hard spanking in front of all the people there. I was shocked because, prior to that day, no one had laid a hand on me in such anger.

Shortly thereafter, Drucilla herself began to heap her abuses on me, a practice that went on until my father sent me to Chicago to live with Eileen four years later.

During those scary years, I had several refuges. Daddy took me to work with him as often as he could, Eileen kept me with her as much as possible, and every night I still had my beautiful French dreams about Gladys, whom I had loved so much.

Believed to be caretaker Gladys with toddler Susan

Photo from Nina's personal effects
Courtesy of The Mark Twain House & Museum
Hartford, CT

CHAPTER 16

SUSAN

1946–1951

STORM CLOUDS GATHERING

IF YOU COULD SAY THAT A CHILD had an idyllic life, then my years growing up in Chicago with Eileen and Russ, might be described in that way. Russell's family owned several photography studios that employed a large number of people. One of the company's specialties was wedding photography, and right after Russ got back from the war, there were plenty of large posh nuptials to photograph in Chicago.

Because most of them took place on Saturdays when school was not in session, Russell loved to take me along. I had my own "little black bag" to carry the light meter, and being in charge of it made me feel very important.

Eileen, for her part, always made sure I had a beautiful, frilly dress and shiny Mary Jane shoes to wear. Russ, an excellent businessman, deliberately dressed us up so that it was hard to distinguish us from the invited guests. The wedding parties made a fuss over me and always involved me in their dances.

Most of the larger weddings involved people of Polish descent so I learned to dance a mean polka before I was nine. I basked in all the loving attention.

One of my other great pleasures was shopping in the Loop (Chicago's downtown area) with Eileen. She was a master at "retail therapy" before that term was ever invented. I especially loved the times when she allowed one of my friends to come with us.

Riding the elevated train toward downtown, I was fascinated that you could see right into peoples' apartments along the "El" route. Just before arriving at the Loop, the train went underground and became a subway. I thrilled at this plunge into the earth.

We would routinely get off at Carson Pirie Scott department store, have lunch there, and then go shopping in any store we wanted. I thought it grand that we never had to go back outside in the freezing weather to get to another store since they could be accessed underground.

We continued to live in Portage Park from the fall of 1946 to the summer of 1950, and I attended the local public elementary school. I had scads of friends in the neighborhood. In my new home, I could just run out the front door and always find someone to play with.

The setup that Russ constructed in our basement certainly helped my popularity as well. He had an ice cream bar built and a little wooden dance floor. Best of all, he installed a full size Wurlitzer bubbler jukebox with all the latest 45 rpm records on it.

Sometimes on Friday or Saturday evenings, I would invite friends, and Russ would stand behind the bar and make us anything we wanted—sundaes, banana splits, malts, ice cream sodas, hot chocolate. He had it all, but I never chose anything other than a vanilla ice cream soda, the treat I had shared with Nina on that frightening but memorable day in Tampa.

We also traveled a lot, going back and forth to Tampa three or four times a year, making trips to Detroit to see Uncle Ira (and, on the three memorable occasions, Clara), and in the summers, going up to Lake Geneva, Wisconsin.

Sometimes Eileen and Russ went on trips without me. On those occasions, they would leave me in Tampa, sometimes with Aunt Bruce, and sometimes with Drucilla. For me, that was a choice between the devil and the deep blue sea. However, I never complained because I had faith that Eileen would always come back for me.

Whenever I was in Florida for longer than a month, either Bruce or Drucilla would enroll me in a Tampa school temporarily. I can recall spending part of 5th grade at Broward Elementary, and part of 6th grade at Cleveland Elementary, both in Tampa. This bouncing around from Illinois to Florida was a situation I took in stride in my young life.

Just before I entered 8th grade in 1950, we moved to a house in Niles, Illinois, another suburb of Chicago, but twenty miles further from the Loop than Portage Park and very rural at the time with lots of farms and horse stables.

I hadn't wanted to move, but the first day we were there I met a girl my age, Barbara Rohner. We did everything together—cheerleading, trick-or-treating, shopping on Saturdays, babysitting—and we had a contest going to see which one of us could hit the 100-pound mark first. We thought that milestone would mean that our impending womanhood had arrived.

She was the first "best friend" that I'd ever had, and we are still friends to this day. I continued to move back and forth to Tampa as the whim caught Eileen, and spent part of my 7th and 8th grade years at Memorial Junior High in Tampa as well as at Niles Elementary.

Eileen didn't see anything wrong with taking me out of school whenever they wanted to travel. I was always able to catch up on my studies when I returned. She, like Nina's mother Clara, thought that taking me to different places was more educational than sitting in a stuffy classroom.

When she and Russ wanted to go somewhere, they just told me to pack my suitcase, and when we got home, I would simply show up again in school with some kind of note of explanation from Eileen.

One such trip was indirectly initiated by me. When my father died, I was nine years old, and I didn't know how to grieve for him. I didn't understand the true implications of death at that age. I didn't realize that I would never see him again. However, one day when I was thirteen, I started thinking about him and just missed him so much that I started crying.

Eileen came into the room and asked me what the matter was. I told her how much I missed my daddy. She said, "Okay, let's take a little trip back home."

So the next day found the two of us again driving to Florida. We went directly to Bay Pines Veteran's Cemetery and found my father's grave marker. She told me to take my time and tell him anything I wanted.

Sitting by that stone, I told him how much I loved him and missed him, but that Eileen was taking good care of me and that I was happy. Eileen was right there beside me holding my hand the whole time.

We then went back across the Bay, spent a few nights with Aunt Bruce, and then made our way back to Chicago. That time we stopped off in

Chattanooga to see Lookout Mountain. Life with Eileen was always an adventure, even on a trip to visit my father's grave.

Around this time, Russ bought Eileen a little two-seater MG, and to my delight, he taught me to drive that fun little racing-green car on the country roads around Niles. When I turned fourteen in the summer of 1951, Eileen and Russ took me to Florida to get a learner's permit—which was legal there, but not available in Illinois.

With that little piece of paper in hand, I drove everywhere in that MG. By terms of the permit, I was supposed to have an adult with me and not drive after dark, but Eileen and Russ didn't place too many restrictions on me as long as they knew where I was going and when I would be home. I never gave them cause to worry, and I was never pulled over. That was to be my last idyllic year with them.

There was never any problem with the laissez-faire approach to my schooling until I got to ninth grade. Then I was required to attend school a specified number of days a year or face having to repeat the grade. Although I was a bright student, missing so much school was starting to take its toll.

In the fall of 1951, I began ninth grade briefly in Niles. Then Eileen and Russ, planning to embark on an extended trip, transferred me to the public high school in St. Petersburg Beach, Florida, where Drucilla was then living. I knew no one in that town, let alone anyone my age at the high school. I was miserable.

Then one day, a few weeks after being enrolled there, I was riding home on the school bus and heard a car honking its horn by the side of the bus. I looked out the window and saw Eileen in her little green MG motioning for the bus driver to pull over. He did, and she got on the bus.

A heated argument ensued. He told her he couldn't let any kids off the bus except at their usual bus stops unless he had a note from a parent. She asked someone for a piece of paper and pencil and she had many offers from the spellbound kids on the bus. Right there, she wrote a note, handed it to him and said to me, "Let's go."

Soon we were speeding along in the MG with the top down. Laughing, the wind in my hair, I was elated to see her and asked where we were going. She said, "Back to Chicago." I asked if we could go get my clothes at

Drucilla's so we stopped there first.

Eileen said, "I supposed we should leave her a note so she won't worry about you." So she wrote Drucilla a little note.

I asked her where Russ was and she told me that they were having a few problems which she would tell me about later. This was a shock as I had never seen them have even a minor argument all the years I had lived with them. I threw my clothes into my suitcase, and we were on our way. Only we didn't go back to Chicago right away.

Eileen had joined the Sports Car Club of America the past year and had made friends there independent of Russell. On the way across Tampa Bay to her mother Bruce's house, she told me we were spending the night with Bruce and then were going to Jacksonville to pick up a Jaguar that was coming in on a ship. She had promised to accept the delivery on behalf of a friend who had ordered the luxury car from England. How exciting that was for a fourteen-year-old girl!

We left Tampa the next morning and got to Jacksonville after lunch. We picked up the beautiful silver Jaguar, and then she told me that I was driving it to Sebring for the races there on Sunday.

I was shocked. I had never driven any car but the MG. The Jag looked like a monster compared to the much smaller MG—and the car wasn't even hers! She assured me that the gears were the same and that it would be a great experience for me to drive it. She said that I could just follow her and there would be no problems.

I didn't want to let her down, so I got behind the wheel of the powerful vehicle.

From the moment we pulled onto the road, I felt as if the car was driving me. I was small, and I could not see out of the windows that well. It had an enormous hood and I felt as if I couldn't see the road.

Eileen was right in front of me though, and not driving at her usual breakneck speed, so I managed to keep up. I maintained an iron grip on the wheel for over one hundred and twenty miles until we got to Lake Monroe in Sanford, Florida.

There, driving along the curving road that wound around the lake, I thought that Jaguar was going to drive me right into the water! I started blowing the horn and flashing the lights so Eileen would know I was stopping.

She saw me and pulled into a restaurant parking lot across from the lake. When I told her I just could not drive it another mile she said, "Okay, you can drive the MG." What a huge relief. We went into the restaurant, had something to eat, and then went on to Sebring with no further upsets.

The next day, the races were preceded by a little parade around the track of some of the sports cars. They asked Eileen to drive the Jaguar, but she said, "No, Susie drove it all the way from Jacksonville, so she deserves to drive it around the track."

So I did! What a thrill. I can guarantee you that I was the only fourteen-year-old driver on that track with all those expensive sports cars. I can also guarantee that if the people running that race knew how old I was, that I only had a restricted license, and that Eileen did not own the car, they would have felt sicker than I did driving around Lake Monroe.

After Sebring, we returned to Tampa and Aunt Bruce's house. I expected to head straight back to Chicago, but Eileen had another plan. We flew to Denver, Colorado, and were met by a man Eileen called Captain Jess, a complete stranger to me. Eileen introduced him as an Air Force pilot from MacDill Air Force Base in Tampa on temporary assignment in Colorado.

Jess took Eileen and me straight to dinner. Even though the unexpected was the norm with Eileen, I had never been out solo with her and any man other than Russ or a relative. Eileen, always outgoing, seemed particularly vivacious.

After dinner, Captain Jess checked us into a hotel where he requested two rooms. I had never slept by myself in a hotel room, and enjoyed the grown-up feeling, but was very uneasy about where Eileen might be sleeping.

Unlike the innocent child who didn't really grasp the implications of her Aunt Bruce's sleepovers at "Uncle" Bob's, I was plenty old enough to wonder if Captain Jess already had a hotel room or whether the second room he had paid for that night was for more than just Eileen.

We spent two days in Colorado before flying back to Tampa and then started the drive home to the Chicago area. En route, Eileen dropped a verbal bomb. While the events in Colorado should have prepared me, they had not.

"I think Russ and I are done, Susie. I think he is cheating on me with a blonde German woman he knows who is a model. You and I have to make plans for a new life without him."

I don't think I really understood the phrase "chilled to the bone" before that moment. With Eileen's words ringing in my ears, I simply could not believe that after over seven years spent in a somewhat bohemian but stable and loving home, the foundations of my family life were yet again showing gaping cracks.

In my young life I had already been uprooted twice, first when I was sent home from Europe as a toddler, and again when my dad sent me to live with Eileen.

I shook with apprehension at the thought that this could be happening again. And this time, where would I go? Eileen had said that "we" needed to plan for a new life, so I trusted that she would not send me back to Drucilla, but where would the two of us live?

I had already missed so much school and was falling behind. Both Eileen and Drucilla had always told me to make good grades because there was money for me to go to college. But how could I make good grades if I wasn't anywhere near a classroom?

More importantly, I loved Russ and didn't want to lose him in my life. There may have been no blood ties, but there were assuredly ties of the heart to the man who had stood in my father's stead since the day of Elwood's death.

For someone who has never been through it, it is hard to describe the impact of the disintegration of a family unit, whether that loss is through divorce or death or even just an extended separation.

When I learned about Nina losing her beloved father Ossip, I felt her pain in a visceral way because I had the misfortune to experience that pain over and over in my life.

CHAPTER 17

SUSAN

1952–1956

THE END OF CHILDHOOD

EILEEN AND I GOT BACK TO CHICAGO, but not to our beautiful house in Niles. She did not prepare me en route for the fact that while I had been in Florida with Drucilla, she and Russell had sold the house in which I thought we had all been so happy. I was relieved that he was still there and thought maybe there was hope for them to reconcile, but surely this sale did not bode well.

Russ and Eileen had moved into the back end of the photography shop—one room for all of us, plus Eileen's dog, Humphrey. There was no shower but only a small restroom with a toilet and sink on the other side of the shop. Russ rigged a shower hose to the sink, got a galvanized washtub, and that was how we had to take our baths.

Eileen and Russ were sleeping on a mattress on the floor. I was sleeping with Humphrey on an Army cot at the foot of their bed.

Even though Eileen and Russ were sleeping in the same bed, the tension between them was electric. The three of us did nothing together anymore. If Eileen went somewhere, she took me. Russ headed to the corner bar every night and brought me along on occasion. The place had great hamburgers and Cokes, and I would eat and play the electronic pinball machines while Russ sat and nursed a couple of beers.

Eileen and Russ would complain to me about each other. This would make me ill, as I loved them both. As an adult now, part of me is appalled that two adults would throw an adolescent into the middle of their marital squabbles. However, I also now know that children can't easily be shielded from family discord no matter how hard parents try. Eileen and Russ were simply so caught up in their own misery that they didn't even try.

Just when I thought things could not get any more strained, Eileen joined the Jehovah's Witnesses—quite a startling development for someone who had barely set foot inside any church for all of her twenty-eight years!

Next thing I knew, I was at a heavily traveled area called Six Corners every Saturday handing out the group's newspaper called *The Watchtower*. Since that was where classmates from my latest school hung out on Saturdays, I got plenty of ribbing about this.

Eileen also took me to the Jehovah's Witness meetings and I found those events truly frightening. I didn't want any part of any of it, but what were my options? Russ just thought she was crazy, but he didn't have any suggestions for me either.

To make matters more complicated, when, with the move back into Chicago, Eileen had enrolled me at Von Steuben High School, the Chicago school system finally noticed the pattern of my many absences and school transfers over the preceding two years. Worse, they had discovered that Eileen and Russ had never officially adopted me.

Somehow, this led them to the decision that in order for me to be reinstated, Russ and Eileen would have to pay tuition. Moreover, those fees would be retroactive to the fourth grade, a whopping sum of money. Despite their relative financial comfort, payment of the required amount was simply beyond their means.

Determined to keep me in Chicago, Eileen first re-enrolled me at Niles Township High School using our old address there, and when that trick was discovered, she enrolled me at another Chicago high school near the photography shop, using the address of another Gooley family property.

Discovered again, Eileen had no choice but to drive me back to Florida to stay with Aunt Bruce. It was a miserable trip for both of us. The whole school year had been so chaotic that I had accumulated almost no credits.

In the spring of 1952, I enrolled at Hillsborough High where I spent part of the second semester. In the meantime, Eileen had pulled some rabbit out of a hat and managed to get me back into Von Steuben High School again, so it was back to the cramped photography studio and the air clouded with marital tension.

With Eileen making frequent trips to avoid Russ, and always pulling me out of school to go with her, I limped through the remainder of what should have been my sophomore year in high school with barely enough credits to qualify me as a sophomore at all.

Then one day in the summer of 1953, I got a letter from Drucilla (a rarity in my life) saying she had recently remarried and would like to get to know me better again. Her new husband, she said, had no children and had always wanted them, so he would welcome me.

Since Drucilla was still raising my brother Bobby, that statement seemed very odd to me. This was such a strange turn of events, that I showed the letter to Eileen, thinking she would understand the oddity of this correspondence.

Almost instantly, Eileen was on top of me on the floor, slapping me with her hands and screaming at me. She said that I was ungrateful, that she had never had any children because of raising me, that just when she needed me the most, I was deserting her.

I was shocked and terrified, as she had never behaved like that. Russ had to pull her off me.

Crying, I tried to talk to her and tell her that I had no intention of going, that I had just wanted to show her the letter. She called me a liar and said that I certainly *was* going. She stormed to the closet, removed a small suitcase, threw in a few of my clothes, and told Russ to take me to the bus station immediately.

He did. Handing me twenty dollars to spend on food, he put me on a bus bound for Tampa. It was as if I were seven years old again, being sent away from Tampa to Chicago, only in reverse this time.

I thought my life was over. I made it as far as Chattanooga before I became so sick with anxiety that I began vomiting violently. Mercifully, the local Traveler's Aid Society stepped in, took me off the bus, and put me up overnight.

The next day, I boarded another bus and arrived in Tampa at three in the morning. Staring around the mostly empty bus station, I saw that no one was there to meet me. I realized then that I had no idea whether Russ had called Drucilla at all or, if he had, if she knew about my changed schedule.

Despite fearing that she might be angry at me for disturbing her in the middle of the night, I had no choice but to find a pay phone and call Drucilla at her home in St. Petersburg.

Groggy, she told me to just take a taxi and they would pay the fare when I got there. I shuddered to think what that nearly forty mile cab ride might cost and how Drucilla would really feel when she had to pay it.

When I arrived in St. Petersburg, I was dismayed to find out that Drucilla and her new husband, Carlson, lived in a two-bedroom trailer with no indoor bathroom. There was a common washroom about fifty yards away. They had one of the bedrooms, and my brother Bobby occupied the other. That left the couch, which was covered with laundry.

I seemed to be falling down a slope. First I had lost my beautiful home in Niles, Illinois. Then I found myself living in the back of a photography shop in Chicago with rigged-up bathroom facilities, but where I was with people I knew and loved.

Now I found myself in a trailer with the woman who had once abused me, a man who was a total stranger, and the brother I loved but had spent only limited time with for most of our lives.

Carlson saw my small bag and asked me where all my clothes were. I told him that what was in the suitcase was all that Eileen had sent with me. He barked, "If you think I'm spending money on clothes for you when you just left your rich relatives, you'd better think again!" Where was the man that Drucilla had described as wanting children?

She put the laundry on the couch into a basket, gave me a pillow, and said we'd talk tomorrow. No welcome home hugs. No "things will be different this time." This woman bore no resemblance to the one who had penned that conciliatory letter.

A voice in my head kept screaming, "How could Eileen do this to me? I never wanted to come back here. I'd rather be anywhere but here."

That fall, Drucilla enrolled me again in St. Petersburg High School as a sophomore. I made friends, became a member of the dance corps, and even won a Charleston contest. And, like Nina, the arts became both a refuge and a source of joy to me.

Life wasn't as bad in that little trailer as I had feared. I loved spending time with Bobby, and Drucilla no longer abused me, but Carlson was cold to me and sometimes, as I was riding home on the bus, I would look out the window, longing for the sight of that little green MG. I missed Eileen and Russ so much, but I was powerless to do anything about it.

Then one day near Christmas, the miracle I had been longing for happened: Eileen just showed up again, this time at the trailer. We hugged and cried, packed like lightning, and hit the road for Chicago.

She told me happily that she and Russ had reconciled, so I thought everything would be all right, and we could go back to being a happy family again.

While I was glad to be back, I soon discovered, however, that the price of reconciliation with Eileen was full membership in the Jehovah's Witnesses—a price Russ had apparently been willing to pay to keep his marriage alive. So now there weren't even the fun nights out at the corner pub with Russ, only meetings at the church center and The *Watchtower* brigade on Saturdays.

Sensing my sadness that the shop contained none of the trappings of Christmas since Eileen's religion frowned upon the secular, on Christmas Eve, Russ snuck out and purchased a small Christmas tree, apparently willing to face Eileen's possible displeasure in the interest of cheering me up.

This reuniting of my family was brief, however, because Eileen was again unable to get me enrolled in a Chicago area high school, so back I went to Florida in January of 1954.

This time I enrolled at Hillsborough High School in Tampa. While I was gone, Drucilla, Bobby, and Carlson had moved out of the St. Petersburg trailer and back into a snug little home in Tampa that Drucilla had built the year after Daddy died. The trailer had only been temporary while Drucilla waited for the lease to run out for the tenants who had been occupying her home.

Since the house had three bedrooms, I was able to have my own room there and assumed that this move would at least make things a little better for me. Unfortunately, I soon discovered that living in this house as opposed to the trailer was not such a good thing for me or for Bobby. There, Carlson's true nature emerged.

Their home in St. Petersburg had been in a trailer park with only a few feet separating it from the next trailer. Drucilla's house, on the other hand, had land separating it from the closest houses.

When Carlson started to beat us, no one could hear us screaming. The man who claimed he wanted children was long gone—or maybe he wanted children for reasons none of us could have imagined.

Carlson had a hair-trigger temper, and we never knew what would set him off. He once knocked Bobby out cold for taking an extra piece of bacon. To Bobby, who had not been subjected to the abuse by Drucilla that I had, this was a devastating new development.

For me, who had escaped to an unconventional but loving home for over nine years, it was a situation that was unbearable. It was a return to the abuse of my childhood, but magnified many times over. Drucilla's abuses had taken the form of whipping, scorn, locking me in closets, and withholding approval and love. Carlson's brutality knew no limits.

Trying to find a way out of the hell into which I had fallen, and out of Carlson's way as much as possible, I worked frantically to catch up in school, taking a required ninth grade English class that I had missed at nearby Memorial Junior High while simultaneously taking junior class Honors English at Hillsborough High. I threw myself into the extra-curricular activities that I loved.

When summer rolled around, I took summer classes at Jefferson High to further close the gap on my credit deficit and ended the summer with nearly enough coursework to earn me the junior status that would have put me back on track.

But Carlson, who was a deacon in the Baptist Church, continued to beat me, once so severely that he put me in the hospital.

When classes began again in fall of 1954, I dug in again on class work and, for the first time in my life, took a job. I was proud of every dime that I earned at the JJ Newberry store. When Christmas season came around, I wanted so badly to do something nice for each member of my household. I spent every penny I had earned on Christmas gifts.

I knew that Bobby would love anything I got him, but for Drucilla and Carlson, part of me thought that if only I could show them that I understood them, and cared enough to spend my hard-earned money on them, they would learn to love me.

I took particular care with Carlson's gift. Knowing that he loved religious music and that the Mormon Tabernacle Choir was particularly gifted, I watched proudly as he opened the package.

He looked at the record and promptly broke it over his knee, saying that they were heathens and not of the right faith, and that they were all going to hell. He then threw the record in the garbage.

The breaking of that record seemed to snap something in Carlson himself as well. The frequency and intensity of the beatings escalated. In the spring of 1955, for the second time, he beat me so badly that Drucilla had to drive me to the hospital. The doctor said I looked like I had fallen out of an airplane and insisted that I be left overnight for observation.

The next day when she came to pick me up, Drucilla told me that she couldn't have me stay with her anymore. Although staying in that nightmarish household was the last thing I wanted, I asked her why. She said, "Because Carlson told me if I bring you back he is leaving me."

She made her choice and it was to stay with her husband. I could understand her choosing him over me, but what about Bobby? Carlson was an equal opportunity abuser and Bobby was the love of her life.

I think that the relief of having a man in her life to help her financially clouded her judgment. Besides, he was never abusive to her, just to Bobby and me. After a lifetime of being let down by this woman, I was not even surprised at her choice.

Drucilla took me straight from the hospital to Aunt Bruce's house. Bruce may have been an alcoholic, but she was rarely abusive. Except for the fact there was not much food in the house, and no money for lunches most days (one day I had only an entire can of coconut to eat and made myself very sick), staying with Bruce seemed like a picnic by comparison to my life at Drucilla's.

At least I lost the fear of being beaten to death while I slept. I worried myself sick about Bobby, but was helpless to intervene. I finished out the school year at Bruce's.

Near the end of the school year, Eileen showed up again. She said she wanted to give me one more chance to come back to Chicago and live with her, and that she would try to get me into Northwestern University which had an outstanding drama department. She said they would buy a new house in Evanston and we wouldn't have to live in the photography shop anymore.

I didn't think that with my checkered academic background that Northwestern would admit me, but I listened to her and got pretty excited about the idea of going back.

Then she said, "Now Susie, you realize that you will have to join the Jehovah's Witnesses. You are not in "the truth," and I'm not even supposed to be speaking to you. You have to come back with me because I want you in the truth with me and Russell."

I just looked at her, this woman who had essentially been my mother since I was seven years old, who had loved me in a way that Drucilla Bailey never had, and who had taken such good care of me all those years, and I knew this was the end of my life with her.

I might talk with her or even see her again, but my time as her "daughter" was at an end. I looked directly into her tearful green eyes and just said, "No!"

She left that day.

That summer, I took more summer classes and stayed on at Bruce's. In the fall of 1955, I continued at Hillsborough High School. Over the course of the previous year and that fall, I was very active in the drama department and landed the lead in several plays. Acting had been the magnet that drew friends to me in all the different schools I'd attended. I was selected two years running to participate in the Florida Drama Festival at the University of Florida, and one year, I won their "Best Actress" award.

These school activities were lifesavers for me, and I spent as many nights as possible in sleepovers at friends' homes. I constantly "adopted" other mothers since I didn't have one of my own.

My high school boyfriend, Chech, lived on a lake and his mother, a very sweet lady, took a liking to me. I spent as much time out at the lake house as I could without wearing out my welcome.

My childhood girlfriend, Yvonne, could also be counted on many nights for a place to sleep. As a child and teenager, I was moved around like a pawn in the lives of others. I learned to make my own family, and those two were as close to my heart as siblings.

As an adult, I lost track of Yvonne when we were both around twenty-two and I moved out of the country. I spent the next forty-plus years fruitlessly searching for her.

When I mentioned this to Deb, she put her sleuthing skills to work and, to my astonishment and delight, found a current address and phone number for Yvonne in a matter of mere minutes by honing in on an obituary for Yvonne's first husband.

In the hours-long phone conversation that followed, I felt an immediate reconnection to this wonderful woman whose friendship had meant so much to me in a troubled time of my life. More importantly, she helped me to recall how well, at least to outward appearances, I had truly stood up to all the challenges of my young life:

I admired you so much for how fearless you were in facing life. My mother used to tell me that she wished I could be more like Susie Bailey.

Partway through the fall semester, my awkward living situation just seemed like an unbearable weight on my shoulders. My friend Elaina was in a terrible situation at home, and living with my Aunt Bruce was like living at a badly run hotel.

So, after I finished my junior year near the end of 1955, we packed our clothes, hit the highway, and stuck out our thumbs.

A kindly looking middle-aged man picked us up right away. When he asked where we were going, Elaina told him we were heading to DeLand where her aunt lived. The man said, "Do you girls have any idea how much trouble you could have gotten in, hitchhiking like this?"

He was right, of course, but he took us straight to DeLand and dropped us off at Elaina's aunt's front door where the woman took both of us in with minimal questioning.

After a few days, Elaina's mother came looking for her, but no one came looking for me, so I just stayed on after Elaina left.

Her aunt lived just a few blocks from Stetson University, a Baptist college that Drucilla had always pushed me to attend. I started using their library and noticed and was fascinated by a student who showed up there regularly.

Fresh off a broken engagement, John, I soon learned, was a junior, big man on campus, president of everything, and had been in the Army four years. To my young eyes, it was equally noteworthy that he was very good-looking.

Thinking I was a fellow college student, John asked me what year I was in. When, I told him that I was eighteen years old but that I hadn't even graduated from high school, John asked probing questions about my circumstances.

He then told me that I might be eligible for the early admissions program if I could pass the entrance exam. Since he knew the university system so well, John tutored me and then arranged for me to take the exam.

I passed! It was January of 1956, and I was officially a college co-ed. All I had to do was get in touch with Drucilla to get the money she always said was available to pay for tuition.

I suffered more than a little trepidation about that, as just about everything else she had ever promised me had turned to dust—but this time she came through.

Drucilla not only sent tuition money, but also funds for all the clothes I needed, and, from then on, she put fifty dollars a month in the Stetson Bank for spending money. That may not sound like a lot today, but in the fifties that was a huge amount of money for a co-ed to have. After all, my tuition and room and board were already paid for as were my books, so that was just spending money. I never understood how Drucilla, who spent her life just scraping by, could have come up with so much money for me.

I didn't know where she got this money, but I had to forgive her everything for doing that for me. Finally my life was under my control and not subject to the whims of one of my mercurial or vicious family members.

I had full intentions of making the most of this chance that I could.

CHAPTER 18

DEB

NINA TAKES CENTER STAGE (1937-1941)

HOME FROM EUROPE IN FEBRUARY 1937, and presumably grieving for the baby daughter she had left behind, Nina got on with her life. The ship's log from her voyage home showed her as living with Clara on Boston Boulevard in Detroit. However, New York still seems to have been her home base.

By July of 1937, Nina had thrown herself back into acting. A July 6 news article mentions her being a student at the Summer Dramatic Workshop run in conjunction with the Westchester Playhouse in Mount Kisco, New York.

That summer Nina had a part in the play *Lysistrada*. Ironically, thirty years later Susan would have a part in that same play!

It is likely there that Nina first met Julius "Jules" Schmidt, Jr. A local, Jules was the son of a well to do architect and a former singer with the Metropolitan Opera. Brilliant, handsome, and musically gifted, Jules was a struggling young actor trying to make it on Broadway.

He took the stage name of John Morny and eventually enjoyed some minor success in the early 1940s with roles in Broadway plays such as *The Great Big Doorstep*, *Hope for a Harvest*, *The Return of the Vagabond*, and *The Man Who Killed Lincoln*.

Jules was to become a lifelong friend, drinking companion, and eventually one of Nina's heirs. In the fall of 1937, a letter written from Nina to Clara (privately held by Schmidt's great-niece Mona K. Vance) described her visits to the Schmidt's home in Mt. Kisco and a series of horseback rides that she and Jules took.

As Susan and I read the letter, we were struck by the flowery language and near-manic tone. At that point in her life, there had been no recorded instances of Nina's seeking treatment for alcoholism or mental health issues.

However, if she was, as we suspect, suffering from bi-polar disorder, such "breaks" routinely begin to occur while an individual is in her twenties as Nina was in 1937. If she had given birth just months before, the stress and hormonal changes, coupled with leaving a child behind, may well have precipitated a manic episode. She wrote:

Last Saturday, Jules...and I drove out to Mount Kisco, and Sunday Jules and I had the most magnificent horseback ride. It was a typical autumn day... and oh, such gorgeous light you never saw... We started at twilight, and it was pitch dark when we got back with thousands of stars above... I just wish you could have seen the fields of long yellow grass blowing in beautiful waves and utter silence everywhere. The light was even more unusual than the week before—it was positively uncanny. It was the kind of light you wouldn't mind dying in—you become hypnotized with the strange beauty of sky and clouds and feel if you concentrated for just a little while, you could will yourself to float right up and become part of them. To die with nature would be infinitely more soothing than to die in a room.

Knowing the end that Nina eventually came to, the last sentence was chilling.

Nina enjoyed the company of Jules's mother Maria who sang German tunes to her:

She also made a few records like the ones you [Clara] made and the other evening Jules and I listened first to all your records and then to hers. She used to sing in the Metropolitan Opera you know.

Nina went on to describe to Clara how Jules was "still desperately trying to get a job." He had headshots made and a screen test set up with Universal Studios courtesy of a local talent agency, but the agency went bankrupt before the screen test could occur.

There is no indication in the letter that the relationship was sexual or romantic in nature despite the later accusations by Jules's first wife Mollie that Nina was his "girlfriend." Nina, in fact, described Jules's lecturing her on some unspecified behaviors:

> *He still gives me long grandfatherly lectures which are a scream, altho there is also a lot of truth in them.*

By midyear in 1938, news articles began to reference Nina's appearances in plays in Los Angeles. While Clara, after much soul-searching, did not decide to close up and sell the Boston Boulevard home in Detroit until 1939, she had already begun to visit California, a state where she and Ossip had enjoyed spending time during his frequent performances at the Hollywood Bowl. Nina, with her acting aspirations, made the same choice.

Using the stage name of Nina Clemens, Nina appeared in late 1938 at the Las Palmas Theatre with Henry Duffy's El Capitan Players in productions of *Pride and Prejudice*, *Little Women*, and a series of Noel Coward plays. Entertainment critic Katherine T. Von Blon, in a critique of "Little Women" had praise for Nina's acting abilities:

> *There was Nina Clemens, daughter of Ossip Gabrilowitsch, famed pianist, and granddaughter of Mark Twain, who proved herself a character actress of precocious gifts in her highly amusing miming of the crotchety Aunt March. Her poise and timing are remarkable and she has a delightful sense of comedy.*

Her time with Duffy's Players continued into 1939. Another review by Von Blon of Claire Boothe's *The Women* again praised Nina:

> *Nina Clemens is unique in style and renders her comedy in cryptic stabs which are effective.*

Nina's Hollywood acting career appears to have been short-lived. Her drinking habits began to interfere with her ability to perform. By this time in her life, the social drinking begun at Barnard had turned to something far more serious.

Years later, mired in depression and under psychiatric treatment, Nina lashed out at Clara, blaming her for not providing sufficient financial support for her career.

Clara's caustic reply was recorded in a letter to Nina:

> *Mr. Duffy said "you were not ready" to the agent, but not for the reason you advance. He had already received from me his desired $3000 for debts, and was willing to "place" you when you had proved sufficient ability.*
>
> *You may remember the agent I arranged for you who told me in your presence he could not possibly take you seriously since you "caroused" at night and failed to meet your appointments in the daytime.*
>
> *You may also recall that Jacques [Clara's second husband] made an appointment in the daytime with a producer, but you sent someone else and did not appear yourself.*

Nina's somewhat cavalier attitude towards her acting career was also expressed in a letter to her friend Ethel ("Mouse Face"). In that correspondence, Nina said:

> *Then a couple of months ago, I got an agent by the name of Leon Lance. I was terribly excited to have an agent, but it turns out he's not much good.*

Nina described how Mr. Lance had selected a particular scene for her to perform:

> *It wasn't my meat at all—terribly romantic, and naturally I did it badly.*

After spending time with a friend working up more scenes to impress the agent, Nina wrote:

We decided we were wasting our time working up things for him so we quit ... He's a Viennese—about 48, who knows all the old masterpieces, but is absolutely ignorant of any plays written since 1910.

Nina's long downhill slide had begun. Originally, mother and daughter had shared quarters at Clara's palatial home at 2005 La Brea Terrace, a home Clara affectionately referred to as "Casa Allegra." Soon, however, Nina's party girl lifestyle began to wear on Clara.

Then in her sixties, Clara was overwhelmed with the constant flow of Nina's friends and the late night parties. The purchase of a home for Nina at 2400 El Contento Drive solved this issue and Nina began to enjoy a freewheeling lifestyle, soon giving up even the pretext of acting.

Nina was clearly a sexually active young woman. If "love-making" can be taken literally then Clara, generally a very conservative woman, appears to have been well aware of, and surprisingly non-judgmental about, this aspect of her daughter's life. In a letter written in response to one of Nina's, Clara wrote:

A's type of love-making would not give me much of a thrill. It sounds rather the way one places a bit of cheese in the corner for a mouse to nibble at after everyone has left the room. Not much spurs and sword for the conquest of a beloved's heart in his method.

Nina displayed a penchant for dating men who were literally or emotionally unavailable. She had viewed with delight the incredible closeness of her parents. Sadly, her own choices virtually assured that she was never to be blessed with such a love.

Letters to friends indicate that sometime prior to October of 1940, Nina had developed an entendre for a married man named Alex.

Research revealed "Alex" to be actor Alexander Lockwood whose career

as a minor Hollywood actor survived a span of over fifty years. Born in Po-
land in 1902, Alex's career spanned stage, movie, and television. He landed
guest roles in such television classics as *Perry Mason*, *Dr. Kildare*, *The Big
Valley*, and *My Three Sons*, and bit roles in popular movies such as *Close
Encounters of the Third Kind*, and *The Sting*.

His last known acting effort took place when, at the age of 86, he landed
a guest role in the television series *The Cavanaughs*. Lockwood died in
Studio City, California, in 1990.

Charming, but moody and temperamental, Alex both fascinated and
infuriated Nina. In one letter, Nina described a longstanding habit of Sunday afternoon drives that she, Alex, Alex's wife Hester, and friend Manon
Krause took to explore the California countryside. Alex apparently acted as
navigator on these trips, poring over road maps as the quartet went along,
and Manon habitually teased him about his "technical" skills.

On one such trip, extended over Memorial Day weekend in 1941, Alex
suddenly decided that he had had enough of Manon's ribbing about his
directional skills and spent the remainder of the weekend surly and uncom-
municative:

> *Alex said in a very sour way that he wasn't going to drive anymore,
> and he got in the back seat. I watched his face in the mirror, and he
> looked cross as a crab.*

When Alex later declared that he was going on a hike alone, and Nina
lobbied to join him, Alex replied, "If you think you can walk where I'm
going to walk you can come along."

Nina's next comment revealed not only her ability to analyze her own
behavior but her nearly painful desire to keep peace among her friends:

> *I realized later what a rude and conceited remark it was, but at
> the time I was so worried about creating harmony again, that I
> just made jokes about not being so weak I couldn't follow where
> he went.*

Much as she had on her trip to Mt. Kisco with Jules Schmidt in 1937, Nina basked in the one-on-one attention of the hike, but transferred her jumbled feelings of mixed joy and unease to descriptions of the landscape around her:

> *The strange twilight as we came back was eerie and strangely lonely yet thrilling. You know how lonely trees can be in a fading light … It was one of those atmospheres you crave to cling to and hold, and you know within an hour will seem like a dream.*

Early in their acquaintance, Alex had confided to Nina that he never drank because, "if there's anyone in the room towards whom I feel amorously inclined, I make a complete fool of myself."

He appears to have strung her along, in the presence of his wife Hester, but never fully acted on the attraction between the two:

> *Now I try to avoid his kisses when he's tight, because they mean nothing to me; when he kisses me when he's sober, it does mean something. Anyway, the craving seems to be in him for sexual satisfaction. It's just the old story—that the thrill of it dies out between married people, and yet they can respond easily to someone new. So, it just boils down to this: first, he believes marriage vows should be observed at any cost; second, that one couldn't keep an affair secret—and that's that!*

Her ambivalence about this situation showed when she continued:

> *So I guess we'll just be very good friends, and that's all. Sometimes I'm very glad—and other times, I'm not. I honestly came back here expecting quite an affair.*

In a final burst of insight, Nina wrote,

And often I wonder if I just dont want him because I can't have him and viceversa.

In the early 1940s, probably not long before she became involved with Alex, Nina also dated a native San Franciscan named Jack. Nina developed strong feelings for Jack, but her hopes were to be dashed in an unforeseen way: in what was an incredible act of courage for the times, Jack came out of the closet.

In a letter to friend Ethel, Nina poured out her feelings about learning of Jack's sexual orientation the previous year.

The letter provides a window into the mores of the time and society's attitude toward homosexuality as a treatable "disease." Jack, she said, had written her a letter which she described as:

> *...a really lovely and courageous letter...Said when he found out he was that way, he almost committed suicide; and that he was sick of lying all those years—condemning people bitterly like himself, for fear his family or friends would find out he was that way.*

In an effort to try to be "normal," Jack sought the services of a Dr. Beaumont to assess whether he was truly homosexual. After visits to the doctor, Jack's friends apparently thought this interest in men was just a temporary aberration. Nina, however, was utterly unconvinced:

> *After talking to Jack for an hour, Beaumont decided there was nothing in the world wrong with him; told him to associate only with normal people. Frances says she thinks that cured him. I doubt it strongly. After all, if he loved me and felt the need of a woman, I certainly was available that last night, and yet he turned to Belmonte. Masculine hormone injections might cure him, but not words. Now things will be even harder for him; he was drafted March 5th.*

Despite sounding upset that she had been used as a cover for Jack's true sexual orientation, Nina did not reject Jack as a friend. Immediately after writing the above, she passed along Jack's service mailing address. World War II service records indicate that Jack enlisted on March 27, 1941.

This was not to be Nina's only romantic involvement with a gay man. Per the same letter, she described a similar relationship. Still in love with married Alex, she sought the services of a fortune teller who told Nina that she would soon meet the man she was going to marry. The man would be 5'11" tall, slim, with very dark hair, dark blue eyes, and an extremely fine person. Nina seemed to know exactly who the man was:

> *She described a man I know, who is definitely a social climber, and I'm sure is a fairy; said he'd ask me to marry him for his future convenience, not for love, and that I shouldn't waste a thot on it.*

The next day, Nina indeed received a call from the man who gave away his game when he asked if Nina had seen a fortune teller and then said, "Did she tell you I was going to ask you to marry me?"

Nina's next line, however is telling:

> *Manon accused him outright of being queer, and since then he's been phoning me and dating me like mad.*

Nina, believing the man to be gay, still "dated him like mad." Perhaps this was an act of kindness on her part, or an attempt to make Alex jealous, but once again, Nina was dating an unavailable man.

What drove Nina to repeat this pattern over and over? Perhaps it was a feeling that she did not truly deserve to be loved or a fear of rejection. If there was no possibility of a successful relationship, she could never be rejected as she had been by her first love, Carl Roters.

As Nina's drinking habits grew worse, the formerly close and loving relationship she shared with her mother began to fray at the edges. By 1941, Clara had begin to spend time socially with Jacques Samossoud, a man who, like her first husband Ossip Gabrilowitsch, was a Russian born musician.

While the two were merely dating, Nina appeared to have seen Jacques as no threat. Her letters convey a convivial attitude towards him. She mentions Jacques expressing his attitudes about war and even his take on the Memorial Day trip episode in which Alex Lockwood had pouted:

> *Samossoud threw back his head and roared with laughter; and said "I never in my life heard of a real he-man acting like that in my life; only a woman would sit and sulk like that for a day and a half; any man would have it out at the moment."*

Per Caroline Harnsberger's *Mark Twain's Clara*, it was Nina who pointed out to Clara that Jacques, twenty years her mother's junior, appeared to be infatuated. Jacques had planted the seed by mentioning his feelings to Nina. It was a seed that was to ultimately bear bitter fruit for Nina.

Nina with unknown actors
Photo held by Susan Bailey

CHAPTER 19

DEB

NINA AND CLARA (1942-1962)

FEW DETAILS ARE KNOWN of Nina herself during the years of World War II, but her friends got on with their lives. Old flame Carl Rotters remarried in March of 1941 and produced three children. Jules Schmidt married in February of 1941 and fathered three children by the end of 1943. It is unknown whether Alex stayed married to wife Hester. Many of Nina's male friends such as actor and artist Bob Skiles volunteered or were drafted and served in World War II.

Nina's life, however, seemed to stagnate. Her drinking grew heavier and heavier. She began inviting a variety of people, including Swedish born actor Sigfrid Tor, to live with her at her El Contento Drive home in an attempt to create a surrogate family for herself.

By early 1944, Clara, probably concluding that her daughter would never be able to support herself, arrived at a decision to make permanent financial provisions for Nina.

On February 25, 1944, she created the Clara Clemens Gabrilowitsch Trust with Nina as the beneficiary. The Trust provided for Nina to receive the proceeds of the interest from the Trust's investments in approximately quarterly allowances for her lifetime. Clara and longtime secretary Phyllis Harrington served as co-trustees. The Trust provided that upon the deaths of both Clara and Nina, the principal of the Trust was to devolve upon Yale University and the American Red Cross.

Creation of this trust may also have been made partly in preparation for Clara's upcoming nuptials. On May 11, 1944, Nina attended Clara's wedding to Jacques Samossoud and seemed to be glad that her mother had found a second chance at happiness.

Born in 1894 in Tiflis, Russia, Samossoud claimed to have conducted the

Grand Opera there as well as in St. Petersburg. Since his brother Samuel was a prominent Russian conductor, some have questioned whether those credentials were authentic.

He was purportedly a member of Czar Nicholas's elite Preobrazhensky regiment and, in any case, fled Russia after the Revolution in 1918. He spent time in Greece, Spain, and Italy before emigrating to the U.S. in 1923.

The ship's passenger log showed him as married, but no wife was sailing with him. Next to him on the list was opera singer Thalia Sabanieeva, also listed as married. Thalia became a diva of some repute at the Metropolitan Opera in New York City, and, sometime prior to the 1930 United States Federal Census, Thalia and Jacques divorced their spouses and married. The length of the marriage is unknown. Thalia resurfaced briefly when Jacques married Clara, asserting claims that he owed her alimony.

Prior to marrying Clara, Jacques served as musical conductor at a small opera house in New York City, at the Chicago Opera House, and at the National Opera House in Washington, D.C. While his Russians credentials might be questionable, evidence exists that he did in fact have a fairly robust career as a musical conductor, primarily of operas.

For example, a November 22, 1937, program from the Chicago Opera House lists Samossoud as conductor for a production of *Norma*.

In 1944, the year he married Clara, Samossoud was musical director on the Nelson Eddy film *Knickerbocker Holiday*. It is interesting to note that during casting the previous year, Jacques, presumably at Clara's behest, made arrangements for talented young Eileen Lucia to try out for a part in the film.

She chose instead to marry Russell Gooley, a fact that Susan indicated Eileen regularly hurled in Russ's face when the two fought: "Marrying you kept me from becoming a famous actress!"

Samossoud's work on the film represented the last sign that could be found of his career as a musical conductor. Jacques had, it seems, found his meal ticket.

In superficial ways, Jacques resembled Clara's beloved first husband Ossip Gabrilowitsch. He was Russian, Jewish, a musical conductor, charming, and well traveled. He had even been acquainted with Ossip.

To Clara, it must have seemed that she was getting a second chance at the great love she had shared with Ossip. To her dying day, Clara considered herself fortunate in this second marriage and would brook no criticism of Jacques.

However, while being an attentive and loving husband to Clara, Samossoud early displayed a penchant for playing the horses and spending Clara's money. From the beginning of their marriage, he seems to have had his eye on accessing the monies generated by the Mark Twain Trust that funded Clara's comfortable lifestyle.

Nina's enchantment with her new stepfather quickly waned. Having had her mother's undivided attention for the eight years since her father had died, Nina was now relegated to the role of second fiddle in her mother's affection.

Perhaps it was this displacement of affection that precipitated Nina's sudden appearance in young Susan Bailey's life in the fall of 1944. Since she knew where to find Susan, the arrangements made for her daughter's care must have been known to Nina, yet she had never before chosen to intrude in the life of Susan and her adoptive family.

She surely must have known that all hell would break loose with her appearance and yet she did nothing to hide who she really was, even telling the principal her name twice.

If this visit to see Susan was a bid to gain Clara's attention, it achieved its purpose in a way that Nina probably did not foresee. Elwood Bailey's swift and harsh response in having her arrested indicates that part of his agreement to raise Susan must have included a stipulation that Nina was to have no part in his daughter's life. He made good on his promise to Susan that "you will never have to see that lady again."

Did Clara have a hand in the new arrangements for Susan's care? It seems nearly certain. Someone picked up the tab for Susan and Eileen's extended stay at the expensive Palmer House Hotel and it surely could not have been the Baileys, who were of limited financial means.

It was also just a few months later that Susan met Clara for the first time. Perhaps Nina threatened to make continued attempts to see Susan until Clara agreed to keep tabs on Susan with regular visits.

It is also conceivable that Clara threatened to revoke the trust she had created to benefit Nina unless her attempts to see Susan ceased. Whether Nina ever knew of Susan's location once she was spirited out of Tampa is unknown.

Nina continued to have contact with married friend Jules Schmidt. In a letter to Jules, Nina expressed her jubilation at the end of World War II. Schmidt it seemed had moved back to New York and been engaged in factory work for the war effort. The letter implies that the two had not seen each other since Schmidt left California:

> I can't tell you how terribly happy I was to get your wonderful letter! I've thought of you so many times—almost constantly—in fact since you left—even started a long letter to you months ago but never finished it. Speaking of that—I wish I could have seen the letter you started to me and tore up?!

The letter also mentions Nina's friends, Genevieve and John Harmon. Like so many of her friends, John Harmon was an actor who had a long successful career in repertory roles. While Nina more or less abandoned the life herself, she continued to surround herself with people in the business.

The letter indicated that with the end of the war, and travel restrictions lifted, the Harmons planned a trip to New York and invited Nina to join them. She jubilantly saw it as a chance to reconnect with Jules:

> There's a world in my heart I'd like to say to you,—but I guess it's better if I don't. I imagine you'll understand by mental telepathy anyway!!... Take good care of yourself—and God willing I'll see you soon. Give my best to Molly [Schmidt's wife], and the children whom I'll meet shortly, and to your family.

Nina's drinking increased exponentially. As early as 1946, her mother's longtime secretary Phyllis Harrington and a man named George Harnagel, Jr., are listed in documents held by The Mark Twain House & Museum as

"Trustees for Nina Gabrilowitsch."

The records show income flowing from dividend bearing stocks, and disbursements made for utilities, taxes, and minor expenses with Nina herself receiving approximately $200 a month in what can only be characterized as an allowance.

Since many of the stocks and bonds are the same as those listed on the inventory of her father's estate, it appears highly likely that these records are simply referring to management of the trust that Clara had set up in 1944.

Jacques continued to burn through Clara's money. In 1947, he racked up $25,000 in debts at The Last Frontier Casino in Las Vegas and bounced two checks that he wrote in repayment of this debt.

Despite the humiliation of having this reported in The *Los Angeles Times*, Clara, per author Caroline Harnsberger, bought into Jacques's story that the $25,000 was a blackmail payment related to a fledgling motion picture company that she had previously loaned him $30,000 to invest in.

The shingles virus that Clara had contracted in 1946 had, by 1948, become a source of crippling pain, and the medication that she took to relieve the symptoms undoubtedly clouded her judgment. The combined effects of her straitened financial circumstances and this disease that rendered her unable to travel probably also account for the cessation of her visits to see Susan in Detroit, Michigan.

In January of 1949, unable to stave off the casino owners' demands for repayment of his substantial debt, Jacques declared personal bankruptcy, an act that he presumably undertook to forestall attempts by his debtors to get directly at the Mark Twain Trust income.

By early 1951, Jacques's compulsive gambling had so decimated the family finances that Clara was forced to auction off her lovely La Brea Terrace home and many of her famous father's items. The auction was, however, so poorly organized and advertised that it netted only $60,000.

Clara, ever conscious of her social image, attempted to put a positive spin on the auction by claiming that she and Jacques had been struck with a case of wanderlust and wished to go "a-gypsying."

Despite moving to La Jolla and far more modest quarters, Jacques still continued to outspend the family's income. It is possible that at this stage,

Nina, who had the income from the beneficial trust Clara had created, was actually better off financially then her mother.

Little is again known of Nina's life from the time of the 1945 letter to Jules Schmidt until, as early as 1952, information reveals she had already undergone psychiatric treatment in Compton and Las Encinas, California. These were to become the first of many stays in "sanitariums" as mental health and rehabilitation facilities were then called.

Clara, who in her later years had a reputation as a tough cookie, was herself no stranger to such facilities. As a young woman, Clara had suffered several stress-related breakdowns. It was not until her happy marriage to Ossip Gabrilowitsch that she achieved a strong sense of self-worth and left her breakdown days behind, although Nina and Ossip still affectionately called her "Nervous."

Nina, however, had no such supportive helpmate in life. By early 1953, Nina's alcohol and mental health issues had again reached a critical stage. While her earlier stays at Compton and Las Encinas appear to have been voluntary, on April 29, 1953, Nina was formally declared mentally incompetent and remanded to Camarillo State Hospital, a psychiatric facility that many claim was the model for the Eagles' famous song, "Hotel California." While members of the Eagles deny this assertion, the outwardly beautiful facility nonetheless had a reputation for overcrowding and poor patient care.

Perhaps due to her famous connections, Nina later described her time there to friends as "not so bad." Other patients were not so fortunate.

One unnamed patient described in writing to Nina his difficulties in trying to land a job after his first release from Camarillo. The patient, clearly undergoing his second or later stint at the facility, indicated that employers refused to hire him as soon as they heard of his time at Camarillo. He urged Nina, should they ever meet outside Camarillo, never to let on that their acquaintance stemmed from their time there.

On May 11, 1953, Phyllis Harrington formally entered in the Superior Court of the County of Los Angeles a petition for appointment as Guardian of Estate and Person for Nina. In her petition, Phyllis referenced Nina's commitment to Camarillo State and asserted:

Said alleged incompetent person is now and has been addicted to the excessive use of alcohol for a long time, has had periods of marked mood swings and great tension, and by reason thereof is unable, un-assisted, properly to manage and take care of herself or her property, and by reason thereof is likely to be deceived or imposed upon by artful or designing persons.

Later in the petition, Phyllis also stated:

For many years petitioner has cared for, advised, and has acted to all intents and purposes, as the guardian of said alleged incompetent person, with the approval and consent of her mother, and has been and now is well acquainted with her character, habits, and require-ments.

The court set May 27, 1953, as the hearing date for consideration of Phyllis's petition and Nina was formally apprised of the hearing. Extant portions of a letter written by Nina to Clara reveal that Nina was outraged to find that Clara (probably at the urging of Jacques) had moved to have Phyllis Harrington appointed as her guardian:

When I entered [Dr. Warrick's] office, Mrs. Harrington was sitting there. She said that you wish her to become my guardian, but she had no papers with her proving that fact. Dr. Warrick asked me if I was agreeable to this plan, and I said I was not—that I would resent anyone acting in that capacity. But because she was sitting right there, I continued acting in the hypocritical manner I have used towards her for years, in order not to hurt her feelings.

In all the interviews conducted when researching this book, this latter aspect of Nina's personality was revealed over and over. She was described as "sweet" and as "never wanting to hurt anyone's feelings." However, her letter went on to express an extreme dislike for Phyllis:

My dislike for her has grown steadily for the last five years (due to things she said to me while I was in Compton, and after I left there)—things I never told you about because you were ill.

She further went on to state:

When I was at Las Encinas, several of my friends asked if she was my guardian. I said I didn't think she was, that I could think of no reason why she should be, when you were alive and I was 42 years old!

Nina's protests against having Phyllis appointed as her guardian were successful, but the court nonetheless, on May 27, 1953, appointed Bank of America as guardian of her estate.

While Nina's railing was directed at Phyllis Harrington, it is clear that she was devastated by what she saw as her mother's betrayal in not only seeking appointment of a guardian but in failing to take on that role herself.

Nina had, in fact, previously begun lashing out at Clara herself, choosing to see her mother as the source of all her problems. In a letter sent in reply to Nina during one of her stays at Las Encinas Sanitarium, Clara had clearly had enough:

I wanted your happiness! Your letter is a startling proof of the injury caused by psychiatrists in their destructive method of inducing the patient to indulge in great stretches of self-dramatization sodden with the evil aggrandizement of trivialities ... and judging by your letter, you, sad to relate, have been a faithful pupil. ... You have dug up phases in your childhood when your parents, according to their views as to the best way to prepare you for the traps and battles of life, were actually, as you seem to think, sowing the seeds of your later misfortunes. A phantastic idea!

It seems possible that the anger evidenced in this letter may have precipitated Clara's move to have Nina declared incompetent, as that action occurred less than three months later. In summing up, Clara went on to lecture:

We cannot with immunity cast the blame of our own failings and weaknesses onto the shoulders of others. If we are not brave enough to admit, at least to ourselves, when our lack of character, or lack of adequate talent has been at fault, but persist in seeking the cause of disappointments in untruths, we are pouring fresh poison into our daily life.

This statement is startling in light of the fact that Clara's husband was, like her daughter, in the stranglehold of an addictive disease. Behavior that Clara could not tolerate in her daughter she willfully turned a blind eye to in her husband.

By that time, Jacques, desperate for money to feed his gambling compulsion, had made more than one attempt to break the terms of the Mark Twain Trust.

Clara's famous father, known for his humor and brilliant pen, was certainly not known for his business acumen. However, in a move designed to protect his remaining daughter, who had no grounding in financial management, Clemens had crafted terms in his will that explicitly prohibited any husband of Clara's from tapping the principal of the trust.

Nina was released from Camarillo State on December 1, 1953, after a stay of approximately seven months. While there, Nina experienced the psychological phenomenon called transference and conceived an infatuation with a psychiatrist named Dr. Warrick. A letter written thereafter to Warrick pours out her feelings. Dashes in the handwritten letter have been removed and replaced here with periods for clarity:

Sometimes, the person you want to write to the most is the hardest to write to because if you think a great deal of them, you don't want them to condemn you. I think the world of you and I don't think you'd condemn me but I don't want to risk it or bore you although you did say to let you know how I was getting along. .

I do get so very lonely for you…And when Friday came, & it was your weekend off, and you drove home the whole place seemed empty, desolate, and dull & I used to wonder if I could last till Monday, just to hear your voice again. There was that kind of sick feeling in my heart when the insides have all gone out of you & you can't cry…. No harm was ever done by loving someone so you won't condemn me for this letter, to use a trite phrase, is a masterpiece of understatement.

On February 3, 1954, Nina was legally declared to be restored to competency. Shortly thereafter, Bank of America was relieved of its appointment as guardian of her estate, effectively returning control of Nina's money to Phyllis Harrington in her capacity as trustee of the funds upon which Nina subsisted.

At the time her assets were turned back over to Nina, the bank valued her estate at approximately $360,000, a sum that clearly included the principal of the Clara Clemens Gabrilowitsch Trust, even though Nina only had rights to the income thereof.

When, on June 16, 1954, Nina signed a receipt for the reclamation of her assets, they included a 1951 Mercury convertible, her half interest in the El Contento Drive property, her interest in the trust, small amounts of cash, and six life insurance policies which appear to have been designed to function as annuities. In addition to her allowance from the trust, Nina thus also had income from those annuities.

Per letters from Bank of America (who held Nina's trust funds), the house at 2400 El Contento Drive was sold in August of 1954, and Nina moved to 1921 North Highland Avenue, which postcards indicated to be the Highland Hotel.

In an undated letter written shortly thereafter, Nina mentions encountering for the first time the stigma associated with having been a patient at a psychiatric facility.

She had attempted to rent a car and gave her contact at the bank as a

financial reference. After the employee spoke with the bank, Nina overheard him tell his boss that the "the young lady has just been released from
Camarillo State." The owner then refused to rent Nina a car. Nina said in
referring to the bank employee:

> *She didn't realize how disastrous a statement like that can be. I*
> *used to hear the kids in the ward complain about trying to get jobs*
> *if any prospective employer found out they'd been in Camarillo, &*
> *I had proof right there when I tried to rent the car.*

Nina's lifestyle at the Highland Hotel was considerably less luxurious
than what she had been accustomed to at her El Contento Drive home.
With her ability to create an ersatz family by taking in friends and struggling young actors severely curtailed, Nina grew even more inward and her
health suffered further.

In an undated letter to friend Jules Schmidt written circa 1957, she wrote:

> *I haven't been feeling well for one thing. In fact I'm so weak I can*
> *hardly walk. You know, almost 3 years of malnutrition doesn't pay*
> *in the end, which is how long I've been at that hotel, always eating*
> *off the hot plate in my room ... So I have to depend more and more*
> *on the dear old whiskey for energy.*

Nina went on to describe to Jules that it was really her state of mind that
drove her to drink, how she craved peace and quiet, and how she could not
tolerate quarreling and arguments or loud voices.

Jacques, meanwhile still had people who were very unhappy with his
failure to pay debts. At one point, the "bill collection" efforts even resulted
in Jacques being roughed up and left in a hotel where Clara's long-time
chauffeur Edgar Glanzer located him the next day. He was tended to by one
of his gambling buddies, a physician named Dr. William Seiler.

The financial situation again became so tight that Clara was forced to
borrow money from Phyllis Harrington. She also sold author and friend

Caroline Harnsberger some additional Twain manuscripts and memorabilia the sale of which Caroline brokered through Parke-Bernet Galleries.

But the items did not even bring enough money for Clara and Jacques to repay Caroline for the shortfall from her purchase price. Ironically, not long after this sale, the income from the Twain Trust began to steadily rise with a resurgence of interest in all things Twain.

On April 14, 1958, Clara wrote a will that dealt Nina a devastating emotional blow: it completely disinherited her.

Not only was Nina not named as one of Clara's principal heirs, but she was not even a contingent beneficiary. Clara stipulated husband Jacques as her primary beneficiary, an unremarkable clause.

But in what must have been a shocking clause from Nina's perspective, Clara's will established that in the event Jacques predeceased her, or after his death if he survived her, the income from the Mark Twain Trust (then re-designated as the Samossoud Trust) would devolve upon Dr. Seiler.

If Nina was insulted and hurt when Clara had encouraged Phyllis Harrington to seek appointment as her guardian, it is hard to imagine how utterly unloved she felt upon learning the terms of Clara's will.

Without giving her daughter the dignity and understanding that might have come from a phone call, Clara explained in a letter that she chose to devise her will as she had because Nina had previously been provided for monetarily with the income from the trust created in 1944, and that she felt any additional money would simply do Nina no good.

The terms of the will went on to state that after the deaths of both Jacques and Dr. Seiler, the principal of the Samossoud Trust would be rolled into a new trust entity to be called The Mark Twain Foundation with the income from the trust to be used for a variety of charitable purposes.

If Clara had simply constructed her will to leave everything to Jacques, and thereafter to the planned Mark Twain Foundation, it would have been consistent with her explanation that she thought the money would do Nina more harm than good. However, the decision to throw Dr. Seiler into the mix as heir to the Samossoud Trust income seems to demonstrate the hand of Jacques.

Clara was a Christian Scientist, and, while there is evidence that she allowed Dr. Seiler to treat her from time to time, he certainly could not be deemed "her doctor," as that was against the tenets of her faith.

There is no evidence that Clara offered Nina, or anyone, an explanation for why she designated Seiler as her heir. An obvious and plausible explanation is that Jacques owed his friend money and the two amicably agreed that the debt could be settled in that manner.

When I interviewed Seiler's widow Reita, a lovely and gracious woman, she indicated that she had married Seiler several years after Clara's death and so was not privy to what had transpired.

She was hurt by an article published in 2003 in the *San Diego Reader* that painted her husband as having somehow acted irresponsibly and unprofessionally. She felt that Clara simply felt affection for husband.

While the true reason for Seiler's inclusion in the will remains a mystery, it is nearly certain that the psychological impact on Nina of her exclusion from Clara's will was significant.

The rift between the two was not complete however as evidenced by a partially extant letter from Clara to Nina. Clara is clearly bed-bound and quite ill, and complains (rightfully) that her pen is jerking all over the page, but expresses a strong desire to see Nina:

> *Yes, dear heart I wish we were together and could amuse ourselves in our private fashion. Of course the bed is not the best locality for any kind of fun however.*
>
> *Mrs. Harrington said your being in the hospital did not mean you were really ill, which of course I was greatly relieved to hear. Don't, for heaven's sake, be ill!! I am doing enough in that line for a whole family.*

Nina's last vestige of family disappeared when, on September 19, 1962, Clara passed away. The stage was set for a major confrontation between Nina and Jacques.

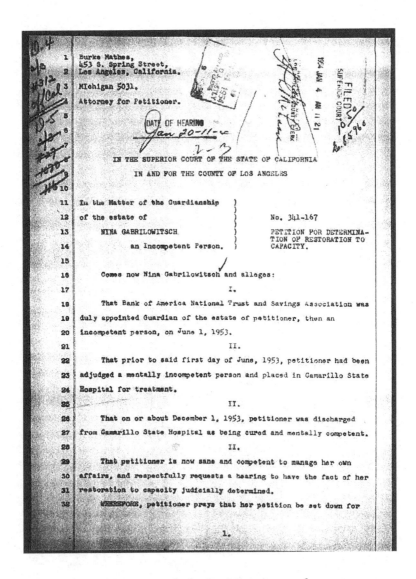

1 Burke Mathes,
2 453 S. Spring Street,
   Los Angeles, California.
3 MIchigan 5031.
4 Attorney for Petitioner.

5

   DATE OF HEARING
   Jan 20-11-c

6

7

8

9

10

   IN THE SUPERIOR COURT OF THE STATE OF CALIFORNIA

   IN AND FOR THE COUNTY OF LOS ANGELES

11 In the Matter of the Guardianship   )
12 of the estate of   )   No. 341-167
13 NINA GABRILOWITSCH   )   PETITION FOR DETERMINA-
)   TION OF RESTORATION TO
14   an Incompetent Person.   )   CAPACITY.

15

16 Comes now Nina Gabrilowitsch and alleges:

17   I.

18   That Bank of America National Trust and Savings Association was
19 duly appointed Guardian of the estate of petitioner, then an
20 incompetent person, on June 1, 1953.

21   II.

22   That prior to said first day of June, 1953, petitioner had been
23 adjudged a mentally incompetent person and placed in Camarillo State
24 Hospital for treatment.

25   II.

26   That on or about December 1, 1953, petitioner was discharged
27 from Camarillo State Hospital as being cured and mentally competent.

28   II.

29   That petitioner is now sane and competent to manage her own
30 affairs, and respectfully requests a hearing to have the fact of her
31 restoration to capacity judicially determined.

32   WHEREFORE, petitioner prays that her petition be set down for

                              1.

Except from 1953 paper declaring Nina restored to competency
Copy of original Court document

CHAPTER 20

SUSAN

1956–1962

A BRIGHT EYED GIRL

WHILE THE QUALITY OF NINA'S LIFE rapidly declined, I was just beginning to spread my wings.

When I started college that January of 1956, I doubt if any other Stetson co-ed appreciated her little bed in a dorm room more than I did. It represented security to me. I knew where I would be sleeping each night and where I would be eating each day. I had nice clothes and money in my little bank account.

I bought myself a camera and a watch, the first ones I had ever owned. Since the day I was sent to Chicago when I was seven, this was the best chance I had been given in life, and I intended to make the most of it.

Other than class schedules, meal schedules, and a nightly curfew, I was on my own. I loved college life and made friends easily. Several of the sororities were rushing me, but that was not part of the course I set for myself. I had a very specific set of goals: land all the acting parts I could, finish college, move to New York, knock Broadway off its feet, and then someday get married and have children.

I know that Nina shared the first goals, but will never know whether she wanted the latter.

I thought about these yet-to-be children often, although I hadn't given much thought to their future father. In my dream future, I knew that I would have at least one boy and one girl and that what I wanted for them was what I had never had: total love and security. I vowed to provide them with unconditional love and a home that they would always know was theirs, a place to which they could always return no matter how old they were.

Though I didn't think specifically about the father necessary to bring these plans to fruition, I did think about him in general terms. I knew he would have to be a professional, a good provider, a loving kind husband, and, most of all, a doting father. In a word, I wanted to prove that I could do "better" than my families (the Baileys and Lucias and, unbeknownst to me at that time, the Gabrilowitsches) had done for me.

I knew that to be a good mother was the most important job in the world. With these principles firmly in mind, I attacked college life with great enthusiasm. I was soon to find out, however, that life has a way of throwing curve balls in our path no matter how well thought out one's plans.

The first round of trouble came in the form of strep throat. This necessitated a visit to the student infirmary where a shot of penicillin was administered. That night I woke up feeling hot. I stumbled to the bathroom, looked in the mirror, and was horrified to see that my face was swollen and covered with a rash.

I remember waking up my roommate and then life went black until I woke up in the hospital several days later. An extreme allergic reaction to the penicillin forced my panicked roommate to call for an ambulance to get me to the hospital.

After I was well enough to be discharged from the hospital itself, I was sent to the infirmary to complete my recovery. During that time John, the student who had helped me get into Stetson, visited me regularly and helped me catch up with missed course work.

Before I met John, he had been engaged to another student. However, when she came back from Christmas vacation in 1955, she broke off their engagement, so John was very much on the rebound when I first met him.

After I got out of the infirmary and was back in my dorm, John kept coming around. We hung out together and he introduced me to a new dimension of the social and intellectual strata of college life that I didn't know existed.

John's IQ was in the stratosphere. He was the de facto leader of the Stetson intellectual crowd and president of both Scroll and Key and Omicron Delta Kappa, the National Honor Society.

On Tuesday nights, students from those groups met at the house of the

Dean of University, Dr. Hugh McEniry, and would sit at the "master's" feet and talk about religion, philosophy, and other erudite subjects that I had never even considered.

After all, most of my teen years up until then had been focused on survival. I felt very out of place there as most of the students were seniors, and I was only a freshman.

However, Dean McEniry was a charismatic leader who included all of the students at Stetson, not just the obviously brilliant ones. He engaged me in a series of questions that made me think, and he always considered my answers and seemed to find some merit in them.

I had made good grades in high school, but had missed so much due to our nomadic lifestyle, I never really thought of myself as one of the "smart ones." At "McEniry's Tuesday nights," he did more for my self-esteem than all the applause I had heard at the end of all the plays I had been in since I was a child.

He made me feel worthy: worthy of being a Stetson student, worthy of holding my own with the brilliant students who surrounded me, and maybe even worthy of being John's girlfriend, a title toward which I seemed to be progressing.

When my first semester ended in June of 1956, I was faced with the problem of where to go for the summer. Going back to Drucilla's was not an option. Since Eileen was still heavily involved with the Jehovah's Witnesses and had forced me to choose between joining her religion or staying out of her life entirely, that door was closed to me as well.

I was saved by my high school friend Yvonne Whitney. Her father was a doctor, and they had a house at Indian Rocks Beach, right on the Gulf of Mexico. She planned to spend the entire summer there and invited me to join her.

That was a wonderful summer. The Whitney's large, beautiful home attracted plenty of young people for almost nightly parties. I met a lot of new young men. However, compared to the maturity and intellect of John, these high school and college boys seemed sadly lacking.

At the end of the summer, when John came down to take me back to Stetson, he arrived with a surprise. Like the hero in a romance novel, he got down on one knee in the sand by the ocean and asked me if I would please do him the honor of marrying him.

Sadly, like Nina, life eventually taught me that men were rarely the heroes they first seemed to be, but nothing that happened later could ever remove the magic of that moment.

We were different in so many ways. I was eighteen years old; he was twenty-six. I had three more years to get a BA; he was headed to medical school in another year. To this day, I honestly don't know if I was in love with John or in love with the idea of my dream husband. Responsible, professional, and, I presumed, set to be a doting father for my children, he fit that role perfectly.

From my perspective of sand and moonlight, the only cloud I could see on the horizon was that I wanted to finish college. Drucilla was still providing tuition and expense money, but would she be able to continue to do that?

I told John that I wanted to marry him, but that I also intended to finish college. He agreed that this was important, so I took a leap of faith and told him I would marry him. In one year, I had gone from a girl without a home whose future prospects looked bleak, to a girl heading back to Stetson for my sophomore year with a ring on my finger from the biggest catch on campus.

John and I were married in February 1957 and settled in a small house on Blue Lake in DeLand, Florida. That June, he graduated from Stetson with a 4.0 average, the highest in his class.

He had decided against becoming a doctor, so in August, we moved to Chapel Hill, where he had been accepted into graduate school in the Philosophy Department of the University of North Carolina. I too had been accepted there as a sophomore majoring in speech and drama.

We rented a small apartment and settled back into classes. We didn't have much money, but Drucilla was still paying my tuition, and John had a fellowship, so we scraped by like all the other students. I got a part time job in the office of the Dean of the Graduate School so that helped out. And, I was accepted into the Carolina Playmakers, the prestigious resident UNC drama company.

In 1958, my world turned upside down—I discovered I was pregnant. While children were part of my long-term dream, the pregnancy was totally unplanned. Since we had only student health insurance, I had to utilize the student health facility to see a doctor.

Everything went well for the first four months of the pregnancy. Then one afternoon, following what can only be described as a brutal physical exam, I lost the baby before I could even get out of the clinic.

It was a boy. Although I had not initially wanted to become pregnant at the time, the loss of this baby sent me into a deep state of grief for the son I would never know. After that, my studies and everything else took a back seat to a driving desire to become a mother. Financially, this would be the worst possible move for us, but something had been triggered in me by the loss of my child, and it would not go away.

Our daughter Karen Lynn was born in 1960, and I immediately found out at a heart level exactly what unconditional love really was. For the week we were in the hospital, I couldn't let go of her. I didn't even want the nurses to take her when they came to return her to the nursery.

During the time of Karen's birth, John showed the first signs of instability in that he disappeared the entire week. He had taken me to the hospital before Karen was born, and then never returned. His parents had to drive up from Mississippi to take me home from the hospital and help me out for a few days until he showed up.

After they left, Drucilla came up to help but got into an argument with John the first night she was there and left immediately. Of course I asked him where he had been and he said in a very hostile voice, "Out of town on business and that is the end of this discussion."

Being brought up without many options and accepting the shelter that I was given by whoever had taken me in at the moment. I accepted this answer without argument. After all, he was providing me and my child with a roof over our heads and the very food we ate. I felt I was in no position to argue.

But none of this really mattered. I was feeling better each day and I was in love with my baby. I often stood in the doorway of her room, just watching her sleep in her little crib, thinking that if I stopped watching her, she might stop breathing. Many nights I fell asleep with her curled up in my arms.

She was a beautiful, smart baby and met all her developmental milestones early. By the time she was ten months old, she was walking and talking so well that we could understand everything she said.

I thanked God for my baby and thought she made up for everything I had gone through in my life before she was born.

John, for his part, was an absentee father. He was in the last year of his PhD program and busy writing his dissertation. His life was largely spent in a study carrel at the library, not at home where there was a crying newborn.

He sometimes held her and pictures taken during her first year show a smiling John looking down on this beautiful child. However, he never fed her or changed a diaper. He did buy me a washing machine, and that was a tremendous advantage over having to take a baby to the Laundromat.

I spent many nights typing theses and dissertations for extra money. After all, I was up with a new baby anyway so I might as well be doing something useful between feedings. The last year in Chapel Hill I got a job as secretary at the local Presbyterian Church. They had playpens in the nursery and let me bring Karen with me and put her next to my desk.

When she was a year old, John received his PhD and was subsequently offered a job as an Assistant Professor at the University of Manitoba in Winnipeg, Canada. He accepted, and our little family of three prepared for the big move.

We had been In Chapel Hill for four years. While John worked toward his degree, I had managed only one more year of college with two pregnancies, part time work, and the money from Drucilla was beginning to dry up.

With the knowledge I now have about Clara, I strongly suspect that she had been the source of this money and that Jacques spendthrift habits had dried up the well.

We arrived in Winnipeg in August of 1961 and rented a fully furnished house in a nice neighborhood from a professor who was on a one-year sabbatical. The neighborhood was a true melting pot. The people on one side of us were from England, on the other side from Scotland. Across the street were families from Italy and France. All the cartoons on TV were in French, so Karen, like her mother, learned that language before the age of two.

In April, 1962, I was in an accident and sustained a concussion and broken left arm. We had to fly to Florida for six weeks and move back in with Drucilla as I could not change a diaper or take care of a toddler with my arm in a cast. I was more than a little nervous about this but just seemed to have no other options.

On the return trip home our plane, Trans Canada, had a problem with the landing gear. It wouldn't come down. We crash landed on foam at the Toronto Airport, went off the runway, broke the right wing and had to exit the plane by sliding down the evacuation slide.

The right side and rear of the plane were non-functional and so it was an uphill climb to even get to the slide. I had to turn Karen over to a serviceman who agreed to hold her going down the slide. I could not hold onto her with one arm.

If I ever thought about being in a plane crash the scenario would have been nothing at all like what actually happened. We knew about the landing gear malfunction since taking off from Tampa. The pilot had kept us well informed. We had first gone out over the Gulf of Mexico to use up fuel and then we were in a holding pattern at the Toronto Airport for over an hour.

The flight attendants relieved everyone of their glasses, pens, shoes without laces, false teeth, hearing aids, and any other objects that might become harmful in a crash. They gave us all pillows and showed us how to clutch our ankles as we came in for a landing.

They also served liquor—free! There was no panic and we all came down that slide safely except for one woman who flipped over the side somehow and broke a bone. As soon as we were on the ground the airport personnel quickly got us into buses and took us to the terminal.

Of course everyone who was going on to another city had missed their connections and we were going to Winnipeg. There wasn't another flight out until the morning so the airline was trying to find a hotel for Karen and me. I was running out of diapers and bottles for her and didn't know how I would manage until morning.

Then a very nice gentleman came up and told me he had a company Lear jet waiting that was just getting ready to take off for Winnipeg and he would gladly give my baby and me a ride if we would like.

I definitely *would* like. I felt I had no other choice. That was one fast and luxurious ride and also the ride that was the beginning of the end of my marriage.

John was not at the Winnipeg Airport to meet us! I called our house several times but there was no answer. I had to take a cab and then ring the doorbell over and over to wake him up to get money to pay the cab driver.

I asked him why he wasn't at the airport and if he knew our plane had crashed. He said he found that out when he called to see if the plane was on time so he never went to the airport. He said he knew someone would call him if anything happened.

He apparently just went to bed, not knowing if his wife and child were dead or alive. How could any sane, loving person even sleep under those circumstances? I decided right then that I had to make a life for myself and Karen that didn't include John.

I almost immediately became more independent than I had ever been. Karen and I started doing some unusual things. I guess traveling so much with Eileen when I was growing up had instilled wanderlust in me. I only know that I was no longer content to just stay home.

In the fall of 1962, John accepted a job as an Associate Professor at the State University of New York at Albany, so we moved again. Shortly after we arrived, I remember reading about Clara's death in the newspaper, and I was saddened. I hadn't seen her since I was a child, but I remembered the kind things she had done for me.

I just wanted to talk with someone else who knew her, so I tried to call Eileen in California. Russell answered the phone and seemed glad to hear from me. He asked me how I was and where I was, but when I asked to speak to Eileen, he told me that she just wouldn't talk with me.

I told him that I had read about Clara's death, news he had not heard. He said they didn't keep up with things like that anymore.

With an incredible sense of sadness, there was nothing to do but hang up. I didn't know anyone else to call who knew her and I felt like I wanted to talk about her with someone.

I never even thought of Nina.

CHAPTER 21

DEB

NINA'S STRUGGLES (1962-1966)

WHILE THE DEATH OF Clara Clemens Gabrilowitsch Samossoud created only a small, sad ripple in Susan's life, it hit Nina like a tsunami.

The reading of Clara's will made it clear that the mother-daughter tie had been severed even before death caused them to part. While Clara had made the terms of her will known to Nina in advance, now her humiliation was public.

Nina did not take the news lying down. She was involved at the time with a man named George Wrentmore who was educated and protective of her. Phyllis Harrington also felt aggrieved by the will.

With the encouragement of those two, as well as that of an attorney, Nina challenged Clara's will both in California and in Connecticut. The suit, in fact, also named the estate of Samuel L. Clemens as Clara's will had modified the terms of the original trust set up by Twain himself.

Since Phyllis had handled all of Clara's day-to-day financial affairs and had no love for Jacques, it is nearly certain that she supplied some of the fiscal information used in the battle.

Phyllis also sued Jacques Samossoud and Dr. Seiler separately. On January 14, 1963, Samossoud and Seiler agreed to set aside a $35,000 fund for the benefit of Phyllis.

As the court battle continued, one ace that Nina had up her sleeve was the promissory notes that Clara had, with the encouragement of Phyllis Harrington, made Jacques sign for some of the sums that she gave to him.

This is perhaps the only sign that she was not as blind to her husband's peccadilloes as she had appeared. Since Clara had spent a lifetime protecting her father's legacy, she likely wanted to assure that as much money as possible was still available to be put to its ultimate charitable use.

In light of those loans, which, with interest, totaled nearly $800,000, Jacques's motivation to see that Nina was not made an heir becomes even clearer. If Clara's estate flowed only to him, then the loans would never need to be repaid. If Nina were also an heir, he would owe the estate for whatever portion of the loan represented her share.

Armed with this knowledge, Nina's attorneys crafted the lawsuit to claim that Jacques and Dr. Seiler had basically coerced Clara into disinheriting Nina by taking advantage of Clara's weakened state and advanced age. Nina also asserted that Jacques had told Clara that Nina did not love her and wasn't worthy of being a beneficiary of the Twain legacy.

Then they pulled out their big guns and stated that Jacques should be required to repay the estate for the vast sums he owed.

Faced with that threat, Jacques caved and negotiated. An Agreement Compromising Will Contests and Claims to Estate was signed by all parties on August 30, 1963. While details dragged on in court for several more months, this agreement essentially settled the probate of the estate of Clara Clemens Samossoud.

The terms of the agreement altered the distribution of Clara's assets in several ways. It formally awarded Phyllis Harrington $300 a month until the deaths of both Samossoud and Seiler, and Nina was cut in for a portion of the distribution of income from the Samossoud (formerly Samuel Clemens) Trust.

For Jacques's lifetime, he was to receive 65 percent of the income of the trust and Nina 35 percent. Upon the death of Jacques, Dr. Seiler was then to receive 55 percent of the income and Nina 45 percent.

It is of note that Nina's share was to go to "Nina Clemens Gabrilowitsch, and to her heirs, administrators, successors, and assigns." Dr. Seiler outlived Nina by over a decade, but there is no evidence in her estate records that the proceeds of her 35-45% share of the Samossoud Trust flowed to her estate.

The agreement also altered the original stipulation in Clara's will that Jacques could never withdraw more than 10 percent of the principal of the Samossoud Trust.

The altered clause provided for Nina to be paid fifteen thousand dollars and for Dr. Seiler to be paid fifteen thousand dollars. The balance of the 10 percent principal was to be paid to Jacques except that, in no event was he to receive more than ten thousand dollars.

He was also directed to pay from his share any creditors of Clara's estate including Phyllis Harrington, author Caroline Harnsberger, the Bahia Hotel where Jacques and Clara had been living, and any medical creditors.

In exchange, Jacques was to be relieved of his responsibility to pay the substantial promissory notes that he signed to Clara.

Nina was required to insure Phyllis Harrington against the death of Dr. Seiler in exchange for Phyllis foregoing the $35,000 that Samossoud and Seiler had agreed to in their separate January 14th settlement with her. It is interesting that Nina was not required to insure against Jacques's life, perhaps because he was already ill with pancreatic cancer.

Any and all proceeds due to Nina as a result of the agreement were to be paid to Security First National Bank into a trust established for that purpose.

It is noted that in the court judgment, finding number six specifically alleges that Nina was "the sole surviving descendant of Samuel L. Clemens."

For Nina, however, it was a Pyrrhic victory. Stress over the extended lawsuit had caused her to sink into further depression and to drink ever more heavily. Shortly after the agreement was signed, on September 23, 1963, an exhausted Nina filed in Los Angeles Probate Court, through the law firm of Smith and Davis, to have a conservator appointed.

She requested that Bank of America be appointed conservator of her estate and that attorney Al Mathews be appointed as conservator of her person. The latter position would entitle Mathews to make medical and personal decisions of Nina's behalf while the former would permit the bank to take care of her financial matters.

It is noteworthy that where she was referred to as "never married," Nina crossed the phrase out and inserted the word "unmarried." She asserted that she had no issue. Neither this document nor any other unearthed in research ever acknowledged the existence of a child.

On October 14, 1963, apparently unhappy with the original law firm, Nina filed to dismiss the original petition and substituted as her attorney,

Mr. Myron Harpole. Harpole, who had been one of Nina's attorneys in the probate battle, was to remain Nina's attorney and staunch defender for the remainder of her life and beyond.

On February 13, 1964, with the assistance of Harpole, Nina wrote a will. Just four days later, she again petitioned the court to have Al Mathews appointed as conservator of her person and Security First National Bank as conservator of her estate. Shortly thereafter, The *Los Angeles Times* reported the granting of her petition:

> *The appointments were made by Superior Court Judge Clyde C. Triplett after Miss Gabrilowitsch, 53, testified that she considered herself too ill to manage her own affairs.*

In an undated letter to friend Jules Schmidt possibly written after this appointment, Nina wrote:

> *I'm bitter now, Jules, so don't mind what I say. All I wanted was to get rid of Mrs. Harrington—now I'm worse off. People are leaping in on me like vultures.*

On February 26, 1964, Nina wrote a letter to Al Mathews thanking him for assisting both her and friend (and presumed lover) George Wrentmore.

In the letter, Nina expresses deep guilt and regret over something she has done that has caused George to be ejected from the apartment that they shared.

> *The picture of George in that bleak room haunts me. The fact that he can't come back to the apartment is all my fault sickens me. I passed out several times from liquor & pills & he was afraid I would die and would have me sent to the hospital.*

The next portion of the letter rambled but implies that either in California or Mexico, Nina got drunk enough to wander the streets and be picked up by the police. She then goes on to explain to Mathews how friend Jules Schmidt hated Wrentmore.

Schmidt, she said was asserting that Wrentmore was borrowing money from her when it was, in fact, the other way around.

> *I think he hates G & you because of that man coming here to thro Jules out. That was my fault too….For 8 long yrs George has been a loyal friend & I can't thro him out like an old shoe.*

Nina was forthright about the degree of her despair.

> *I'm sober now but my mind isn't tracking at all. Everything depresses me. I've lost my sense of humor.….All I want is to sleep.*

In another telling revelation, Nina disclosed that Jules Schmidt, apparently divorced from wife Mollie, had been to visit.

> *Jules came out here to marry me—hoping that I would be willing & take me back east with him but I can't do it. Sex drive is dead in me & in 1937 I did love him.*

With Susan Bailey's birth in late 1936, or possibly in early to mid 1937, this clearly placed Jules Schmidt as more than just a friend in Nina's life at the time.

Nina then went on to describe how George Wrentmore discovered that Phyllis Harrington had, in his estimation, been abusing a joint checking account that Nina claimed to be unaware of. Her description of the situation is so unfocused that it is difficult to determine whether there was any validity to the claim.

Nina's love-hate relationship with Phyllis continued. She described how Harrington had kept from her the news of the death of Bank of America attorney George Harnagel whom she barely knew.

*...she did not want to shock me...& yet she didn't mind telling me
that Bruno W. [long-time Gabrilowitsch family friend and conductor Bruno Walter] had died which was a real shock. B.W. said he
never saw such a case of hypnosis as Jacques had over mother.*

In the ensuing months, Nina's continued companionship with ailing
George Wrentmore provided a certain amount of stability in her life, but
even that disappeared when George, thirteen years her senior, passed away
on May 3, 1965.

On September 13, 1965, Nina wrote a letter to Jules Schmidt and his wife
Helen. It is unknown when Schmidt remarried but presumably sometime
after Nina had refused him in February 1964.

Nina indicated to Schmidt that she was living in Twenty-Nine Palms,
California, at an adobe house owned by a Mrs. Lova Dolle. She said that she
moved there because of the need to get away from Los Angeles.

*I was getting close to a nervous breakdown at the Highland Tow-
ers. The psychologist was getting on my nerves a good part of the
time and I miss George's affection so terribly.*

Nina referenced a twenty-page letter which she had written but not
mailed and cautioned Jules against sending anything to her Highland Towers address for fear that her live-in nurse, Sig Fritschel, might open and read
it. Al Mathews, Nina indicated, had sent Fritschel to live with her.

*At first I thought he was a gem, but after 8 months I've changed
my mind. His German attitude of "Deutschland Deutschland uber
alles" is devastating—although he does mean well.*

Nina mentioned having lived at some point, presumably not long before,
in Scottsdale, Arizona, and not particularly liking it, "but maybe George's
illness was on my mind."

Her long-time friendship with Pat Gleason was also on the ropes.

I can't count on Pat Gleason because he's become moody, & lives like a hermit except 2 nights a week bar-tending. He's right across the street & rarely comes to see me.

With the lease on her Highland Towers apartment coming up for re-newal, Nina was wrestling with whether or not to renew it. She expressed interest to Schmidt in going to Florida to meet his wife and also inquired about moving to Fort Lauderdale where Jules was planning to settle. She seemed unsure of her welcome however.

Maybe you have changed your plans, & don't want me to come. If so, please say so. I shall understand. I don't want to be a burden to anyone. I can keep myself entertained.

On November 29, 1965, Nina placed a call to The *Los Angeles Herald-Examiner* indicating that she urgently needed to talk to a reporter. Even though it had been more than half a century since Mark Twain's death, she probably banked on the fact that throwing out the name of her famous grandfather virtually guaranteed that she would get a response.

The following day, columnist Dick Horning published an article entitled "Mark Twain's Kin Lives as Pauper." A photograph accompanying the ar-ticle shows that Nina had prepared carefully for the interview with nearly theatrical make-up and a stylish blouse and jacket.

This picture is in sharp contrast to other photographs of the period that show her with heavy bags under eyes, unkempt hair, and little to no make-up. No one viewing the photo would have seen her as down and out.

By contrast, in the interview, Nina claimed that despite receiving 35 percent of her mother's estate, she was living like a pauper and that all the clothes she had to her name were two print dresses, an overcoat, one pair of shoes, and a few miscellaneous items.

Nina bounced around from topic to topic, showing off sketches she had drawn, along with an autobiography she was writing. She even touched on first love Carl Roters:

This one's Carl Roters, my first husband. I married him in 1932 when I was a student at Barnard College. We divorced in 1935—no children.

As previously mentioned, there is no factual evidence that Nina married Carl, and he himself denied it. Her reference to him as her "first husband" is even more interesting. This perhaps relates to a claim she sometimes made that she and George Wrentmore had married while on one of their trips to Mexico. The Wrentmore family does not believe that such a marriage took place.

In the interview, Nina also mentioned wanting to travel and to visit her cousin Olivia Lada-Mocarski at Quarry Farm where her grandfather, Mark Twain, spent so many happy hours. She talked about the weather being bad for her bangs. She mentioned her early acting days.

The tone of the article is respectful, but it is clear that Horning was struggling to impose some structure on an unfocused interview that clearly had not been "urgent" in nature.

Reading the article is nearly painful. It seems a desperate cry for attention and for acknowledgment that she had once been an active vibrant woman and part of an important family.

Saddened by what she had read in the article, friend Rochelle Vickey dropped Nina a letter that read:

My mother recently sent me that awful article from the Herald— about YOU...Despite what little we have to offer one another, it's good to communicate while we have life and limb to do so,—the little notes and get-togethers often spark those happy moments that none of us can manage to keep!

Whether Nina responded is unknown. The end was drawing near.

CHAPTER 22

DEB

THE DEATH OF NINA (1966)

"When I die, I want artificial flowers, jitterbug music and a bottle of vodka at my grave."

NINA CLEMENS GABRILOWITSCH
JANUARY 15, 1966

ON JANUARY 19, 1966, a *New York Times* article headline reported: "Nina Clemens Gabrilowitsch, 55, Twain's Last Direct Heir, Dies."

Nina, the article stated, had been found dead at "a Los Angeles motel where she often stayed. Several bottles of pills and alcohol were found." The autopsy and police report confirm the presence of those articles in the room.

The years of drinking, and mood swings, and a profound sense of aloneness had culminated in that moment.

Bartender William Shaw, who had spoken with Nina on Saturday, January 15, 1966, just hours before her body was found, reported the jitterbug music quip. It became the signature detail that thereafter served to indelibly define Nina Clemens Gabrilowitsch in Mark Twain lore.

Her bright mind, mercurial wit, and unflagging devotion to her friends were lost to history. She became the drunk who killed herself with pills.

The call came into the Los Angeles Police department at 5:50 p.m. on January 16, 1966. Detective George Sobota took the call and headed to Apartment 206 of the Hyatt Lodge at 2011 North Highland Avenue in Hollywood.

His three-page LAPD Death Report, filed at 4:33 a.m. on January 17,

1966, indicated that Nina's body had been found nearly an hour and twenty minutes prior to the time the call was placed to the department.

A Dr. Laurence Stuppy placed the call to report Nina's death. Stuppy, a Harvard educated physician, indicated in his witness statement that he had known Nina since 1960, as both a patient and a friend.

Stuppy's daughter, when contacted in 2010, reported that while Nina had been a holiday guest of the family on more than one occasion, her father never discussed the circumstances surrounding Nina's death. He was, she said, a man who took doctor-patient confidentiality very seriously and would never have discussed such a delicate matter with his family.

By the time Detective Sobota arrived on the scene, it was clear that a number of people including Richard Francis Gleason (who had discovered the body), hotel desk clerk John Harlan Pekins, Dr. Stuppy, attorney and personal conservator Al Matthews, and possibly Sig Fritschel (who represented himself as Nina's guardian) had already entered the room.

A paucity of detail exists concerning the nearly hour and a half time period between the discovery of Nina's body at 4:30 p.m. and Dr. Stuppy's 5:50 p.m. call to the LAPD.

Why was Dr. Stuppy called to the scene? Why was attorney Al Matthews present and who called him? Why didn't anyone call the police sooner?

The events of the days and hours preceding Nina's death and the events of the on-scene investigation at the Hyatt Lodge on the day she died are reconstructed per Detective Sobota's Death Report and witness statements contained therein.

Richard Francis Gleason indicated that he knocked on the door of Apartment 206 at about 4:30 p.m. on January 16 to retrieve a model ship that was the apparent subject of a financial dispute between Sig Fritschel and another party (possibly Gleason himself).

When Nina did not answer the door, Mr. Gleason called desk clerk John Pekins to let him in. Had Nina called Gleason some time prior to this? If not, why had he expected her to be in the room?

While Nina frequently stayed at the Hyatt Lodge, her usual residence was at nearby 1922 North Highland where she shared apartments 61 and 63 with Sig Fritschel. From photographs at The Mark Twain House & Museum in Hartford, Connecticut, it appears that Nina had known members of the Gleason family for many years.

In her will, she left a small annuity to Pat Gleason. It is unknown whether Pat was a nickname for this Richard Francis Gleason or whether he was another member of that family.

When Gleason and Pekins tried to open the door, they found it jammed by a blue chair that had been turned on its side. Shoving the door open, they discovered Nina lying on the floor and called Dr. Stuppy to the scene. Dr. Stuppy pronounced her deceased of causes unknown.

Upon arrival, Detective Sobota entered the room with Gleason, Stuppy, apartment manager Jack Tierney, and attorney Al Mathews.

Sobota described finding Nina lying on her back on the floor near the dressing room with her arms at her side. On the table were two glasses with a white granular substance around the rims, an empty martini glass, and an empty prescription pill bottle for a non-steroidal anti-inflammatory drug called Indolin.

Sobota remarked that a four-foot by five-foot sliding glass door next to the front door was "closed but unlocked with a screen installed that could be easily removed."

Her purse lay about five feet away, its contents strewn on the floor. Among the contents were two admission slips from St. Vincent Hospital dated January 7 and 9. The blue chair lay on its back near the door and a picture over the bed hung at an angle. A partially full bottle of Wolfschmidt vodka was observed under the bed.

In the nightstand were two vials of pills, prescribed by a Dr. Boken on January 11. The first (erroneously described as "Corbrital" in the report) was Carbrital, a sleeping pill containing a combination of pentobarbital and carbromal. The second vial contained the methamphetamine Desoxyn.

Dr. Stuppy described visiting Nina on January 12 and administering a penicillin shot for an apparent pulmonary condition. He described Nina to Detective Sobota as "lacking the responsibility to take care of herself."

He also indicated that Dr. Boken, a colleague of his, had prescribed sleeping pills for Nina in the week preceding her death. He did not mention the prescription for Desoxyn, an "upper" which would not ordinarily be prescribed with a barbiturate such as Carbrital.

The doctor also stated that he hospitalized Nina in San Diego in December of 1965 due to a "violent episode." He then transferred her to St. Vincent Hospital in Los Angeles and indicated that he frequently gave Nina passes to leave the hospital.

Sig Fritschel, who claimed to be Nina's "guardian," told Detective Sobota that he met Nina in November of 1964 and moved in with her in December 1964. Per her September 13, 1965 letter, Fritschel was, in fact, appointed by Al Mathews to be her live-in nurse.

Sig described Nina as "incompetent, of average intelligence, but emotionally age 8 and a heavy drinker." He also described Nina appearing at the residence they shared at about midnight on January 13 and telling him that she was AWOL from the hospital.

She stayed until 10 a.m. the next day and then told him she was going to stay with "the Dahls" in Santa Monica overnight. It seems very likely that this reference was to her friend Lova Dolle.

The final witness was Al Mathews, her conservator and a well known Los Angeles attorney famous for his defenses in such cases as the Barbara Graham and Caryl Chessman ("Red Light Bandit") murder trials. He was a founder, along with *Perry Mason* author Erle Stanley Gardner, of the famed Court of Last Resort.

Mathews indicated to Detective Sobota that he was an attorney and executor of Nina's estate. This claim is interesting as Al Mathews was not, in fact, Nina's executor. As previously mentioned, Nina's will of February 13, 1964, named attorney Myron Harpole for that role.

Perhaps she made a previous will that named Mathews as her executor and he was unaware of the 1964 will, or he was deliberately misrepresenting his role. It is also possible that the term "executor" was simply confused with his role as conservator.

Al Mathews certainly played a significant role in Nina's life. Besides his role as conservator of her person, in the 1964 will, she left "my friend Al Mathews such of my personal effects as he may desire, including but not limited to my books, furniture and furnishings, jewelry and other personal items of this nature."

George Wrentmore, Jr. believes that the relationship between Nina and Al Mathews had deteriorated by the time of her death. His father had passed away about eight months prior to that time.

In an email, George said, *"My dad kept the dogs off Nina's back. When he died, the Mathews boys, et al, swarmed in like vultures. Nina was ready to be plucked."*

While inflammatory, and inaccurate in the sense that Mathews already had a conservator's role in Nina's life, it nonetheless indicates a tension that George sensed.

He even went so far as to state that he felt that a "triple toe loop" down a set of stairs that Nina had taken shortly before her death—in the presence of Mathews—was suspicious.

It would appear there was a minor dispute between Dr. Stuppy and Al Mathews at the scene of Nina's death. Mathews told Detective Sobota that he had called a mortuary as Stuppy was prepared to sign the death certificate.

Stuppy, however, told Mathews that he did not know the cause of death, and therefore, could not sign a death certificate.

The L.A. County Coroner's Office was called in, and Nina's body was taken for autopsy.

2/13/64

LAST WILL AND TESTAMENT
OF
NINA CLEMENS GABRILOWITSCH   50...53

I, NINA CLEMENS GABRILOWITSCH, of Hollywood, California, declare this to be my last Will and Testament, and revoke all other wills and codicils which I have made.

FIRST: I direct my executor to pay as soon after my death as is convenient my expenses of last illness, funeral expenses and just debts.

SECOND: I declare that I am a single woman and that I have no descendants.

THIRD: It is my intent by this Will to dispose of all property whatsoever and wheresoever located that I may have a power to dispose of or to appoint by will or otherwise.

FOURTH: If he survives me, I give, devise and bequeath to my friend Al Matthews such of my personal effects as he may desire, including but not limited to my books, furniture and furnishings, jewelry and other personal items of this nature.   BOOK 1748 PAGE 527

FIFTH: I hereby direct my executor to pay the following annuities from my estate, and I give, devise and bequeath the residue of my estate, real and personal, wherever situated, including all failed and lapsed gifts, to my executor, in trust, to hold, manage and distribute as hereinafter provided in order to pay said annuities and to finally dispose of my estate:

There shall be paid out of first the income and then the principal of the said trust the following sums: /

1. The sum of One Hundred Dollars ($100.00) per month

Excerpt from Nina's will
Copy of original court document

CHAPTER 23

DEB

NO PEACE IN DEATH: NINA (1966-1989)

PERHAPS, I THOUGHT, Nina's sad death might have a silver lining in the search for proof that Nina had given birth to a child. The Death Report filed by Detective Sobota clearly indicated that the coroner's office had been called in to determine cause of death.

Since there was a more than reasonable likelihood that the autopsy would address the issue of whether Nina had ever given birth, a copy of that document was obtained in 2008.

To my surprise, the segment of the autopsy dealing with the genital area simply stated "no evidence of tumor, inflammation, or recent pregnancy," thereby begging the question of whether Nina had previously given birth. Since she was fifty-five years old at the time of her death, a "recent pregnancy" would indeed have been an oddity.

The autopsy did, however, shed light on other aspects of her death. By 11 p.m. on the evening of Nina's demise, the coroner's office reported to Detective Sobota that there were no visible external marks on the body, but that the stomach showed several pills, possibly indicative of an overdose.

Deputy Medical Examiner Eugene McClellan in completing the initial Autopsy Check Sheet at 9:15 p.m. on the night of Nina's death, wrote, "Mode sui?" in the Gross Impression section of the sheet, indicating that he suspected suicide. Cause of death was eventually ruled as "acute barbiturate poisoning, ingested overdose."

It appears that there was some internal disagreement in the coroner's office as to whether the overdose was accidental or suicidal. More than one date is listed as "final" in report copies obtained from that office.

For example, one line indicates January 23, 1964, as the date of finalization of the report. Another box lower on the sheet shows the "Accident" box checked and initialed on January 27. Next to it, the "Suicide" box is checked and initialed by another party on January 31.

Yet another copy of the same sheet bears a typed notation indicating that the verdict of suicide was finalized on February 4. It is that date and verdict that appear on the final death certificate of Nina Clemens Gabrilowitsch.

Was Nina suicidal? Much has been made of her comment to the bartender on the night before she died, yet also contained in his statement was his assessment that Nina was acting "flighty," an adjective that seems inconsistent with the depressive behavior generally displayed by a suicidal person.

Throughout her adult life, Nina was in and out of various treatment facilities, so her stay at St. Vincent just a few days before her death was not significant in the way it might have been for another person.

When contacted via email in late 2007, her executor, attorney Myron Harpole wrote, "The report is that she committed suicide; however, I firmly believe that her sad death could have been by inadvertent use of a prescription drug with alcohol … Of course, I do not really know; but Nina had friends and enjoyment of life. She was an intelligent and pleasant woman."

Attempts to reach Detective Sobota to discuss his impressions of the scene were initially unsuccessful. When reached in late 2010, he displayed a reluctance to discuss the matter.

Given the forty-four years that had passed since Nina's death, his reticence was probably simply based on lack of memory of any details of the scene or, perhaps, a sense that confidentially was still an issue. He said it was best to deal directly with the current Los Angeles Police Department to get any additional details.

Perhaps most telling are words written by Nina herself in an undated letter:

> *Up in that garage of my house I loved so well, I would sleep all day, waken at dusk, have some drinks; Pat or Sigurd Tor the Swede or one of the innumerable couples who lived there with me would fix dinner by candlelight and then to me everything was cozy (My key word to living is the word "cozy").*

When the evening was over, & those people went home (or to bed), then I was in my element, alone with my drinks & my music, particularly the latter. And when the dawn came, cold reality, I would creep into bed oh so gratefully in that garage to the dreams that never deserted me. The Harmons said to me while I was staying with them in Tarzania recently: We used to wonder when we were living with you why you took those drinks so late at night when you were so sleepy you could hardly stand up. We knew you weren't enjoying them, & we finally figured you must be afraid of dying in your sleep. Was that it? Because if it was, you were doing everything in your power to die faster.

They were wrong—it was my waking dream world alone I wanted so badly & I didn't want to go to sleep & miss it. But I am petrified of dying—they were right in that sense.

Harpole filed Nina's will on January 21, 1966, just days after her death. In the will, Nina explicitly stated, "I declare that I am a single woman and that I have no descendants."

However, a later clause stated, "Except as otherwise provided in this will, I have intentionally and with full knowledge neglected to provide for my heirs who may be living at the time of my death."

Perhaps the latter clause was simply legal boilerplate used to cover all eventualities, but it strikes an odd note in light of the explicit statement that she had no descendants.

Nearing the end of her life, and bereft of any close family, Nina chose to leave small annuities to four friends: George Wrentmore, Pat Gleason, Marie Weston, and Jules Schmidt.

Each was to receive a monthly stipend of $75 to $100 a month for the remainder of their lives. The will further provided that after those four were deceased, any remaining monies be "distributed to the American Cancer Society in memory of my father Ossip Gabrilowitsch." She made no provision for her child.

Between the time Nina wrote her will on February 13, 1964, and the time of its admission to the Superior Court of the County of Los Angeles for probate nearly two years later, both George Wrentmore and Marie Weston had died.

Despite Nina having died testate, California law apparently required notifying next of kin of her probate proceedings. The original petition named only her second cousin Olivia (Loomis) Lada-Mocarski.

A February 7, 1966 Supplemental Petition for Probate of Will indicates that executor Harpole requested the sending of additional notices to Jervis Langdon, Mrs. Eleanore [sic] Pennock, and Mrs. Virginia Schieffelin.

The court document listed these individuals as Nina's second cousins. Their grandfather, Charles Langdon, was the only brother of Mark Twain's wife Olivia.

On April 8, 1966, the first startling development in the probate of Nina's estate occurred. Filing through the law firm of Cooney & Cooney, Sigfrid Tor filed a Statement of Claim of Interest asserting that he was "the surviving husband of said decedent and her heir at law" and that he was thus entitled to one-half of her property.

Attorney Harpole almost immediately filed a request to take a deposition from Tor. Tor then filed a request to act as his own attorney, probably because he was unable to afford the legal fees to have representation at the deposition.

It seemed that Nina was to have no peace even after her death. The next challenge to her will came on July 5, 1966, when, filing through attorney Harry E. Rice, a C.A. Huffine requested special notice of all proceedings.

Presenting himself/herself as an heir at law, Huffine's address was given only as care of Rice. No information was provided concerning Huffine's basis for claim of heirship. Nina's probate records give no indication of Huffine ever dropping the claim of heirship, but references to this individual disappear shortly thereafter.

On August 15, 1966, the battle heated up further when Nina's four Langdon relatives petitioned for revocation of her will and for determination of heirship. Listed as defendants were heirs Pat Gleason, Jules Schmidt, Al Matthews, and the American Cancer Society, as well as attorney Myron Harpole and "Does I through X." The significance of the latter term is unclear but implied that there were other potential heirs.

In their challenge, Jervis Langdon, Virginia Schieffelin, Olivia Lada-Mocarski, and Eleanor Pennock claimed that of Nina's great-grandparents, only Jervis and Olivia (Lewis) Langdon and John Marshall and Jane (Lampton) Clemens had left any living issue and that the four of them were thus "the decedent's only next of kin and her only heirs at law."

They challenged Nina's will on the grounds that "the decedent's purported last will is not and never was decedent's will and was made at the time of its execution as a direct result of the undue influence of George Wrentmore, Pat Gleason, Jules Schmidt, and other persons whose identities are yet to be discovered . . ."

They further claimed that Wrentmore and the others had "exploited their confidential relationships" with Nina.

The latter argument is puzzling in light of the fact that Wrentmore, Gleason, Schmidt, and Weston stood to inherit only modest sums of money under the terms of Nina's will, certainly not of sufficient value to coerce her into the will that she created.

The second cousins further claimed that Nina was incompetent because her "continual intemperance and continuous use of intoxicating liquors, barbiturates, and other habit-forming drugs...so weakened [Nina's] physical and mental powers as to cause her to be in such a fixed and continued condition of mental unsoundness as to be mentally deranged" and incapable of executing a will.

The Langdon relatives then claimed that at the time her will was created, Nina did not recollect or understand what monies she possessed or "remember her relations to her next of kin."

Somewhere in the next few days, the attorneys for the Langdon family claimants acknowledged that an Andrew Gabrilowitsch of Silver Springs, Maryland was a next of kin of equal standing with the Langdons. Andrew was the grandson of Eugene Gabrilowitsch, brother of Nina's grandfather Solomon Gabrilowitsch.

Since Solomon is believed to have had nine siblings, it is nearly certain that there were many other second cousins on the Gabrilowitsch side, but none others were named. It is possible that the "Does I through X" referenced in earlier petitions was an attempt on the part of Nina's attorney to acknowledge that there were likely to be additional kin located.

On September 22, 1966, Harpole filed a vigorous rebuttal of the Langdon claims that Nina was incompetent at the time she executed her will. On September 8, the American Cancer Society had also filed to dispute the Langdon assertions as did heir Pat Gleason on September 5 and heir (and attorney) Al Mathews on September 20.

On October 21, Sigfrid Tor weighed in, agreeing with the Langdons that Nina "was incompetent to make a will on the date of said instrument, and he verily believes that she was unduly influenced in the making of said purported will."

He went on to state that he had married Nina on May 14, 1951 in Tijuana, Mexico, and was never divorced from her. He, therefore, requested that the will be revoked and he be declared her sole heir.

On December 15, 1966, the Langdon family members formally withdrew their petition for revocation of Nina's will. Why had they filed in the first place and why did they withdraw their petition?

The Langdons were wealthy but Nina, at the time of her death, possessed an estate of only modest value. She had some Treasury bonds and several small insurance policies, but the major source of her income had been from the proceeds of the Gabrilowitsch Trust that her mother had created in 1944.

Provisions of that trust were such that the principal devolved upon Yale University and The American Red Cross after Nina's death. Despite her successful contest of her mother's will, it is unclear whether she ever received any income from her thirty-five to forty-five percent share of the Samossoud (formerly Samuel Clemens) Trust.

For the next fourteen months, other than one payment to a creditor, no public documents were filed regarding the probate of Nina's will. However, Sigfrid Tor had clearly not dropped his claim of being Nina's husband.

On February 5, 1968, Myron Harpole filed a document that indicates he had been investigating Tor's claim. Harpole sought admissions from Tor that both he and Nina consistently indicated that they were single on their driver's licenses, that Tor had filed as a single man on his income tax records, that he was collecting $80 a month rent from Nina for a room she occasionally used from 1960 to 1964, that he had made in excess of $3000 in claims against Nina's trust fund for "nursing services," that they never publically claimed to be husband and wife, and other similar facts.

Harpole further sought admission from Tor that in 1966 he had testified under oath that he had been drinking for some time and was drunk at the time he alleged to have married Nina in Tijuana. The document also indicates that Nina had testified under oath in San Diego in 1964 to the effect that she knew Tor but had never married him.

Harpole also wanted Tor to admit that Nina was competent when she executed her will. In a move clearly designed to pressure Tor to drop his suit, Harpole had also requested Tor to turn over half of his property and earnings from the period of his alleged marriage to Nina, presumably knowing that Tor's finances would not enable him to do so.

Tor fired back a response on February 25, 1968. He acknowledged that he had been listing himself as a single man on his driver's license and tax returns, but claimed that he and Nina had, from time to time, registered themselves at hotels as Mr. & Mrs. Sigfrid Tor.

He claimed he did not recall testifying under oath that he was drunk when he married Nina. As to Nina's competency at the time she executed her will, his language had softened from earlier documents to indicate that he could not say whether or not Nina understood the decisions she was making in 1964 when she drew up her will.

Nina's life was checkered with men whom she claimed to have married or vice versa. So who was this man claiming to have married her in 1951? Research revealed that Sigfrid Tor was born Eric Ostlin on June 12, 1901, in Sweden and was naturalized in Los Angeles on June 28, 1935. A subsequent notation on his naturalization card indicates a name change to Sigfrid Tor in March of 1935.

Tor, an actor, had a brief career in film, appearing in at least twenty-four movies, almost all in the 1940s. The majority of the roles were uncredited bit parts, often as a Nazi.

A November 8, 1951, incoming passenger log for the ship *Oslofjord* shows Tor claiming 2400 El Contento Drive in Hollywood (Nina's address) as his own. However, he lists himself as single.

Since Nina, per interviews conducted by author Caroline Harnsberger, regularly allowed her acting friends to live at the house, this ship log is significant primarily as proof that Nina's friendship with Tor extended back at least as far as 1951, the year that Tor claimed he had married her. Tor eventually returned to Sweden where he died on July 30, 1990.

In an e-conversation with George Wrentmore, Jr., the question was posed whether he had any knowledge of a marriage between Nina and Sigfrid Tor. Wrentmore found the idea amusing as he responded that Tor was "flagrantly gay."

For the next several years, the probate case languished with Tor apparently refusing to withdraw his protest of the will.

Then, on August 30, 1971, without changing his claim that he had been married to Nina, Tor signed a brief document (drafted by Harpole's law firm) withdrawing his objection to probate of Nina's will. For reasons unknown, this document was not filed in court until July 18, 1972.

Activity on Nina's probate file after the withdrawal of Tor's claim slowly came to a close. However, a document filed on September 27, 1972, by attorney Charles W. Wolfe shed light on the nature of the Langdon challenges and the settling of Sigfrid Tor's claim.

The September 1972 document revealed that the Langdon family members had challenged not only Nina's will, but also caused the estate of her mother, Clara Clemens Samossoud, to be reopened.

Because the challenge regarding Clara's estate was pressed in San Diego County, and Nina's attorney, Myron Harpole, was named in the suit, he retained the services of Wolfe to defend him and Nina's estate.

In Wolfe's petition, filed on behalf of Harpole, the Langdons motivation becomes clear:

> The contestants [Langdons] initially believed that the decedent [Nina] had potential rights against the estate of her grandfather and undertook extensive discovery including five day deposition of petitioner [Harpole] to find evidence in support of their contest and also in support of their belief of additional assets. The matter had

THE TWAIN SHALL MEET   169

been gone into by petitioner [Harpole] on behalf of decedent [Nina] during her lifetime several years before her death. The decedent had no right to such interest and the contestants upon learning all of the facts concerning the validity of the will and decedents property withdrew their contest.

Upon learning that the income from the estate of Mark Twain himself was not in play, the Langdons had withdrawn their challenge of Nina's will. There is no indication how Nina's share of the Samossoud Trust came into play.

The petition also went on to indicate that, "Finally the heirs made a settlement with Sigfried [sic] Tor and he withdrew his contest."

The nature of the settlement with Tor is unknown. While speculative, since neither Pat Gleason nor Jules Schmidt stood to inherit enough to warrant making a settlement with Tor, it seems likely that The American Cancer Society negotiated the withdrawal of his challenge. The Wolfe petition also flatly rejected C.A. Huffine as having any standing with regard to Nina's will.

Financial probate information shows that Nina's estate, originally valued at around $48,000 in June of 1966, had, through claims and attorney fees, dwindled down to just over $38,000 by June of 1973.

From that remainder, Wolfe was still owed over $5800 for his services, and Al Mathews over $1000 for acting as Nina's conservator.

Of the original four heirs whom Nina had stipulated to receive monthly stipends, only Pat Gleason was still alive as of a June 7, 1973, probate document ordering final settlement of Nina's will.

The final probate document, dated August 3, 1989, is an ex parte court order to terminate a blocked depositary account in Nina's name.

Over twenty years after her death, Nina's affairs were finally laid to rest.

Excerpt from Nina's autopsy report showing a difference of opinion about the cause of death.

Copy of original from Los Angeles County, Office of Chief Medical Examiner

CHAPTER 24

DEB

2008–2009

A FUTILE HUNT FOR NINA'S DNA

THE EXAMINATION OF THE LIVES of both Nina and Susan had turned up a number of interesting parallels and a wealth of circumstantial evidence of a mother-daughter relationship between Nina and Susan.

The genealogist in me, however, wanted hard proof if it were possible to find it. In such cases, absent specific documents such as a birth certificate, DNA provides the gold standard of proof (or disproof) of a relationship between two individuals.

For tracing the ancestry of males, the Y chromosome has been fully mapped and can thus be used with a high degree of specificity. For females, however, evidence relies on mitochondrial DNA, often called simply mtDNA.

Minor mutations aside, mtDNA is passed down from mother to daughter in an unbroken chain. Therefore, Nina would have the same mtDNA as her mother Clara, grandmother Olivia, great-grandmother (also named Olivia), and so on.

The sisters of all of those women would also have identical mtDNA as would their daughters, granddaughters, etc.

mtDNA also passes to a woman's son, but he cannot pass it in turn to his children (male or female). The mtDNA in any specific ancestral line thus dies out with each female who does not produce a daughter.

Therefore, in seeking genetic proof of Susan's mother-daughter relationship with Nina, my task was to locate a living woman who met specific criteria. She had to share a common female ancestor with Nina *and* she had to descend from that woman in an all-female line.

Alternatively, a living man whose mother met the criteria would also share the required mtDNA.

As a famous example of using genetics in this manner, testing the mtDNA of Prince Philip of England provided the proof that the claims of a woman who believed herself to be Anastasia, daughter of murdered Russian Czar Nicholas and his wife Alexandra, were false.

Czarina Alexandra and Philip's maternal grandmother, Princess Victoria, were sisters and therefore shared the same mtDNA. Victoria passed that mtDNA to daughter Victoria Alice and thence to grandson Philip.

Alexandra's mtDNA likewise passed to daughter Anastasia. Had the woman claiming to be Anastasia actually been so, her mtDNA would, therefore, have been identical to Philip's—it was not.

If a man or woman with the right ancestry could be located and expressed willingness to have his or her mtDNA tested for comparison to Susan's, we could have our proof. If they matched, it would provide nearly overwhelming evidence that Susan was Nina's daughter.

With over thirty-five years of genealogical research experience, I thought that finding one or more such distant relatives of Nina's would be a straightforward task, but I had not counted on the scarcity of females in her maternal ancestry.

Essentially, my task was to locate sisters of the women in Nina's direct female line and then to track their daughters' (if any) lines forward, following only female lines.

Having just spent two years delving for information on Nina herself, I knew that she had no sisters. That meant the first mtDNA dead-end and a move back one generation to search for sisters of her mother Clara.

Clara, daughter of Mark Twain, had indeed had two sisters. However, sister Susy died of meningitis and sister Jean drowned in a bathtub during an epileptic seizure. Neither had lived long enough to marry or to produce children.

This meant dead-end number two and a need to move back to the generation of Clara's mother, Mark Twain's beloved wife Olivia.

Never having had any reason to search Olivia's ancestry before, I was hopeful that she had had sisters who lived to marry and produce daughters. I recalled, in fact, mention of a sister whose married name was Susan Crane.

In what was coming to be a familiar pattern, however, Olivia turned out to have had only one biological sibling, a brother named Charles J. Langdon. Prior to Olivia's birth on November 27, 1845, her parents, Jervis Langdon and wife Olivia (Lewis) Langdon, had adopted Susan who, as it turned out, had not produced children in any case.

This meant yet another generation in which the females in Nina's direct line had no sisters who produced children.

Moving back another generation, information began to get scantier, and I was entering an era in which public records were not kept in most states.

Per records focused on the Langdon family, Olivia (Langdon) Clemens's mother (Mark Twain's mother-in-law) was born Olivia Lewis on August 19, 1810, in Lenox, New York, to Edward Lewis and Olivia Barnard.

With no original source materials to consult, I relied on online trees, which indicated that Olivia Lewis had at least three sisters. Hopeful, I began digging for evidence that those sisters had left daughters.

The oldest, Philissa, was born circa 1797 and married a man named David Fowler. Family trees mentioned a slew of daughters for this couple—Ann, Polly, Betsy, Catherine, Sarah Ann, Orpha, and Electa.

Surely, I thought, there would be living female descendants from one of those! However, after much research, it appeared nearly certain that all of these daughters, born prior to 1830, were in fact not Philissa's biological offspring, but rather her stepchildren.

Philissa's grave inscription clearly refers to her as "second wife" of David Fowler. More telling, the University of California's Mark Twain Project papers include a December 15, 1830, letter addressed to Philissa Lewis, indicating that she did not become Philissa Fowler until after that date, i.e. until at least eight years after the birth of David Fowler's youngest known daughter, Electa. While Philissa and David had at least one son together, no evidence has emerged to suggest that they had any daughters.

Moving on to Olivia Lewis's sister Susan, born circa 1802, online family trees claimed that she died November 12, 1830. No husband was mentioned. Attempts to clarify this information with the Town Historian for the City of Lenox, Massachusetts, elicited the response that records from that era had been lost.

Possibilities of finding an mtDNA trail to follow brightened with the discovery that Olivia Lewis's twin sister Louisa had married a man named Shepard Marsh. The 1850 United States Federal Census record for Elmira, New York, showed a thirteen-year-old daughter Anna in the household of Shepard and Louisa Marsh. At last, a possibility!

By the 1860 United States Federal Census, the entire family had moved to Des Moines, Iowa, and daughter Anna had married a man named Tallmadge Brown. Also in the multi-generational household was one-year-old Louisa Brown, presumed to be the daughter of Tallmadge and Anna. The mtDNA chain was continuing forward.

But by the 1870 United States Federal Census, little Louisa Brown had died, as had her infant sister Anna May Brown (confirmed by the Woodland Cemetery records of Des Moines, Iowa).

New to the household, however, was Tallmadge and Anna's daughter, Carrie, age eight. Hope brightened.

On May 23, 1889, Carrie married a man named B.F. Holcomb, but by the 1900 United States Federal Census, Carrie was listed as a thirty-nine-year-old widow with no children.

Subsequent census records show no evidence that she ever remarried. Yet another trail mtDNA trail had come to an end.

Investigations further back up Nina's maternal line met with an equal lack of success. Even for those cases where possible trails were identified and researched, data was highly questionable and deemed unreliable.

Attempts to locate DNA from Nina herself (perhaps from a hair sample or similar source) were equally unsuccessful.

The idea of finding proof of the mother-daughter relationship between Nina and Susan via the use of DNA was reluctantly shelved until 2010, but then I will let Susan tell that story!

CHAPTER 25

DEB

2009–2011

NINA'S HEIRS AND ACQUAINTANCES

WITH THE SEARCH FOR DNA in Nina's direct maternal line coming up empty, I turned to tracking down living individuals who might have knowledge of Nina and the issue of Susan's parentage. Since Drucilla Bailey and Eileen Lucia had taken their knowledge to the grave, the net needed to be cast wider.

Susan crafted a website entitled marktwainonline.com to try to elicit information about Nina, and I added a blog to my ancestryhelper.com genealogy website to cast for further information.

I also began to search for information about Nina's four heirs. How did Nina know these individuals, and might they have been privy to her deepest secret?

George Wrentmore, it transpired, was a native of Ann Arbor, Michigan, and son of Clarence and Mattie Wrentmore. Clarence, a civil engineer and faculty member at the University of Michigan, was instrumental in development of the university's program in the Philippines. George, therefore, spent many of his formative years in that country.

A 1920 passport application shows a solemn, handsome young man. George worked briefly in real estate before following in his father's footsteps as a civil engineer. He also undertook work as a geologist. He fit the profile of most of the men in Nina's life—older, charming, with a cosmopolitan background and alcohol issues.

Contact with the Wrentmore family came when a woman named Gayle, one of George's granddaughters, responded to an inquiry on the ancestryhelper.com blog. George, as we had discovered from Nina's letters, had been the last significant man in Nina's life.

Gayle recalled visiting Nina at a treatment facility where Judy Garland was also staying. She put me in touch with her father, George Wrentmore, Jr.

George turned out to be a man of definite opinions. He indicated that Nina and his father had been steady companions for a number of years. Occupying the penthouse at what he referred to as "The Hollywood Towers," Nina and his father made frequent trips to Mexico together.

They had, he said, even claimed to have married on one of those trips, but he did not believe that to be true. When asked how his father and Nina met, George offered an intriguing tale:

> My dad was "a cool dude" in his day (Annapolis Navy, geologist, civil engineer and on and on). He was prospecting gold in Central America, came back to the US to find investors for a rich strike there, met Nina and hung it all up. Guess his energy was running low and he decided to settle down. The strike was worked per a politico down there. A subsidiary of an oil co. ended up with the option after the politico was assassinated. Reportedly took over 100 million in gold out of the strike . . . He met Nina around 1958 in Hollywood. I think Nina felt attached to the H/wood crowd. I was married to a "showgirl trophy wife" at that time. Nina seemed somehow attracted to/fascinated with her as she [was] definitely a showstopper and was plugged in with a lot of show biz folks.

He recalled Nina with fondness, but remarked, "Too bad about Nina. She just didn't have the right stuff to overcome her thirst. Maybe if her lifestyle hadn't been subsidized and she had to work, she'd have been a different person. Possibly cold and hunger would have been the motivators to dry out via gainful employment."

George also shared that Nina's relationship with attorney Al Mathews had a love-hate element. While the two were often at odds, Al used his influence to get cases involving Nina's frequent driving while intoxicated charges heard by friendly judges.

George said, "Nina kept getting her driver's license back despite numerous DUI charges. I think she finally left it running one nite, it tore down the hill in Hollywonk and crashed thru a house. Permanently revoked."

When asked if he thought it was possible that Nina had ever had a child, he replied that he had "heard rumblings to that effect and that supposedly was why she drank."

Here, finally, was someone who had known Nina and actually had vague knowledge of a child!

Looking at pictures of Susan's grandson Kyle, George's reaction was swift and certain if a bit confused on the generation:

> *That kid is, without any doubt, Nina's kid. I've reviewed that (photo) a few times ... a definite Xerox copy. DNA would validate that 1000 percent.*

After being so close to the subject for so long, there were times when Susan and I would think that we were just seeing those astounding resemblances where perhaps there were none. Except for the one incident when Susan met Nina at age seven, neither of us had known the living, breathing Nina. This man, however, a man who had known Nina well, clearly saw the resemblances.

Of Marie Weston and Pat Gleason, two of Nina's remaining heirs, little is known. Photos at The Mark Twain House & Museum show photos of a Pat Gleason. The man who discovered her body on that sad day in January of 1966 was listed as Richard Patrick Gleason. His friendship with Nina spanned over two decades per his statement to LAPD Detective Sobota.

It is unknown whether "Pat" was a nickname for this man or whether they were brothers or other relatives. George Wrentmore, Jr. referred to Pat as "a bartender in Hollywood." Pat appears to have been single at the time of Nina's death.

For heir Marie Weston, little additional information is known. No one interviewed recognized her name. Marie was alive at the time Nina executed her will in February of 1964 and deceased by the time the will was entered for probate in January of 1966.

Based on that window of time for her death, this heir is believed to be the Marie Z. Weston who died April 27, 1965, in Los Angeles. Research revealed that woman to be Marie (Zorn) Weston, mother of Doug Weston who founded the famous Troubadour nightclub in Los Angeles.

Doug passed away with no survivors in 1999. Attempts to locate the survivors (if any) of Marie's daughter Lucille (Weston) Varney were unsuccessful. The nature of Nina's friendship with Marie (who was seventeen years her senior) is unknown.

Reaching out to other people whose lives had crossed paths with Nina yielded no additional clues as to whether Susan could be Nina's daughter, but did yield a few more bits of information about her life.

The daughter of Dr. Lawrence Stuppy, the doctor who treated Nina at the end of her life and who was called to the scene of her death, was located and interviewed. She recalled Nina as a quiet woman, pleasant and well dressed, who shared two or three holidays as a guest in the Stuppy's home.

Stuppy's daughter said that her father often "brought home strays" for the holidays. When I asked if her father had ever spoken of Nina mentioning a child, she said he was very strict about professional ethics and would never have talked about such a thing, even to his family.

Miggie Warms, whose mother Dorothy and Nina were friends in their young adult years, said that her mother described Nina as a good friend and that all of Nina's friends thought Clara was "a bitch."

Rita Seiler, widow of the Dr. Seiler who had been named as successor heir in Clara's will, said she never met either Clara or Nina, as both had died before the time of her marriage to Seiler. She said she was aware, through her husband, of the rift between Clara and Nina.

An elderly woman whose father was Phyllis Harrington's steady companion for decades had also never met Nina. She was, however, aware of Phyllis' role as Nina's informal guardian.

She conveyed that while Phyllis was immensely loyal to Clara, she also found it difficult to work for her. I explained our belief that Susan is Nina's daughter and asked if she thought Clara could have hidden something like that from Phyllis.

With no hesitation, she said, "Absolutely not. Phyllis did *everything* for

Clara. Clara could never have covered it up without Phyllis's help."

She went on to describe an incident in which Clara called looking for Phyllis because she had gotten the notion in her head that she wanted to go to a bank. Apparently Clara had never set foot in a bank in her life and wanted Phyllis to take her to one!

The woman also recounted how Phyllis had known of Jacques's gambling habits. He had, she said, invented a story for Clara of how he needed money to help fund a training facility for police dogs. This purported facility just happened to be in Las Vegas where Jacques was amassing significant gambling debts.

Jacques was, she said, protected by mobster Lucky Luciano from casino owners dunning him for debt. If true, it is possible that the two met in Jacques's early days in New York when Luciano's power was at its peak. Despite being exiled from the U.S. since 1946, Luciano had continued to wield tremendous power in organized crime in America.

After Luciano's death on January 26, 1962, the woman said that casino owners came after Jacques full force to recover approximately $30,000 in gambling debts. It was then that he went hat in hand to Clara for money to pay off those debts.

Phyllis, she said, was instrumental in convincing Clara that Jacques should sign a promissory note for repayment of the funds. It is such notes that ultimately provided the leverage Nina needed to contest her mother's will.

The woman also recounted that Phyllis had never shared her concerns about Jacques's behavior with Clara. As long as the two had known each other, Phyllis still feared that criticizing Jacques would lead to her dismissal as Clara had a blind spot where her second husband was concerned and would not tolerate criticism of him. Bruno Walter, it seems, was correct about Jacques' "hypnotic power" over Clara.

A final bit of information shared by this woman was that Phyllis herself had a drinking problem. While Phyllis could perform perfectly well at her job, she was, the woman said, an evening drinker.

How ironic, I thought, that the woman tasked with watching out for Nina because of her alcohol problems should have similar issues. The fox, it appears, was guarding the hen house.

The two daughters of Lova Dolle, the woman whose house Nina was living in shortly before her death, were also located. Both believed that "the Dahls" who were mentioned in the police report concerning Nina's death referred to their family. Nina, they said, died very shortly after her last visit to them.

When asked how Nina and their mother knew each other, the daughters both indicated independently that their mother was bi-sexual and that they believed her to have been Nina's lover. Although Nina had many gay friends over the years, this was the first time that anyone who knew her actually said that she might have been bi-sexual.

Only one heir remained to be researched in detail—Nina's long-time friend Julius "Jules" Schmidt.

CHAPTER 26

DEB

2009–2011

THE MYSTERY OF JULES SCHMIDT

SINCE ITS INCEPTION, the marktwainonline.com website had gener ated a number of interesting but routine contacts, mostly from people trying to determine whether they were related to Mark Twain. Then, on June 8, 2009, Susan, who manages the website, received an email from Maren Rectenwald, niece of Jules Schmidt. It was far from routine.

At the time that Rechtenwald made the contact, nothing on the website indicated our belief that Nina was Susan's mother. Neither did it mention Jules Schmidt. Maren had not, in fact, even looked at the photographs showing the resemblances between Susan's family and Nina's. That was what made the contact all the more startling.

Rechtenwald had e-mailed simply because, she said, she wanted to share a story about Nina that she had always kept private and felt that it was time to share. She had been conducting an Internet search looking for someone with an interest in Nina when she came across the marktwainonline website.

Her Uncle Jules, Maren's email said, had fathered a child with Nina Clemens Gabrilowitsch.

After receiving the email, Susan contacted me, very upset. Confronted with the possibility that Jules Schmidt and not Elwood Bailey might be her biological father, it seemed like too much to bear. She asked me to just deal with it.

Maren, daughter of Jules's brother Lawrence Schmidt, said that she had known that Nina and her Uncle Jules had a long-term friendship, but whenever she tried to ask her father about it, he refused to discuss the matter. Maren indicated that as a young girl, she been fascinated by and idolized her Uncle Jules.

In an effort to discourage this hero-worship, her father produced examples of what he deemed to be Jules's shortcomings. On one occasion, he told Maren that Jules had "fathered an out of wedlock child with the granddaughter of someone famous."

Maren's inquisitiveness continued. One day, while in her twenties and visiting her father, Maren noticed a box sitting on a hall table that contained papers of her father's. Without permission, she borrowed the box.

On the top was a copy of Nina's will naming her Uncle Jules as Nina's heir. When her father discovered the loss of the box a few hours later, he called and angrily demanded that Maren return the box immediately. Maren did so, without ever examining the remainder of the papers in the box.

Tersely, Lawrence stated that Jules and Nina had had a child together and that was why he never liked to discuss their relationship. He was deeply bothered by the lifestyle of his brilliant but troubled brother and ashamed that Jules had been responsible for the birth of an out of wedlock child.

Once the information about Jules and Nina was known to Maren, on more than one occasion later in life, Lawrence Schmidt wondered aloud whether it might be possible to find "the child." He did not, he told Maren, know the sex of the child or other details.

After Lawrence Schmidt's death, the papers Maren had seen did not resurface. She had, she said, always had the feeling that her father knew more about the purported child that Jules and Nina had produced than what he ever shared with her.

Maren then put me in touch with her cousin, Jules's daughter Maria. After explaining our hunt for proof that Nina was Susan's mother, I gently asked if she thought it was possible that her father and Nina could have had a child together.

Maria said that her mother disliked Nina and saw her as a rival, but felt that with all the drinking her parents did, and all the accusations that they hurled at one another, surely an accusation concerning a child would have slipped out at some point.

Maria shared one of her favorite memories of Nina. She said that Nina was always kind to her and to her brother Brian and their sister Rachel, and would pay them a dollar to brush her hair.

What a poignant picture that painted! Kind-hearted Nina helped the children earn a little money while buying for herself some of the gentle attention that was so lacking in her life.

Maria also said that she recalled Nina wearing "corduroy pants and tailored shirts. Her hair was always kind of a greasy looking mess … Nina was always very nice to us. My father seemed more content when he was around Nina. I always remember him as being very sad otherwise. He and my mother were always having violent fights with each other."

Maria then put me in contact with her older brother Brian. She said that he had been very close to Nina. In response to my inquiries Brian wrote via email:

> As far as my father and Nina having children I suppose it is possible as they were very close for many years. Nina was always very close to me and she never mentioned that she had any children with my father or with anyone else for that matter.
>
> I spent many days with her when we lived in Hollywood. I could do no wrong and during those years as a teenager I was pretty wild. She just always stood by me. Her only problem was the drinking which was nonstop during the fifties.
>
> An example of her ways was to let me use her car, buy me cigarettes, give me money for going out and things like that. She hardly ever left her apartment and was almost like a recluse. It was really hard to see her that way but that was Nina.
>
> She lived on Highland Ave just up and across the street from the Highland Hotel. She drank Jim Beam [later corrected by Brian to Seagram's] and smoked Pall Mall unfiltered cigarettes. Her hair was black and fairly short. She probably was only about 100 lbs. She rarely ate much and was really not in very good condition.

Brian echoed his sister's sentiments, saying that he doubted that his father was capable of keeping a secret such as having had a child with Nina, as it would have made too good of a weapon in the fights between his parents.

When I asked Maria about Jules Schmidt's remaining child, daughter Rachel, she became emotional. Maria said that they had last spoken to the younger sister whom she called "Rachie" when she called her to tell her of their mother's death.

Rachel, who had married and divorced at a young age and subsequently left California, said she was on the road, fleeing with her children from an abusive second husband and headed to Florida. In the thirty years that had passed since that conversation, Rachel had never been heard from again. Maria said it broke her heart not to know whether Rachel was alive or dead.

I found no woman named Rachel in the Social Security death records who matched the birth date provided by Maria, so I was convinced that she was still alive. After months of digging, I located Rachel, happily remarried, and surrounded by a loving family.

Immensely relieved to know that her sister was still alive, Maria asked me to make the initial contact in case Rachel did not want to have communication with her for some reason. I agreed as it would also give me a chance to elicit any memories that Rachel might have of Nina.

When I spoke to Rachel, she indicated that she had married as a teenager primarily to get away from her turbulent home life. She said that living with two alcoholic parents who fought constantly was simply more than she could bear.

The years that followed with her second husband and then as a single mother were even tougher, but once she met her third husband, she said, her life became stable and happy.

How like Susan's life, I thought! Rachel had avoided reaching out to her siblings for fear that somehow she would be drawn back into memories of the unhappy life she had put behind her.

Rachel remembered Nina but had no thoughts on whether or not her father and Nina could have produced a child together. She did remember that the man Nina was living with was gay. That reference was probably to Sigfrid Tor, also described by George Wrentmore, Jr. as gay.

Rachel said she was willing to talk to Maria. The long silence between the two siblings was broken at last. While finding Rachel brought little new knowledge of Nina, it certainly brought a smile to my face to know I had helped mend this particular broken fence!

With the help of Maren's niece, Mona K. Vance, a professional archivist, Susan and I were then able to look at several photographs of Jules Schmidt at a variety of ages. Both of us had the same response to viewing the photos: there did not seem to be even the slightest physical resemblance between Susan and Jules.

Susan's visceral response was, "There is absolutely no way I am related to that man!" I commented in an offhand manner that he looked more like he could be her brother Bobby's father than hers.

We in turn provided childhood photographs of Susan and her brother Bobby to Maria and Brian Schmidt. Both responded that Susan did not look in the least like their father but remarked, as I had, that Bobby did bear some slight resemblance.

Susan and I briefly discussed the wild idea that Nina had had more than one illegitimate child and that she and Bobby were those two children, with Elwood as her father and Jules as Bobby's.

For a sexually active woman in an era with only crude birth control, it was not inconceivable that Nina could have gotten "caught" more than once.

However, if Drucilla had disliked Susan, her husband's love child, being foisted upon her, it was hard to imagine that she would have taken in a second child of Nina's and raised him with love as she did. Susan and I finally decided that we would never know where Bobby came from and just put that issue aside.

I suggested DNA testing to rule out the possibility of Jules as Susan's father. Both Maria and Brian were amenable, but Susan was so utterly convinced that Jules was not her father, that she, for a period of over two years, opted not to pursue it.

Julius "Jules" Schmidt
Photo Courtesy of Maren Rectenwald and Mona Vance

CHAPTER 27

SUSAN

2011

DNA REVISITED

I KNEW THAT IN MANY WAYS it was hard for Deb to understand why, in the two years since Maren Rechtenwald had first contacted us, I was still resisting doing the DNA testing.

By this point I knew in my heart that my long search for my mother was over. There was simply no one else but Nina who fit everything I knew and that Deb and I together had discovered.

I did realize that without positive DNA proof, many people would cast doubt on my conclusion. Personally, obtaining such proof for the sake of the general public was not a high priority for me, but I wanted my children to know with as much certainty as possible where they came from—the reason I started this journey of discovery in the first place.

I had a bad feeling about doing a DNA test with Jules Schmidt's children because, although I wanted DNA to prove that Nina was indeed my mother, I certainly didn't want the results to take away my father, Elwood Bailey, from me.

I understood that if my DNA matched that of Jules Schmidt's children, then that would prove that Jules was my biological father—and all but prove that Nina was my mother. The second result of that testing would be wonderful.

But I resisted doing DNA with them for two years because I just didn't feel that I could risk losing the only parent I had ever had, even if I believed that there was only the slightest chance that I could be the daughter of Jules Schmidt. I was not prepared to take that emotional risk.

Finally though, after two years and with our research all but finished,

Deb convinced me that I needed to submit my DNA for comparison with the Schmidt offspring to see if there was a half sibling match.

By this time we had acquired a New York literary agent for the book we had drafted, and she too was weighing in on the importance of this testing if for no other reason than to rule Jules out as my father.

I finally relented and Brian, Maria, and I all sent our DNA samples to the University of New Mexico DNA lab, one of the most reputable DNA facilities in the country.

Deb explained that what we were doing was called a sibling match test, but was essentially the same as a paternity test. After sending it off, I forgot about it for awhile and made plans for an extended retreat at a health resort in Florida.

The night before I left, I had a dream. In it, we had gotten the results of the DNA testing and they were positive, proving that I was Brian and Maria's half sister. But then there turned out to be some sort of a problem with the results.

I called Deb immediately and told her about this dream. I also told her where she could get in touch with me for the next three weeks in case she got the results back from the lab.

The second week I was in Florida, Deb called me and asked if I was sitting down. Then she told me the DNA results were back and there was a 60-64% chance that I was the half sibling of Maria and Brian Schmidt. When I heard that I sunk to the floor!

I asked her if she was positive.

Ever-cautious Deb said that she was totally astounded that the percentages had so far exceeded what we had been led to expect for two unrelated individuals, but also confused that they were so far below the 90-plus percent results that would be expected if the Schmidts and I were half-siblings. Brian and Maria themselves were deemed to be full siblings at a 99.96% certainty level.

Because the results seemed gray, Deb said she had called and talked to a lab technician who gave her an explanation of the science behind the testing.

In a nutshell, he told her they had tested sixteen marker sites, looked at genetic information called alleles, and compared how Maria, Brian, and I matched up.

I was still so much in shock that I barely processed the technical information that Deb was reporting. I did vividly remember that, years before when Lula Joughin, Bob Joughin's daughter and I had tested to see if we were related in any way, our match probability had been less than 1%.

Yet there I was, matching the Schmidts at over 60%. And I had grown up thinking Lula was my cousin!

Deb said she then pressed the lab analyst to explain what the 60-64% results meant. The analyst cautiously told Deb that scores above the 50th percentile were very seldom seen in unrelated individuals.

The technician also said that since we were quite sure that Brian, Maria, and I were either half-siblings or totally unrelated, the results supported the idea that the Schmidts and I were half-siblings.

Still unsatisfied, Deb said she had left a message for the lab manager to call her but he failed to do so.

When that call went unanswered, Deb called back and talked to a different lab analyst than the first. Unlike the cautious reply from the first technician, this individual told Deb that the reports certainly meant that I was a half-sibling to Brian and Maria as match scores as high as mine and theirs "simply did not happen by chance."

So it was true, then. Jules Schmidt must be my father.

Proving Nina was my mother but losing my father, Elwood, in the process was not a fair trade for me. My dad had been a loving presence in my life until his death when I was nine years old. Nina had been in my life for exactly one day, when she took me out of school when I was a second grader.

And though I have pictures of Nina and a newborn baby that I believe to be me, I, of course, have no memory of that time. The emotional attachment I felt to Elwood Bailey was intense. I had *no* emotional attachment to Nina.

And now this stranger, Jules Schmidt, was supposedly my real father? I didn't know Jules Schmidt, had never met him, and now I had three new siblings to deal with when, after the death of my brother Bobby, I had come to think of myself as an only child.

I couldn't wrap my mind around this. I felt as if my daddy had died all over again! I was sorry I had ever done DNA or started this damn book!

I had grown up in the Bailey family thinking I was one of them and now I was being told that I didn't have an ounce of Bailey blood in me! It was almost more than I could bear. Had I not been at a health institute when I got this news, I don't think I could have dealt with it alone.

They had a slew of psychologists. I immediately made an appointment with one and saw him once or twice a day for the rest of my stay.

The counselor listened to me, made helpful suggestions, and also ordered daily massages and swimming in a heated salt water pool. He helped me to see that, even though I didn't share one drop of Bailey blood, Elwood Bailey clearly thought I had.

He said that my relationship with Elwood and memories of growing up with him were still valid, that he was the father of my heart and always would be.

I can't tell you that I felt 100% OK, but I started to feel that I might be able to cope with what I had first considered tragic news.

If Jules Schmidt was my father, I wanted to know more about him. I began to do some research and found that he had been an accomplished pianist, Broadway actor, and mathematician.

I also found out through talking with his daughter (and now my half sister) Maria, that she adored her father, but that he was an alcoholic and that life growing up with him had been very difficult.

I began to be even more grateful that I was placed in the home of Elwood Bailey, also an accomplished man and mathematician, but with none of Jules' darker traits.

I sat down at my computer and composed a letter to my children and grandchildren explaining what had happened and that they now had a new, albeit deceased, grandfather. I included all the positive information I had learned about Jules but none of the negative behavior that I heard from his children. I also included one of the pictures of him that his niece, Mona Vance, had furnished us. He was a handsome man.

Then I got another call from Deb!

She explained that, still unsatisfied with the inconsistent responses from the university lab we had used, she had called Mr. Bennett Greenspan, head of the highly respected Family Tree DNA company.

After explaining, without using full names, that the test was done to try to determine, indirectly, whether I was Mark Twain's great-grandchild, he was intrigued and generously offered to have his lab chief analyze the report results she furnished. He soon called Deb back.

Greenspan told her that his laboratory head scientist had examined the test results and stated unequivocally that I could *not* be related to the Schmidt children. Because one of our alleles, called Penta D, didn't match when viewed as a triple, he said that it was a *complete rule out*.

He said that the laboratory we had used must have only compared me to Maria and Brian one at a time, but never looked at all three of our results together.

Deb then called back the original lab who agreed that their program was indeed not set up to assess more than two people at a time, that the Family Tree DNA analyst was "very good" to have caught the Penta D issue, and that it "almost certainly" ruled out Jules Schmidt as my father.

However, he did say that it was not, in his opinion, a *100 percent* rule-out because either Maria or I could have a mutation on our Penta D allele. So, though the possibility was small, it still was not out of the question.

So there I was, left in the god-awful position of having moved from a "probably yes" to an "almost certainly no" with regard to the question of whether Jules Schmidt was my father.

At that point, my faith in DNA was moving towards zero.

Deb asked Greenspan how the 60-64% match happened if the Schmidts and I weren't related at all. She had, by that time, shared the ethnic background of both the Schmidts and of my believed parents.

He told her the reason the match was so high was probably due to the fact that Molly Schmidt, Jules' wife and the mother of the children I tested against, was of Eastern European Jewish origin as was Ossip Gabrilowitsch, Nina's father.

In other words, we might simply share the same tight gene pool which could make us look closely related when we are not.

He called it being "identical by state" rather than "identical by descent."

So while it appeared to disprove that Jules Schmidt was my father, I realized that it gave indirect support to Nina's father, Ossip Gabrilowitsch, being my grandfather.

Greenspan suggested testing again with his laboratory and told Deb that great strides had been made in DNA just in the past year. He said that while he already trusted his lab analyst's opinion, that what we got back from their more elaborate DNA test would give me an absolute answer to the question of whether Jules was my father. I would have to test again with one or both of the Schmidt children!

Can you imagine how Deb felt when she had to make this call to me? Can you imagine how I felt when I received it?

I had that dream before we ever received the results that they would be positive but that something would be wrong with that conclusion. That dream was turning out to be painfully accurate.

I had started out accepting the original results and even informed my family about it. Now though, the final evidence seemed to rule out Jules Schmidt as my father (a result I was thrilled with), but point only indirectly by ethnicity toward Nina as my mother.

When I thought Jules was my father, my big consolation had been that I felt I had nearly positive proof of Nina as my mother, and now that certainty was taken away from me again.

I was as numb as a tennis ball in the final match at Wimbledon! Deb asked me to immediately submit my DNA to the Family Tree DNA lab for further testing. Fat chance!

CHAPTER 28

DEB

2012

A DISCOVERY THAT CHANGES EVERYTHING

I N ESSENCE, WITH REGARD TO TECHNICAL PROOF concerning who fathered Susan, we were, at the end of 2011, back to where we started before ever undertaking the DNA testing.

Neither of us knew with absolute certainty whether or not Jules Schmidt did or did not father Susan. However, whether or not he actually fathered her, we both concurred that Jules Schmidt, undeniably a long-time companion of Nina's, *believed* he had done so. He would have had no reason to fabricate the story for his brother.

More importantly, we suddenly realized that Jules Schmidt's statements to his brother Lawrence provided the long sought, and now nearly indisputable evidence, that Nina had, in fact, conceived a child.

Whether that child was Susan, or whether there was also out there somewhere another child belonging to Nina, we simply had no way of knowing.

I believed that there were undoubtedly many additional living individuals who knew Nina and could shed light on her life, but with that critical bit of evidence in hand, the search seemed to be grinding to a halt.

Letting go of Nina proved difficult. The five year long search for letters, photographs, wills, court documents, and people who had known the living breathing Nina seemed to be drawing to a close.

While Jeffrey Mainville, then Assistant Curator of the Mark Twain House and Museum in Hartford, charitably remarked that the research completed made me the "foremost expert in the world on Nina Clemens Gabrilowitsch," I felt frustrated that I had not delivered to Susan the essence of the woman that she had come to accept as her mother.

We had a few precious letters in Nina's own words, but everything else we knew consisted of facts and impressions gleaned from and seen through the eyes of others.

But what was Nina really like as a child, I wondered. When did her mental health issues first manifest themselves? How did she feel about her parents? Those were questions with no answers.

A genealogist never knows when to quit. We are driven by an endless thirst for data, data, and ever more data. I continued to search online for materials, managing to turn up old press photographs of Nina and Clara from time to time that Susan could purchase and treasure. Her friends and family continued to marvel at the startling physical resemblances.

Then, on October 24, 2012, on an internet search for the phrase 'Nina Gabrilowitsch,' a new web page result appeared. The L. Tom Perry Special Collections of the Harold B. Lee Library at Brigham Young University held the "Nina Gabrilowitsch Diaries." The manuscript summary read:

Handwritten diaries from 1921 to 1941 with typescripts of the materials. Gabrilowitsch writes about her travels, her family, school, concerts held by her father, and other daily activities. She also relates some family stories about Mark Twain. She lived in Detroit, Michigan, California, and New York State.

Twenty years worth of material in Nina's own words. 3 boxes of material. 1.5 linear feet of material.

No matter how I tried to process the collection description, I knew an astonishing gift of information when I saw one. In her book *Mark Twain's Clara*, author Caroline Harnsberger had made references to Nina diaries but, frustratingly, had not listed where she had seen them.

And now, here they were. I left a long voicemail for Mr. John Murphy, curator of the library's 20th Century and Mormon Manuscripts.

Murphy, it transpired, was on sabbatical in Europe and my message was received by staff. Library policy, it turned out, generally restricted extensive copying of special collections material.

However, after explaining how important it was to Susan to see for herself what Nina had written, and how we needed to carefully review the manuscript for any evidence of Nina having been pregnant, the special collections staff extended themselves above and beyond, contacting Murphy by email, to seek permission to send copies of the entire set of diaries.

On September 25, 2012, Reference Specialist Cindy Brightenburg emailed:

> *To photocopy every diary would be too labor intensive for our staff, however, there are typescripts for each diary that are easily photocopied, and my supervisor has approved copying of all the typescripts for you. This is unusual as our policy is to copy on 10% of each folder, not the entire collection!*

It was a decision for which Susan and I will be forever grateful. We promptly sent copy fees.

The diaries had been donated to the Harold B. Lee Library by Hollywood screenwriter and author Cynthia Lindsay. Research revealed that Lindsay, who began her career as a stunt double for such famous figures as Claudette Colbert and Sonia Henie, was sidelined by a horseback riding incident and turned to writing.

It is unknown how she came into possession of the diaries although it is possible that Lindsay's first husband, actor Russell Gleason, was somehow related to Nina's friend and heir, Patrick Gleason.

A short time later, the diaries arrived. The front page of the 954 pages of typed transcript read, "Loaned by Hazel R. Palter 10/8/52 Fr 8834." Attempts to locate information about Palter were frustratingly fruitless as were efforts to determine to whom they had been loaned prior to Lindsay's donation.

If 10/8/52 referenced a date, it meant someone had loaned Nina's diaries out during her lifetime.

Digesting the diaries was to consume my life, and Susan's, for the next year. Quotations from the diary that appear here are as originally written, warts and all.

Nina's voice was about to be heard.

CHAPTER 29

DEB

ADVENTURES IN EUROPE: NINA (1921)

*"After that we went home and had tea and then I had my supper
and I went to bed but dont you think I spent a lovely afternoon?
dont you wish you had been me?"*

NINA CLEMENS GABRILOWITSCH, MAY 24, 1921

WHILE TEN-YEAR-OLD NINA NEVER MET a punctuation mark that she liked, her precocious intensity leapt off the pages of her diaries. The opening entry on May 21, 1921, found her in London, England on the very trip that, two months later, spawned the London *Times* article that sung her praises.

While most young girls keep their diaries under lock and key, hidden from the prying eyes of siblings, parents, and friends, young Nina seemed to be conscious that her entries might someday be read. Her writing style, like that of her famous grandfather, was peppered with detail, and sometimes with a dry sense of humor.

The picture that quickly emerged was of an intelligent, intensely interior young girl, fascinated with the books, music, and cultural opportunities afforded her, but profoundly isolated from the company of children her own age.

Here at last was a Nina whose heart Susan could truly come to identify with as, in many ways, she had a similar childhood.

Nina embarked on a whirlwind tour of the sights of London, taking in such attractions as the changing of the guard at Buckingham Palace, the Museum of Natural History, the Tate Gallery, the Tower of London, and the Royal Zoo.

She watched in fascination a theatre production called *Chu Chin Chow* (the *Cats* of its time), visited the British Museum, the Royal Botanical Gardens, Westminster Abbey, the Victoria and Albert Museum, Hampton Court Palace, Kensington Gardens, the National Portrait Gallery, and a plethora of other tourist attractions, most of which are hardly typical fare for a ten-year-old.

Keenly observant, Nina displayed a nearly photographic memory. After visiting Madame Tussauds Wax Museum, Nina named over twenty-five of the museum's figures. She likewise detailed every article of clothing worn by the Buckingham Palace Guards, and recited a list of over seventeen rooms in the Hampton Court Palace.

With rare exception, Nina's adventures took place not in the company of her parents, but under the supervision of a family maid named Margaret or of Ossip's secretary, a Miss Rix.

It seems clear that Clara and Ossip, whom Nina referred to as "Mutti" and "Vati" (holdover terms of address from her early childhood in Germany), loved their daughter. It seems equally apparent that time spent with Nina usually occurred when Clara and Ossip felt inclined to take her along to concerts or to theatre productions, activities that they both loved and where her inclusion did not impinge upon their ability to relax and enjoy themselves.

Nina's luck did not always hold in this regard. On one occasion, longing to visit the Royal Tournament with her parents, and initially bouncing with delight at the thought of this family outing, Nina related:

> *Vatti said that he thought we would go and I thought he would go in the afternoon with Mutti and I and this is what I said to Mutti when I hooked up her dress: oh Mutti wont it be fun when we all go to the Royal Tournament? and Mutti said: well Vatti dozent want to go in the afternoon because it spoils his nap but he wants to go with me in the evening but Mutti continued you and Margaret can go this afternoon and Im sure she'd like to see it.*

Nina generally handled her parents' frequent absences from her life with equanimity, mentioning their comings and goings in the most casual of terms.

> *This morning we had breakfast earlier than usal because Mutti and Vatti were going to Paris soon.*

Sometimes, however, a tone of resentment crept in:

> *Father told me that Mother had gone on to Switzerland with Tante Olga and I was very much surprised.*

On those infrequent occasions when Nina was included in a family outing, her entire writing tone changed and glimpses of an ordinary childlike pleasure in her parents' company emerged:

> *Mutti, Vati, and I went together to the movies to see A Yankee in King Arthur's Court written by my grandfather Mark Twain and really it was perfectly lovely I liked it best of all the movies I have ever seen.*

On the one occasion when Clara and Ossip arranged a play date in London for Nina with children of a musical acquaintance, they did not even go along, but instead sent her off to strangers in the company of a casual acquaintance.

The Gabrilowitsch family dynamic often placed Nina in the odd position of acting more parent than child, more servant than daughter. Her brilliant, busy parents seemed woefully ill-equipped to handle the vagaries of day to day life.

If the maid was unavailable, Nina brought Clara her breakfast, left warm water for washing up outside Clara's door in the morning, and "fixed Mutti on her balcony for a nap." She regularly had to retrieve walking sticks and articles of clothing that her forgetful parents left behind on trains, boats, and at the homes of friends. Nina was regularly dispatched, along with maid

Margaret, to purchase everything from stockings, to corset laces, to spirit lamps, and even alcohol.

Despite the success of Ossip's career, and Clara's income from The Mark Twain Trust, the two displayed an odd streak of frugality. Clara in particular would spend extravagant amounts of money on clothing and gifts and then fret over the cost of a hotel room. This generated anxiety in Nina who would solemnly report that the family was moving to another hotel "because this one was too expensive" or cause her to worry over the cost of train and boat tickets.

Spending countless hours alone in her room, Nina became a voracious reader. Having consumed every book brought along on the ocean journey, she sent Margaret to purchase more. Numerous trips to London's famous Mudie's Lending Library enabled her to feed her appetite with such classics as Dickens's *Barnaby Rudge* as well as more popular fiction such as a Peter Pan tale.

Two of Nina's other lifetime passions, photography and letter writing, were already evident at this tender age. Nina haunted the parks and streets of London, snapping photographs at will and eagerly writing letters to friends and family to tell them of her adventures.

To pay for film, Nina approached Clara and told her she would like to earn some money. Seeing an opportunity to correct Nina's tendency to walk pigeon-toed, Clara agreed that Nina would get money for each two day period in which she managed to walk with her feet properly turned out.

Clara, for some reason obsessed with educating Nina in a manner which she deemed proper, also spent time home-schooling Nina. Clara seemed, however, to have no understanding of the level of material appropriate for a young girl. At a time when most children would simply be enjoying a summer vacation, Nina was tasked with reading a history of England.

While Ossip took Nina with some regularity to a nearby pond for walks, rowing, and feeding the ducks, Clara is never mentioned as joining her husband and daughter on these excursions. Clara, Nina revealed, skipped these excursions not out of lack of interest, but due to a physical malady:

This morning at breakfast Vatti said he would take me to the zoo,

and I was delighted but Mutti couldn't go because she said there
was too much walking to do and I said if there was a wheelchair
there Vatti and I would wheel you and Mutti laughed.

Eventually thought to be parasitic in origin, Clara's medical condition caused difficulties in walking that persisted for a period of several years.

To Nina's great delight, after a stay of nearly two months in London, the family took a train to Weisbaden, Germany to spend time with Ossip's mother, Rosa Segal Gabrilowitsch, as well as Nina's beloved "Tante Pock," Ossip's younger sister Pauline.

Nina suffered from a paucity of relatives in general and a virtual dearth of any near her age. Rosa, well into her eighties, was Nina's only living grandparent. Samuel and Olivia Clemens had died before her birth and Ossip's father Solomon had passed away circa 1915 when Nina was only five years old. Since Clara's siblings had all died without marrying, there were no aunts, uncles, or cousins on Nina's mother's side.

While Ossip was fortunate to have three siblings (middle-aged brothers Arthur and George, and sister Pauline), none had married, sealing Nina's status as the sole child in a small circle of much older family.

Because spending time with relatives was a rarity for Nina, she treasured her time in Weisbaden:

Vatti said he is going to take me to my Aunts and then to my grand-
mother so...I thought I would change my dress for a sunday dress
so I put on my yellow silk one then we went to Tante Pock and then
we went together to Grandmother and we were so delighted to see
each other!

Tante Pock plied Nina with gifts of jewelry including a coral necklace and a small green cat on a chain to be worn around the neck. In true aunt fashion, Pock dragged out pictures of Nina as a child and showed her pictures of her parents.

After a stay of only four days, Ossip, Clara, Nina, Pock, and maid Margaret set out for St. Moritz, Switzerland where they met family friend Olga

Samaroff, wife of Philadelphia Orchestra leader Leopold Stokowski. Because the Stokowski couple had long been close friends of the Gabrilowitsches, Nina affectionately referred to Olga as "aunt." Conductor and pianist Bruno Walter and his wife Elsa also joined the party intermittently.

Nina's adventures as a world traveler continued. Perhaps due to Tante Pock's influence, Nina was included in trips to the ice grotto at Lucerne, Alp Grum, and Lake Silvaplana (which Nina erroneously called Silver Plana). Nina was enchanted with the glaciers and lakes.

In mid-July, Nina was afforded an opportunity to simply relax and act like a child when a Mr. Hecht of San Francisco, California, arrived with his young son and daughter, Frederick and Dorothy. Nina and Dorothy happily played with dolls and five-year-old Frederick joined them for games of hide-and-go-seek and tennis, and for rambles around the countryside.

Two weeks into the trip to Switzerland, Ossip left the group to undertake a far more solemn task, that of attempting to affect the release of his brothers George and Arthur from their native St. Petersburg. While Ossip had been fortunate to escape from Germany at the outbreak of War I, George and Arthur had become virtual prisoners in their own apartments, held hostage to the upheavals of the civil war between the "Red" (Bolshevik) and "White" (non-Bolshevik) factions.

Ossip's efforts failed. It was not until several months later, in October of 1921, that Ossip, with Clara's help, managed to smuggle in the funds needed to bribe his brothers' way out of Russia. Nina's reunion with her two uncles was delayed indefinitely.

Nina celebrated her eleventh birthday in St. Moritz. Ossip had not yet returned, but sent a telegram reading, "Happy birthday, greetings to a dear little rat. Father." A deluge of gifts ranged from educational to whimsical. Nina was clearly as delighted with the prosaic writing portfolio, paper cutter, and pencil "to ware around my neck," as she was with a ball, small wooden carved box, and a miniature carriage set replete with bride and groom and a menagerie of toy animals.

Tante Pock presented Nina with a traveling magnifier in a monogrammed red case as well as a leather book mark embossed with her name, a gift sent along from the "Hofkapellmeister," Nina's pet name for master conductor Stokowski.

A few weeks later, on September 21, 1921, the Gabrilowitsch family headed back to England, boarded the ship *Olympic*, and set sail to return to their home at 5456 Cass Avenue in Detroit, Michigan.

Ossip and his sister, Polya "Pock" Gabrilowitsch

Photo from Nina's personal effects
Courtesy of The Mark Twain House & Museum
Hartford, CT

CHAPTER 30
DEB
CHANGES: NINA (1923)

"My silver pencil had my initials on it, N.G.. Father says N.G. suits me perfectly because I am no good."

NINA CLEMENS GABRILOWITSCH, UNDATED DIARY ENTRY.

WHILE SHIP RECORDS REVEAL that the Gabrilowitsch family again spent the summer of 1922 in Europe, Nina's sole diary entry for 1922 was a brief description of dancing with Harold Emmons, the ten-year-old brother of her friend, Mary Margaret Emmons.

Hired help in the Gabrilowitsch household had changed. Margaret, the maid with whom Nina spent a great deal of time in 1921, appears to have left service as had the secretary, Miss Rix. The latter had been replaced sometime in mid 1921 by a Miss Claire Shover.

While fifty-five-year-old Shover's primary responsibility appears to have been to act as Ossip's secretary, she also played a role in Nina's life. Resenting her overbearing presence in the household, Nina launched a diatribe:

I think Miss Shover is a very tiresome person and I wish she was not in our House. Mother and Father are the only ones that like her. They think I do too, but I am far from it. The maids can't stand her. She loves to command everybody. She should have been an officer or a king.

The true nature of Nina's resentment was further revealed:

...but just because she is there I can't eat supper with Mutti and Vatti. I would feel more like sacrificing that last pleasure if she was interesting...

Two other staff members who also took service somewhere prior to 1923 were to become surrogate family members, providing lonely Nina with a constancy she did not receive from her parents.

Affable and artistic British-born Edgar Glanzer joined the family as chauffeur, a position he held until his death in 1955. Glanzer's grandson, Bill Winter, kindly shared the story of how Edgar came to be part of the household.

Ossip, in the market for a car, went for a ride in a Hudson with salesman Edgar at the wheel. Impressed with Glanzer's driving skills, Ossip promptly offered Edgar a job. Driving young Nina to school or special events fell within the purview of Edgar's duties.

It was nursemaid Sophie Pruischutz, however, who became Nina's constant companion and tutor. Nina referred to her simply and affectionately as "Mademoiselle." Like Marie Koehn, Nina's childhood nurse, Sophie was German and multi-lingual. Forty-five-year-old Sophie's duties included meeting Nina after school several days a week, entertaining Nina, and giving her German and French lessons. Nina spent far more time with Mademoiselle than she did with her mother.

Mademoiselle did not live in the Gabrilowitsch household, but was frequently called upon to spend the night when Nina's parents were away. Nina, who declared, "I love to tease her," regularly pulled childish pranks such as taking Mademoiselle's gloves and hiding them in a drawer.

Mademoiselle did not hesitate to tease Nina in return. One night when Nina, not gifted with her father's talent, was hammering away at piano lessons, she reported that Mademoiselle "said to me. If I have to listen to this much longer I will certainly not feel well."

Clara and Ossip's lives continued to pull them away from home for weeks at a stretch. Clara had returned to giving vocal concert tours. Ossip was not only handling full-time duties as conductor of the Detroit Symphony Orchestra but also engaged in regular piano performance tours. Even when Ossip was in residence, Nina said: "at lunch is nearly the only time I see Father."

Susan commented, "Russ Gooley was not my father and yet, after reading Nina's diaries I realize that I probably spent more time with him than she even spent with her own beloved Vati. And I certainly had the love and attention of my father, Elwood Bailey, every day of my life until I was sent to Chicago."

Nina, highly self-conscious about her own looks, admired her mother's beauty. Remarking one night to Clara about how much trouble she always took to dress herself for dinner, Clara replied:

That is one reason why husbands get sick of their wives so soon. They dress up in their best before they are married but afterwards they think they can put on any old thing and look as untidy as they wish so that when the husband comes home he has to eat with a wife that is not clean or properly dressed.

Attending the exclusive Liggett School, Nina's classmates were children of Detroit's wealthiest and progressive families.

Harriet Hughes, two years Nina's junior, was Nina's best friend. Harriet's father, Charles A. Hughes, was founder and publisher of the *DAC News*, a monthly magazine of the Detroit Athletic Club. The magazine, which featured not only top-flight sports reporting but also essays and humorous pieces, endures to the present.

Nina also idolized beautiful Virginia Booth. Two classes ahead of Nina, Virginia was the daughter of Ralph Booth, manager of Booth Newspapers, Inc. prior to his appointment as U.S. Minister to Denmark.

Frequently mentioned friends Gina Mary and Edith Jane Scotten's father Walter was a powerful and wealthy member of the Scotten Tobacco family. Twin friends Aileen and Kathleen Keena were the daughters of a bank manager.

While still heavily engaged in solitary reading, Nina played ball, dominoes, tiddlywinks, and other popular games with friends and with Mademoiselle. She also began to display an athletic streak, a talent that was to bring her a great deal of pleasure through her childhood and young adult years until alcoholism began to takes its toll on her health.

In the summer of 1923, rather than heading to Europe, the family chose instead to go to California. The opportunity for Clara to seek medical treatment there provided primary motivation for this change from the family's usual summer travel pattern.

Like young Susan en route to Chicago so many years later, Nina rejoiced in watching the passing scenery and sleeping on the train that provided the family's transportation westward.

From the minute Nina saw California, she was hooked. She fell in love with the heat, lakes, and flora and fauna and was particularly taken with Santa Barbara:

> *I love these days at Santa Barbara, they are so peaceful and quiet and in later years I shall love to think of them.*

Nina was thrilled to be given both swimming and horseback riding lessons. The latter provided a double bonus for Nina: it both suited her love of the outdoors and afforded her more of the one-on-one time with her father that she so craved. Nina declared horseback riding to be "more fun than anything I have ever done before."

Clara and Ossip did not allow Nina to simply enjoy her summer vacation. Every morning, she took French, German, or piano lessons, followed by a walk or ride, and then swimming lessons. Her time with Clara was especially limited.

While Nina generally displayed a caring nature, a series of small incidents in 1923 signaled the slow development of a personality marked by an innate inability to relate to the sufferings of others or to feel responsibility for causing others pain. She could also, with complete dispassion, describe death:

> *We cantered on the sand and saw four dead pelicans somebody must have shot them.*

Similarly, Nina not only calmly described a scene that would horrify most thirteen-year-olds, but also, in the next sentence, simply changed the subject:

While we were having our lunch we saw the seven American war ships that had been wrecked on the coast. They pointed out to us the coffins of the sailors that had drowned. We played checkers and dominoes.

This indifference could even extent to those she most loved. Despite learning that the cure for Clara's illnesses was likely to be extremely painful, Nina displayed more concern about having to leave Santa Barbara than she did for her mother's suffering.

Even Nina's reading material displayed the dichotomy between the childlike and overly-adult facets of her nature. While she read about her famous grandfather in Albert Bigelow Paine's *The Boys Life of Mark Twain* and enjoyed again Twain's *A Connecticut Yankee In King Arthur's Court*, she also read *Death and Its Mystery* by French astronomer and author Camille Flamarrion.

The latter, an advanced and dreary tome on psychical research into manifestations occurring at the time of death, could not have been further from the typical reading list of a young teenager.

As in Europe, Nina took the opportunity in the waning months of summer to explore many famous California tourist destinations including San Francisco's Chinatown, Redwood Forest, Capitola by the Sea, San Carlos Mission of Monterey, Pebble Beach, the Booth Sardine Factory, Fox Studios, and Douglas Fairbanks's studio.

In August, another family event of note occurred: Clara took up the practice of Christian Science. With her painful treatment apparently unsuccessful, on August 22, Clara declared that she "couldn't stand being sick any longer" and engaged the services of her first Christian Science Healer.

For the next several days, Nina marveled as Clara grew progressively better.

Clara, who had until this point displayed no religious leanings whatsoever, began to spend time with Nina doing readings from the Bible. She also encouraged Nina to read Christian Science tracts and books and apparently saw to it that Nina followed the precepts of the religion:

> *I don't take the ice bag any more because you can't mix Christian Science and Medecine.*

It seems likely that classes had already resumed at the Liggett School by this time, but the Gabrilowitsch family did not return to their home in Detroit until September 28. There, Nina immersed herself again in activities at the Liggett School, adding participation in track and field events to her growing list of athletic activities. She begrudgingly threw the javelin, but loved the fierce competitiveness of high-speed events such as the fifty-yard dash.

Nina fretted that, for her, physical maturation lagged behind that of her classmates. Her failure to start what she referred to as 'the modern curse,' when all but one of her fellow eighth graders had done so was a source of embarrassment.

She continued to vacillate between pranks such as throwing pencils at the pantry door to startle the servants and far less charitable actions.

In November, Nina made her first attempt at taking the stage, albeit only for giving a speech. She related that her speech went well but that she "nearly died" when she mounted the platform and that she had an unfortunate tendency to swallow in the middle of a word.

As Christmas drew near, Nina also faced a new and, to her not particularly welcome change. Ossip and Clara had purchased the new home at 611 Boston Boulevard that was to become the family's home for the next thirteen years.

While Nina solemnly reported that, "Everyone says we have made a very good investment," she clearly was torn about leaving the house on Cass Avenue that had been her home since the age of nine.

Nina was left to face this change alone as both Clara and Ossip took off on tour. Beneath her brave words, hints of sadness emerge:

> *I saw my bedroom for the last time when all the furniture was gone, my but it looked queer. A taxi came at exactly 10:10 A.M.*

and I descended the stairs and closed the front door for the last time in four long years.

Nina and Ossip

Photo from Nina's personal effects
Courtesy of The Mark Twain House & Museum
Hartford, CT

CHAPTER 31

DEB

A PERSONALITY SHIFT: NINA (1925)

"I lost my trunk key and Mother said not on any account to tell Father because he would have a perfect fit and believe me I didn't."
NINA CLEMENS GABRILOWITSCH, JUNE 20, 1925

N
O DIARY ENTRIES SURVIVED for 1924 or early 1925. By the time they resumed on April, 1925, gone were the last traces of the child. A full-blown teenager had emerged.

The missing diaries from the previous sixteen months are probably simply explained. Nina continued to spend a lot of time with close friend Harriet Hughes:

Harriet read in two of my diarys and some of the things were so far gone that I don't see how I ever could have written them so I tore them up.

Nina was also wrestling with the beginnings of romantic interest. By attending the all-girl Liggett School, and with a social life otherwise dictated by the interests of her much older parents, Nina sole exposure to males her own age consisted of occasional brief time spent with her friends' brothers.

This lack seemed to bother her not at all. Her diaries are virtually absent of any longings to spend more time with boys.

From research done before obtaining the diaries, I had observed that Nina had a penchant for going after men who were somehow unattainable (perhaps married) or emotionally or physically unavailable (e.g. gay men). There were also puzzling hints in that early research of possible bi-sexuality.

Reading the diaries, I began to understand that the genesis of Nina's patterns of emotional behavior began in her teenage years and never changed.

She was, quite simply, starving for one on one attention, particularly from adults. Ossip and Clara's lives were busy and filled with travel. While loving their daughter, they never hesitated to leave her for weeks at a time in the hands of nursemaids or other family help.

While outwardly supporting her parents' right to live their own lives, inside Nina was beginning to internalize the idea that perhaps she was not worthy of her parents—or anyone's—undivided love and attention.

This belief became a self-fulfilling prophecy and resulted in a heartbreaking inability to engage in an ordinary romantic or sexual relationship.

Instead, Nina began to demand attention. She would focus with desperate laser intensity on a person as the object of her affection, becoming obsessively fixated on that person for a period of time. The failure of that person to return her affection had no bearing on Nina's actions.

Since she longed for, but never really *expected*, her affections to be returned, the lack of reciprocity did not change her behavior one iota as long as the object of her affection was in her sight. However, the moment the person became physically absent from her life, Nina simply set that particular person aside and moved on to the next.

The first recorded instance of such an obsession involved Nina's music teacher, Mrs. Martha Wiest. Nina wrote:

> *I love her so well and mostly always one will do a lot more for a person one loves then for one one doesn't care a snap about.*

Wiest, a widow just a few years younger than Clara, was almost universally disliked by the other students at the Liggett School. By turns sarcastic and kind, Wiest seemed to enjoy Nina's obsession with her, alternately flattering and insulting her.

Nina spent a great deal of her time trying to put herself in Wiest's path, including cutting other classes. On one occasion, Nina was being chauffeured home by the ever-faithful Edgar when she spied Mrs. Wiest walking down the street lugging a board and a pot of flowers:

I hopped out and asked her to come in the car and we'd take her
home. After hesitating for a moment she consented and I was so
happy that as I got in I closed the door with a bang and lo the
glass cracked! Mrs. Wiest laughed and said I might as well be a
boy. Edgar almost had a conniption fit and we were sure that Miss
Shover would have one.

Nina was envious whenever Mrs. Wiest paid attention to another student. At a much anticipated outing to the recreational facilities on Detroit's
Belle Isle and a nearby amusement park called Luna Park, Nina became
jealous of Wiest's comforting of Harriet Hughes who became nervous on a
roller coaster:

...all through the wonderful ride she kept patting her because she
said Harriet looked absolutely as if she were going to faint or die! I
wish she said that about me.

Wiest seemed more than aware that Nina, unlike her world class pianist
father, did not possess a great deal of musical talent. She resisted taking on
Nina as a pupil, probably out of fear that Nina's mediocre or poor performance would be seen as a reflection on her.

However, the juggernaut that was Clara rolled over Wiest, with Clara
assuring her that she only wanted Nina to have "some idea of music."

While Weist remained Nina's primary obsession for an extended period
of time, Nina also developed a fascination with Djina Ostrowska, harpist
for the Detroit Symphony Orchestra, and friend of composer Aaron Cop-
land. Ostrowska was endlessly kind and patient with Nina.

Nina's adulation of Wiest and Ostrowska conveyed no overtones of
sexual attraction. In fact, she seemed remarkably absent of sexual desire for
a fifteen-year-old girl. The only hint of sexual attraction expressed at this
time was an observation that while she and friend Harriet played together
in an alley, "We talked the while and kept moving closer and closer together,
till finally there was hardly any space between us."

While Harriet Hughes was, in fact, a high-spirited, bright young girl who as an adult went on to a distinguished career in journalism, Nina confided that Harriet had "an awful reputation at school" with teachers and said that the headmistress wished she would be expelled. The two climbed up on roofs, and pulled pranks like leaving stones painted with teachers' names under their windows.

Nina continued to earn excellent grades in everything except math. When it came to algebraic equations, she declared that, "I had no more idea how to go about those problems than I have of how to make an airship; in fact I have less."

However, her behavior at school became increasing erratic, providing Clara, Ossip, and her teachers cause for increasing concern. Nina displayed an inability to concentrate for any length of time and often burst into bouts of uncontrollable laughter which she simply described as "giggles." The behavior she describes would probably be diagnosed today as attention deficit disorder.

School head mistress Jeannette Liggett and Mrs. Wiest called Clara in for a parent-teacher conference. Nina, in what was to become her trademark way of dealing with criticism, listened politely and then determined to change just enough to take the heat off herself:

> Both of them said I don't concentrate half enough and that I waste lots of time wandering around in the halls. Also that I never keep my mind for very long on what I am doing and missed lots that goes on. They said that it was very serious and that something would have to be done. I shall try because I am sick of hearing about it.

Nina grew progressively more irritated that her reputation as someone who did not concentrate became widespread knowledge. She was particularly incensed that even the grade school children seemed to be aware of her behavior.

Her propensity to cut class and go wait in Mrs. Wiest's classroom in the hope of spending time with her only added fuel to the fire. Because she claimed to use that time to study, Nina was insulted that this was viewed as slacking. She hated to be criticized in any way, declaring that it "makes me so mad I could swear."

As the school year drew to a close, and the family packed for yet another European vacation, Nina experienced a rare episode of getting in trouble with her parents. She and friend Harriet had gone to play ball in a nearby alley and, when they became too hot, climbed onto the top of a nearby pergola to catch a cool breeze.

When another classmate called to leave a message at the house and Ossip realized Nina was not at home, he sent out Edgar and three other members of the household staff to look for her. Ossip was on the verge of calling the police when Nina reappeared. Nina angrily wrote:

> *Father said we couldn't go there anymore but Mutti had given me permission before and I am sure she won't object now because we aren't babies that can't go five feet by themselves.*

Just prior to leaving, the family learned that Ossip's secretary, Miss Shover, had been diagnosed with cancer. Clara, who often displayed a certain degree of callousness towards the family help, visited Shover in an attempt to cheer her up. She told Shover that she would need to apply the same willpower she brought to her work if she wanted to get better.

Clara was unnerved by Shover's suffering. Despite her dislike of Shover, Nina said, "It is awful to have a cancer. I hope I never get one. People out of her family have died of it, that is why she is afraid."

In late June, with the courtesy of one free ship's cabin furnished by newspaperman Ralph Booth, the Gabrilowitsch family again embarked for Europe.

Ossip planned to seek treatment in the spa town of Gastein, Austria, for problems he had been experiencing with his arm. Clara and Nina were to meet Ossip's siblings and visit Venice.

Nina hated traveling by ship, declaring that, "I have a perfect horror of any kind of boat or ship, except a canoe and I would rather spend fifty days on the train than two days on the ocean." I could not help but recall Susan describing the extreme sea sickness she had experienced when making a sea voyage as a toddler.

Another familial pattern continued on the sea voyage. In virtually every description of time spent traveling, and even when both were at home, Ossip and Clara failed to share a bedroom. Clara and Nina stayed in a spacious room with private bath while Ossip stayed in a small cramped cabin that would clearly have been more suitable to the short, slight Nina.

In another shipboard incident, a cabin steward repeatedly asked to enter Nina and Clara's room to shut the porthole. Clara screamed at him to go away. She left the porthole open and soaked their cabin with water.

Still, the next night, she again left the porthole open, allowing water to not only flood their cabin but to also cascade down the hallway outside their cabin. There was no evidence of remorse by either Clara or Nina for the inconvenience and discomfort they caused themselves, the cabin stewards, or their fellow passengers.

While her concern for Miss Shover showed that she was capable of being considerate, in this case it seemed more important to Clara to refuse to take orders from someone she saw as her social inferior than to act in her own best interest.

Echoing in my head was Susan's story from a childhood dinner with Clara in which a fork was dropped at a restaurant and Clara airily said to "let the servant get it."

The family had been on land for only two days when, in Frankfurt, they received news of Miss Shover's death. In a role reversal, both Clara and Nina were horrified by the news while the usually affable Ossip took it in an entirely selfish manner:

> *Father is just having the worst fit because she knew where everything was and in what condition things were in etc. and now he will have to hunt up someone and teach her everything all over again.*

In Frankfort, Nina was delighted to again be reunited with her Aunt Pock and Uncles George and Arthur. Pock, who seems to have been a bit of hypochondriac, had been on a cleanse of some sort and was violently sick. In true sibling fashion, Pock lashed out at Ossip when he made fun of her, saying that it was obvious that he was full of poison.

Ossip responded with a laughing fit and Pock was not amused. George was in a panic at Pock's illness but Clara told him that it was natural after someone had not been eating for two weeks.

As Ossip prepared to depart for Gastein in the company of friend Bruno Walter and his wife, Nina watched with envy as the crowd of family and friends gathered at the train platform.

Ossip and his brothers Arthur and George were chattering away in Russian. Clara and Mrs. Walter were trading whispered secrets. Pock and Bruno Walter were conversing on a subject that Nina knew nothing about.

Nina wistfully wrote, "At times like these I wish heartily that I had a brother or sister because then we could go by ourselves but that will never be."

Nina especially loved her Uncle George whom she found incredibly funny. George, like his brother Ossip, was apparently very absent minded. Nina laughingly described an incident in which Uncle George put marmalade in his tea and almost broke a plate while cutting toast with a knife.

Nina was by turns amused and aggravated with Pock who ran perennially late. While in Venice, they missed mass at the Church of San Marcos because Pock was not dressed by the mass start time of 10:30 a.m. Pock regularly begged off activities due to headaches or was holed up in her room writing letters and endlessly packing.

With Ossip off in Gastein, the remaining party traveled throughout Italy, hitting the sights of Venice, Bozen, Milan, Genoa, Alassio, and Laigueglia before going onto the tiny country of Andorra.

Nina fell in love with the canals of Venice. With her vivid imagination, she envisioned men in the abutting ancient stone palaces "masked and cloaked whispering secrets and killing passersby."

Her fascination with death and the macabre continued. At Venice's Palazzo di Brera, her favorite paintings were of Laocoon and his two sons being strangled by serpents and another of a prisoner in a dungeon.

At a cemetery in Milan, Nina was intrigued with the Italian tradition of placing on graves pictures of the deceased or statues of the person and their relatives. Clara found them too theatrical, saying that relatives should be too grief stricken to care how they looked.

By late July, the travelers returned via Munich, Berlin, and Hamburg,

Germany, and then to the port of Cuxhaven. The ship stopped at Cherbourg and Boulogne, France, and Plymouth, England, before setting sail for the United States.

On the return voyage, Nina was afforded an opportunity to simply act like a young girl when she found a ten-year-old boy and his fifteen-year-old sister as well as several other young people with whom she could spend time. She played shuffle board, deck tennis, and spent time in a gym.

While Clara and Ossip were horrified, Nina described as exciting an incident in which the ten-year-old threw a temper tantrum and started pummeling his fifteen-year-old sister. Nina stepped in and gave the young boy a whack, whereupon he kicked Nina, pulled her hair, broke her glasses in two, and bit her arm.

Just before landing in New York, Clara had received word that her best friend, Elsa Strauss, was dangerously ill. Upon arrival, Clara immediately took off for Massachusetts to be with her.

Ossip turned his attention to finding a new secretary and deputized Nina to compose fifteen letters to potential applicants. The following day, Ossip kissed Nina good-bye, and put her on a train with a plan of hopefully making connections with Clara in Albany.

Being allowed to go anywhere by herself was a first for Nina who said: "I felt very important and grown up traveling all by myself, but was hoping Mother would get on at Albany."

It would be years later when Susan was living in Albany, New York, that both Clara and Nina decided to "get off at Albany." Susan moved to Albany the year Clara died and left there the year Nina died.

Ossip and Clara

Photo from Nina's personal effects
Courtesy of The Mark Twain House & Museum
Hartford, CT

CHAPTER 32

DEB

A CAREFREE VISIT TO MACKINAC ISLAND: NINA (1925)

"I wish I could always stay twelve years old because then one is old enough to understand whats going on and yet one doesn't have to act too grown up."

NINA CLEMENS GABRILOWITSCH ON HER 15TH BIRTHDAY, AUGUST 18, 1925

MICHIGAN'S SCENIC MACKINAC ISLAND prohibits motorized vehicles and its beautiful Victorian cottages have long served to house a summer colony of wealthy and cultured families. For the first time, in the summer of 1925, the Gabrilowitsch family joined the ranks of those families.

Nina had only been home from Europe for a single day when she and Mademoiselle, with family cat Gavotte in tow, were dispatched to the island to open their rented house, what today is known as the Burnham Cottage.

Most homes available for rental were too small to accommodate anyone beyond the immediate family, so Nina was excited to find that the cottage contained enough rooms to allow Mademoiselle to stay in residence.

Less than a week later, both Ossip and Clara had joined Nina on the island. Due to Mackinac's physical isolation, the family relaxed into the rhythms of an ordinary family on vacation.

This late summer sojourn on Mackinac Island, and those that were to follow in the years ahead, were precious to Nina. Being in residence there afforded her large blocks of time with her parents, both singly and together.

Nina and Ossip rode almost daily. After a particularly long ride, Nina wrote, "We stayed out two hours and I was so happy I almost split."

Nina found it funny that Ossip rode so fast that he was oblivious to his surroundings. She joked that she needed to carry a megaphone so that she could let him know when anything worth seeing was coming up.

Ossip and Clara often took walks alone, managing to get lost on more than one occasion. The resourceful Nina continued to find her parents' difficulty with managing such ordinary skills to be amusing.

Even Gavotte found the island entertaining. A house cat who rarely wandered far from the back door at home, Gavotte got the yen to wander one day and went missing for over five and a half hours.

Mademoiselle and Nina were ready to give up in despair when they heard a plaintive meow from the undergrowth near the cottage porch. The "fat ball of yellow fur," as Nina dubbed him, had managed to find his way back.

Gavotte continued his hi-jinks by making a game of jumping on and off the sideboard in the parlor of the cottage and managed to knock a crystal candleholder off a side table and break it.

Clara and Nina discovered the joys of a new sport: croquet. Clara, not usually interested in anything athletic, gleefully took to the game. She particularly loved to roquet competitor's balls, a process whereby a player's own ball was held firmly under foot while placed against the competitor's ball. With a stroke of the croquet mallet, the competitor's ball could then be hit off the course.

Clara would whack so hard that she regularly broke balls in two. She excelled at the game and played at every opportunity. Nina basked in the attention that their mutual skill brought and also in the sheer joy of finding a fun activity that she could share with her mother.

They were regularly joined at croquet by Mademoiselle and Ossip's new secretary, Frederick Post. Unlike Miss Shover, Nina adored Post and his witty, urbane sense of humor.

Also on island was Nina's friend from home, Horatia "Ray" Gleason and her mother. That pair were drafted into the ranks of croquet play as well. Even Gavotte tried to join in and poor Mademoiselle spent a great deal of her time simply trying to remove the cat from the path of the balls.

Nina hated to lose and apparently allowed it to show:

Mother gave me a lecture on not getting annoyed when I don't win the croquet games because she said no game is worth getting up such feeling about and it isn't being a good sport....She said she didn't like to see a disagreeable look on my face and I suppose I have because it does irritate me when I make stupid blows and don't win.

As a measure of how isolated the island really was, Nina wrote in her diary on August 28 that she was catching up entries back to August 5. She had filled up her last diary and had nothing to write in until Ossip made a day trip to Detroit and brought her back a new one.

Susan and I had observed by this point that Nina regularly fudged entries, clearly entering material after the fact when she got busy and even accidentally duplicating entries.

She also made passing references that hinted at having more than one set of diaries. Clearly the ones that survived were the "main" set, but perhaps she kept a shortened and even more personal second set.

Nina loved Burnham Cottage itself and looked forward to family evenings spent curled up on couches and reading Mark Twain's *Innocents Abroad* aloud. Ossip found it so funny that he often laughed until tears ran down his face, and Nina admitted to sneaking the book off the shelf and reading ahead as she could not wait to see what happened next.

She was enchanted with the cottage's paint scheme in which every room had a different color scheme and furniture style:

If I ever have a house of my own I shall have all the rooms different colored just like this and I shall have three or four guest rooms so I can have visitors. I also want a stone terrace at the back where one can sit and read and beyond a garden with a fountain all cosily shut in by a thick hedge or stone wall.

Living in such a small community, Nina got a small taste of what it was like for someone to be recognized wherever she went. On one outing she was startled first by a young girl calling out "Hello, Nina" and then by a couple riding by in a buggy and doing the same.

Nina remarked that she had no idea of who any of the people were and said she finally understood what her mother and father dealt with on a regular basis. Susan had seen firsthand the kind of adulation and demand for attention that Clara received on the occasions when the two attended the Detroit Symphony together.

On another occasion, the sexually innocent Nina was also startled by quite another matter. She and Mademoiselle were walking back to the cottage after playing tennis at a neighbor's when they passed by another cottage:

> *Above us on the steps were two women sitting so you could see right up through their legs! Isn't that shocking. And one had nothing on.*

Nina also developed a playful habit of lightly punching on the arm anyone who came up to her. Mademoiselle, uncertain how to take it, sometimes hit Nina back. Clara found it amusing and called Nina a "silly Gump from Gumpdom."

The entire family enjoyed their time on the island so greatly that well before their stay ended, plans were made to rent a cottage again the following summer.

Nina, never good at leaving a place, grew melancholy as the she walked around one day in mid-September and noticed boarded up cottages and nearly empty streets, all signs of summer's end.

She, Mademoiselle and Gavotte were the first to leave as Nina needed to get back to Detroit for school. Ossip followed a few days later, stopping home just long enough to say hello to Nina before heading off to a performance in New York. Clara still remained on the island, soaking in the last beautiful days at a haven the family had so quickly come to love.

Ossip and Clara might not have shared a bedroom on a regular basis. They also seemed perfectly comfortable running on separate but parallel lives for weeks at a time. But small incidents can often say the most about the true foundation of a marriage.

Getting to and from Mackinac Island requires a ferry ride from the Michigan mainland to the island, a ride that today takes around sixteen minutes but was probably longer in 1925. When Ossip arrived home he caught Nina up on news from the island and described an action of Clara's that spoke volumes about the underlying core of love between Nina's parents:

He told me some things which happened on Mackinac after our departure and how Mother turned the electric lights on all over the house so he could see it from the boat all the way across when he left.

I could just envision Clara, ensconced in the cottage, sad that that her husband was leaving, and sending her love by lighting his way across the water.

Nina on horse "Lass" with father Ossip

Photo from Nina's personal effects
Courtesy of The Mark Twain House & Museum
Hartford, CT

CHAPTER 33

DEB

LESSONS LEARNED: NINA (1925-1927)

"That's why I could never bear to be a writer. Half the time I wouldn't feel like writing books & what would I do the rest of the time? Oh I'm just dying to be an actress, but Mother doesn't want me to be one very much."

NINA CLEMENS GABRILOWITSCH, NOVEMBER 25, 1926

NINA RESUMED HER SCHOOL LIFE and the much-coveted piano lessons with Mrs. Wiest began. Wiest's worse fears about Nina's skills were realized. Declaring that Nina played as if her joints were made of steel, Wiest blamed Nina's former teacher for never teaching Nina how to relax.

Despite the fact that she idolized Mrs. Wiest, Nina did not seem in the least bothered when Wiest told her that she was lazy or was wasting her time by not practicing enough. Nina, whose ear should have been finely tuned after years of watching her father's performances, displayed a very cavalier attitude towards her own skill set:

I practiced on three pages of it last night and there were only three or four chords I couldn't get. All I do in a case like that is to leave out the least important note.

Susan chuckled when she read that and said, "I used to think the black ones weren't all that important."

Nina fretted about her looks, declaring her face to be fat and her nose to be too hooked. She also loathed her glasses and orthodontic retainer.

Nina watched with a mixture of love and envy as her mother, then over fifty, continued to be credited as a beauty. Clara worked diligently with a combination of diet, beauty regime, and plastic surgery, to maintain her vaunted appearance.

Clara saw to it that Nina dressed well, monitoring her clothing. Mademoiselle regularly sewed clothes for Nina. On one occasion, she made Nina a dress with a black background and different colored designs but Clara declared it "vulgar" and would not let Nina wear it.

On one shopping trip to the fashionable J.L. Hudson's Department store, Clara bought Nina a lovely blue coat with fur cuffs and collar.

When Susan read that, she recalled again the time that she was eight years old and Clara also took *her* shopping for a blue coat at a boutique in Detroit. She wondered if, on that occasion so many years later, Clara remembered this very shopping trip with Nina.

Because Clara so strongly believed in the importance of appearance, she also carefully monitored what Nina ate. While others saw Nina as thin, Clara clearly feared her gaining weight, adding to what Clara saw as Nina's list of physical shortcomings. Under such supervision, Nina therefore ate very little in the company of others but sometimes gorged when left alone.

One time Nina admitted to eating six sandwiches and, on another occasion, to eating a breakfast of four pieces of toast, two muffins, and four hard-boiled eggs.

Ossip, most often irritated that he saw Nina as eating too little, nonetheless said that her face looked fat while her body looked thin, describing her as a "pumpkin on a match!"

Susan made a very astute observation when she commented: "I believe this may have been the genesis of Nina's addictive behavior. At this age, she ate to make herself feel good. Later, she drank for the same reason."

Ossip weighed in on other aspects of his daughter's appearance as well. Nina's hair was a constant source of irritation to her. She waffled regularly between the desire to cut or to grow it.

When she finally worked up the nerve to cut it into a shingled bob, a very popular haircut, Ossip told her: "for heavens sake, you look just like a hippopotamus, in fact I'd much rather look at one."

While likely said in a spirit of jest, the remark must certainly have undermined Nina's already flagging confidence.

When Susan read this part of the diary, she grew visibly upset and commented:

> *Eileen and Russ were just the opposite, praising me at every turn. I sometimes felt I couldn't be as good at everything as they said I was. Drucilla, on the other hand, took me down every chance she got. It kills your soul. And to do it in a joking manner is even worse because then the jokester can say, "I was only joking," or "You can't take a joke." I now wonder if Eileen wasn't so effusive because she was trying to undo what Drucilla had done. Who did Nina have to praise her? Who did Nina have to build her up?*

Ossip, like all good fathers, tried to give Nina a sense of direction in life, stressing to her the importance of being responsible:

> *He said that you can't get along in life with no sense of responsibility and that when I have been told to do something I should see that it's accomplished and not leave it to other people. He said "sometimes you act so sleepy. Wake up and know what's going on around you!"*

While Nina often pretended not to care about her parents' rules of deportment and appearance, she was horrified when Mrs. Wiest confided that another teacher had accused Nina of having bad manners. As Clara's daughter, this was a cardinal sin.

Nina said, "That remark hurt. It is always sad to hear that somebody thinks you are going down. I shall keep a good watch on manners now."

Susan also recalled how much emphasis Clara put on manners. In the few times Susan was with her, Clara insisted on impeccable table manners, sitting up straight, not crossing her legs, putting the napkin in her lap, setting her knife on the edge of a plate, taking only one or two sips of water at a time, not picking up dropped utensils and "a lady always leaves a little something on her plate."

Susan felt sorry for Nina having to be so very careful to be on her best manners every day of her life.

Nina's social life began to revolve almost exclusively around attending cultural events. She went almost nightly to plays, the symphony, opera, or movies, at places such as the Bonstelle Theatre, the Masonic Temple, and the Symphony Orchestra. At one Symphony performance, Nina remarked:

> *Mother and Mrs. Strauss, and I sat in the front row as usual, and also as usual every last seat was taken, to our joy.*

Reading that, Susan said,

> *This is uncanny. The time Clara took me to that very same symphony she insisted on sitting in the front row. Eileen also sat only in the first row at every movie and play we attended. I wonder if this started with Clara taking Eileen to the symphony when she was a child spending her summers in Detroit.*

Nina's fascination with things theatrical seems to have coincided with Clara's decision to produce and star in a stage version of the story of Joan of Arc, loosely based on Mark Twain's *Personal Recollections of Joan of Arc*. Fifty-two-year-old Clara, never lacking in self-esteem, saw nothing odd about playing the nineteen-year-old Joan.

For the next year and a half, the play consumed most of Clara's attention, again leaving Nina in the primary care of Mademoiselle Pruischutz. Even when not on tour, Clara regularly left Ossip and Nina to their own devices after a symphony performance or theatre production while she headed out with friends to dance the night away.

While Nina clearly loved Mademoiselle, she grew embarrassed by her constant presence, worrying that her friends were think her "babyish" for always being with a governess while they were free to go about on their own.

She began to stay late at school, leaving poor Mademoiselle to stand alone outside waiting for her to come out. In exasperation, Mademoiselle once declared that if it happened again, she was simply not going to come to school again to meet Nina. Perhaps that was Nina's hope!

Nina clearly understood that the life she led in no way resembled that of her friends:

> *Come to think of it my life is very different in some ways from all my friends. I don't drive a car; I am not allowed to go freely around the city with other girls or in their cars; I don't go to dancing school; I don't know or entertain any boys; I don't sleep at girl's houses or invite them; I don't play bridge; I don't give parties; and I don't go to the football games. Therefore there are so many girls that wouldn't want me for a friend, because these things are the main features in their lives and I don't do them.*

Nina's parents and teachers tried to encourage her to become friends with some of the more popular girls, but Nina had no desire to force herself on those girls who showed no interest at all in her.

She began to evidence an unhealthy fascination with fainting and illness, repeatedly wishing that she could see people faint or get sick or be so stricken herself. This desire extended to her friends, family, actors, and teachers:

> *I was wishing the other night in bed that if I said "I wish" 100 times in one breath any person I desired would faint, and that if I said "I wish" 50 times in one breath any person I desired to would get sick.*

This sentiment was an odd combination of wishing people ill, coupled with a desire to be able to come to the person's rescue. Nina particularly longed to see Mrs. Wiest faint and wished that another teacher, a Miss Bogan, would become ill so that she could take care of her.

Nina also showed a similar affinity for people who looked sad or tired. When watching a movie or theatre production, she invariably raved about actors, particularly older men, with deep lines under their eyes or ones who looked sad and tired.

Clara was totally flummoxed by her daughter's odd taste in men. Nina gleefully reported that the men she found the best looking were the ones her mother found the worst looking.

These bouts of concentration on things gloomy alternated with light-hearted behavior. Nina adored spending time with her father who loved to tell jokes, pull pranks, and tease her. Away from Detroit, she seemed to relax, blossom, and soak up family time.

A return trip to California with both parents in the summer of 1926 was followed by a second stay on Mackinac Island. Clara, off working on the production of *Joan of Arc*, left Ossip and Nina to take the latter trip alone.

While on island, Nina got briefly sick and Ossip, away from the watchful eyes of Clara, brought Nina pills. With a twinkle in his eye, he said he was going to send in the best Christian Science practitioner he knew—and then sent in his secretary, Mr. Post!

By late 1926, Nina's diary entries became distinctly angrier. She felt that everyone was constantly criticizing her, complaining that: "It's a wonder somebody doesn't criticize me for breathing."

When she told one of her teachers that Mrs. Wiest sometimes hugged her during piano practice, the teacher remarked, "That's probably to keep from hitting you."

More and more, Nina began to compartmentalize feelings. She described an incident in which her homework was disturbed when a woman was struck by a car just outside the Gabrilowitsch home. The bleeding and unconscious woman was carried into the house to wait for an ambulance to arrive.

After first saying that she could not imagine working in an emergency room where someone saw blood and damaged bodies all the time, Nina then described going back to her homework with the statement: "Such a pleasant little intermission."

Nina began to work off her pent up emotions with extreme physical exertion. She made a regular habit of going to her room, stripping down to her underclothes and dancing until she was dripping with sweat and totally exhausted.

Susan remarked that, since childhood, she also used rigorous dancing to relieve stress. Once, in her sixties, she took a five hour dance class, drove an hour to attend a contra dance, and then danced another three hours straight before driving back up the mountain to home at midnight. She understood perfectly why Nina would choose this method to relieve stress.

Teachers had to constantly upbraid Nina for her compulsive giggling, and her friends began to slowly pull away. Teachers also remarked on how sad Nina looked, but she could not comprehend why they thought so. She got angry when forced to do things she did not like.

Nina's mood was considerably lightened when, in the spring of 1927, Ossip's sister Pock and his brother Arthur paid a visit. In the presence of the aunt and uncle she loved, Nina took to playing pranks such as putting a plaster head of Joan of Arc in her bed and stuffing clothes under the covers to form a "body."

Aunt Pock teased Nina in much the same manner as Ossip. When someone complimented Nina on her intelligence, Pock "thought it would be only kind to let her think that, so she didn't tell her how stupid I am, but she thinks Mme. O. isn't so smart if she thinks I am intelligent."

Nina also mentioned both Pock and Arthur speaking French to communicate with Clara and Ossip's friends. If, as Susan and I believe, those two raised Susan for the first two or more years of her life, French may have provided the means for them to communicate with Susan's English speaking nanny, Gladys. It was certainly the language Susan remembered and dreamt in for years.

Family friends kept the pair well entertained, but even with Pock and Arthur in Detroit for what is believed to be their one and only trip to the United States, both Clara and Ossip nonetheless left to go out of town on performances.

As the time for her departure drew close, Pock set aside her teasing manner and told Nina how very much she enjoyed the time they had spent together and how she loved her more than ever before. Nina grew unhappy saying:

It was very sad to see them go. I just feasted my eyes on Aunty be-
cause it will be over a year before I see her again. She is the sweet-
est, kindest aunt anyone could wish for.... I tried to feel cheerful,
but I never felt quite so lonely before.

Susan recalled feeling those very same feelings whenever Eileen dropped
her off with Drucilla Bailey or with her Aunt Bruce.

Summer of 1927 saw the family on yet another trip to California. Despite again being assigned lessons (typing and cooking) while on vacation,
Nina thrived on the warm weather, travel adventures, and family outings.

She spent time with a gentleman who "knew grandfather and said I had
eyes like his. Mother says I haven't at all. She said her father's eyes were
grey, rounder than mine & the expression wasn't the same."

The family focused more than usual that summer on things Twain. While
the family were driving around Lake Tahoe, the driver started to tell them
about Mark Twain. Ossip told Nina to tell the driver who Clara was.

The surprised driver remarked that he probably couldn't tell his passengers anything about Twain, but then proceeded to explain to Nina that
Twain used to live in Carson City and that the old tavern where he went
was still standing.

Clara was also the guest of honor at a ladies' tea given by the League of
American Penwomen. One of the guests began to tell stories about Twain.
She related an incident in which a fan kept the ashes from Twain's cigar and
wanted him to autograph the box so she would have proof they were his.
Twain wrote: "positively these are my ashes."

Clara obliged the ladies by performing a song but initially demurred at
giving any sort of speech, saying, "it is very hard for me to talk about my
Father because I saw him only from the personal side at home."

When pressed, however, Clara then related an incident in which Twain
and good friend W.D. Howells were arguing over who was more famous.
To settle the argument, they stopped at a store that sold pictures of musicians, actors, and writers.

Twain said "Show me a picture of Mark Twain." And the girl looked
horrified and asked: "what does he act in?"

In September, the trio went on a trek to trace Twain's movements in Nevada. In Carson City, "Father dug up one old fossil after another, trying to find someone who had known Grandfather." Their search led to a Miss Annie Martin.

Miss Martin, who was about six years old when Twain visited, recalled him being in love with a certain girl at whose house he had dinner. While she washed dishes, Twain demanded a toll in the form of a kiss before she was allowed to put them away in another room.

Martin also recalled an incident in which a young girl listening to one of Twain's lectures complained about feeling faint from cold air blowing into the hot lecture. Twain gallantly carried her home but three days later, the girl was dead of spinal meningitis.

The trio next went to Virginia City and stopped at the Crystal Bar where Mark Twain and other luminaries such as General Sherman had imbibed. They attempted to see the office and printing press that Twain had worked on, but the office was locked and no one had a key. Nina found the place "dreary."

Besides educating Nina in the history of her family, Clara also taught Nina life lessons that were often completely at odds with the conservative, chaperoned lifestyle usually imposed upon her.

For example, Clara took Nina along when she performed at the House of Corrections in Detroit. Nina found the inmates terribly pathetic. When learning that visiting relatives smuggled in dope, she remarked: "That's a lovely way for the relatives to help the prisoners to overcome the habit they are in prison for—by giving them more of the stuff they shouldn't have."

Sadly, years later Nina had a friend do exactly that for her while in a rehabilitation facility.

Similarly, while in San Francisco, Clara's idea of broadening Nina's horizons was odd. She worried about Nina going to a Midshipman's ball, but then took her along on a tour of the seamy side of Chinatown with stops at a former opium den filled with rubbish, tenement houses, and a sweatshop telephone exchange. Yet, she insisted on going with Nina in a taxi to her first two cooking lessons.

While most of Nina's activities were chosen for her by her parents or teachers, or by herself to draw attention, acting seemed to be the one enterprise that she undertook purely out of her own fascination with the stage. She persevered despite, like her mother, suffering from stage fright.

Nina described going to the performers' rooms at the symphony and pretending they were actors' rooms. She said: "I love any place or any bare room that savours of the stage."

She was thrilled when she landed the part of Orlando in the school's production of Shakespeare's "As You Like It." She felt it suited her because she could wear tights rather than skirts and she avoided having to learn the long "all the world's a stage" soliloquy of the character Jaques.

On performance days, after getting over her stage fright, Nina was in her element. She loved the back stage madness, the costumes, and the audience reaction.

Perhaps best of all, she loved that her mother attended a performance one night with Theodore Hecht, her leading man from *Joan of Arc*. Nina referred to them as "Ma and her cavalier."

The play went well and Clara and Hecht took off for a drive while Nina got dressed back stage. In true Clara fashion, she lost track of time, leaving Nina to wait with friends until she and Hecht reappeared.

Reading the pure joy that radiated from Nina's words," Gee I love the smells of paint and scenery and I love the confusion that goes on behind the scenes," I found myself saddened that this love of the stage had not turned into the salvation that it became for Susan her entire life.

CHAPTER 34

SUSAN

1962–1969

THE ACTRESS

"I won't work for music - not one inch - that's certain, and I'm not crazy about school work, but I swear I'd work for acting - and also for dancing."

NINA GABRILOWITSCH, SEPTEMBER 23, 1927

ACTING WAS INDEED MY SALVATION from a very young age. It was both my escape from the sometimes harsh reality around me and a source of tremendous pride. The stage was a place where I could control what happened and where I could shine in my own right.

My life on the stage began at the end of my fourth grade year in Chicago. We were learning about the 48 states that then comprised the United States. All the children from both fourth grade classrooms were involved putting on a skit with props and music. Parents were going to be invited.

I had no idea what a skit was all about but I thought it sounded like fun and was eager to do my part. The art teacher was tasked with helping us make costumes to represent the state we were assigned. The music teacher was also to participate by helping us compose and learn a song about our state.

I wanted to be Florida because I had lived there and could think of palm trees, and sea gulls and sand. I thought I could make up a pretty good song about that.

I was assigned Mississippi!

I didn't know a thing about that state and I surely couldn't spell it. When

I told the teacher this, she came up with a song about spelling Mississippi that was to be my song.

How boring! I was not happy. All the other children were singing original songs that described their state. My song went like this:

M-I-S-S-I-S-S-I-P-P-I,
That used to be so hard to spell
It used to make me cry.
But now that I've learned spelling
It's easy as apple pie.
M-I-S-S-I-S-S-I-P-P-I.

So I decided that, if I had to sing that stupid spelling song then I would just add a little extra to it. I had been taking dance lessons ever since getting out of the hospital after having polio. I had also been taking piano lessons with a member of Russell's band and doing a little singing.

The day of the show came and the teacher staged us just like the 48 states. As Mississippi, I was right in the front and almost center. Florida, Georgia, and Alabama each sang their songs, standing in one place.

Then it was my turn. This Mississippi gig would be my first real 'performance' in front of an audience and I was determined to make it memorable.

I acted my way through every note of that song. Eileen, also a dancer, had helped me choreograph it. I used facial expressions, hand gestures, twists and turns, cried on cue, and, in general, was a great little cheerleader for the state of Mississippi during the few minutes I had.

That was the first time that I had ever heard of a standing ovation. It was just a little auditorium in Portage Park Elementary School, and just our small end-of-year assembly program, but that crowd stood up and roared its approval—and I was hooked for life.

After that day, Eileen went out of her way to find local performances I could be in. For the next seven years, whenever I enrolled in a new school, I immediately headed for the drama department to see if I could get cast in a play.

Drama was part of the glue that held me together for a lot of those years.

I invariably managed to get a very good part, often the lead, in any play being cast. I went to the Florida Drama Festival in Gainesville twice and one year won the Best Actress award. If there was some kind of award associated with any of the plays, I usually won it.

During my middle and high school years, we moved around so much that it was hard for me to make friends. But being good at acting was my way into the local clique. I was naturally bashful, but on the stage I guess my true personality would come out because I was never shy, afraid, or experienced stage fright. Nina may have, but not me!

Sometimes I wondered where this acting ability came from as there was not one actor in my family. Although Eileen was very supportive, Drucilla told me it was the devil's work and I would go straight to hell. She never saw one play I was in—ever!

But I had decided as a child that there was something mentally wrong with her so I paid no attention to her proclamations and just auditioned for one play after another wherever I could find one. It was acting, and Eileen, that sustained me.

After I married John, during the time we were at the University of North Carolina at Chapel Hill, I discovered they had an excellent theater group called the Carolina Playmakers. I learned that Thomas Wolfe hung out with the Players when he was a student there.

During my time at UNC, I managed to land a few roles and begin my education on other aspects of the theater like lighting and set design. But we only had one car, I was working part-time and taking classes, Karen had been born, and we lived on a farm out in the country, so it was difficult to be as involved in the Playmakers as I would like to have been.

Then my life changed when John landed his position at the State University of New York at Albany. It meant that I didn't have to work anymore, and that we could buy a house.

We purchased our first home in Colonie, New York, and in 1964, our son Greg was born. Except for singing in the Capital Hill Choral Society, I temporarily shelved my singing and acting career.

I was incredibly happy about this new baby and hoped against hope that it would be a new start in our marriage and our lives together. This time

John didn't dessert me at the hospital but was there to take me home with our new baby boy.

I had prepared Karen for the new baby by reading her books about big sisters and by role playing with her dolls. But the day we brought him home from the hospital, I laid him down beside her on the sofa and she said, "Mama, I think he thinks he's real."

We all had a laugh over that. Apparently Karen just thought she was getting a new doll.

We soon found out that he was very real indeed, this little fellow who grew up to have such a startling resemblance to Ossip Gabrilowitsch. He stole my heart and Karen's.

John, however, increasingly distanced himself from his family. As he was moving up in the academic world and becoming one of America's foremost logicians, he more and more just ignored us.

We had only one car, and naturally he took it to work each day. At night, he began to stay out later and later. Part of this could be accounted for by conferences and lectures, but not all of it. I had my hands full with a toddler and a baby.

One day, Karen had a doctor's appointment and John was supposed to pick us up and take us there. He never came. He didn't answer the phone at his office when I tried to reach him.

My friend Doris drove us to the pediatrician, and then dropped me off at John's office. I knew he was in class and would be able to drive us home when he got out.

When we got to his office, Karen wanted to color, so I opened his drawer to get her a piece of paper. There was a card addressed to "the love of my life." Of course I opened it and read it. It was from a student professing her love for John.

I realized in that moment just how bad things had become in my marriage. Later, at home, I showed the card to John and tried to talk to him about it, but he was belligerent and accusatory about my "going through his private things."

My stable world was once again shattered. I still hadn't finished my college degree and knew I had no way to support my children. I thought back to the way I had grown up and was determined that, no matter what, my children would not be brought up with that kind of instability.

So I made a decision that night. I would stay until I had that college degree in hand but I promised myself I would leave with my children the very day I received it.

I had a long talk with John and, for once, I did most of the talking. My only trump card was that he didn't want a divorce because he was climbing the academic ladder and in those days a divorce was a blight on career prospects.

John agreed to help me get the degree if I would just stay with him through the process. Since I had no way now to obtain it without him, we made a truce. He said to me that night: "These children are much more like you than me anyway!"

He thought he was hurling an insult at me. I just thanked him.

So I started taking courses again and auditioning for plays at the Slingerlands Players. My return to acting fed something in my soul, and as long as I got the children in bed before I left, John didn't care. Thereafter, many of my nights were spent in rehearsals and plays.

That theater was really where I honed my craft in acting, singing, dancing, and every other aspect of theater including set design and building, costumes, lighting, stage managing, and directing.

At first I just considered myself lucky to have gotten into this group. The director was gruff and most people were a little scared of him. For some reason I really liked him because he expected a lot and I thought this was an excellent trait to have if you were trying to create something of quality with a large group of people.

I remember the night I auditioned. The director, and other members of the group, were in the audience. All of us would-be actors were on the stage and, one by one, he gave us a set piece to read. After reading, the actor would be told to either come sit in the audience or just a simple, "Thank you."

When my turn came I was handed a sheet and told the age and circumstances of the character I was about to read. My part was a seventy-two-year-old lady that was a bit hysterical. Hmmmm. This was a challenge.

All the parts I ever had were mostly typecast, meaning I was playing a character much the same age and similar to me.

Just off stage I had seen some props; among them was a cane. I ran and got the cane and came back and limped a bit across the stage, all the while reading my part in a loud but kind of gravelly voice, mimicking what I heard when I was listening to older people.

I was asked to sit down in the audience. I hoped that meant I was in but when I sat right in front of some members of the crew one of the women said to me, "We hate you!"

That was like a stab to my heart and I turned around in my seat and asked, "Was I that bad?" She said, "No, you were that good!"

During the first year I was in The Slingerlands Players I was cast in one lead after the other. Then I tried out for a new play and didn't even get a minor part.

In tears I went to the director and asked him why. He told me that he just had someone else in mind, that I couldn't expect to have a part in every play, and that I had to pay my dues by building sets, painting, etc.

I told him I was only interested in acting and started to walk out of the theater. As I was leaving he said that if I walked out and refused to work backstage, "don't bother to come back." That stopped me!

Unlike Nina, who wanted things only if they came easily, I had not grown up with servants so I never shied away from doing the work it took to become a success.

During the rest of the time I was a member of this troupe, I had many more opportunities to act and they were wonderful. But oh my God, I fell in love with backstage work. I learned how to age a twenty-year-old to an eighty-year-old through makeup and costumes.

I learned how to set up and run a light board and spotlight and how to design and build a set. I learned about backdrops and scrims. I learned how to cue an orchestra. I learned how to be a stage manager, the most difficult and most important job of all.

In general, I learned every aspect of how to run a theater and, by osmosis, I even learned about directing. The director would give me small scenes to work on backstage and then we would add those to the play. He sometimes, but not often, changed my direction.

If he did make changes, I could see how it made a scene better so I was learning, learning, learning. This would all come in handy when I owned my own musical theater years later!

After four years in Albany, in January of 1966, John accepted a job back at Stetson University in DeLand, Florida, where we had met and married ten years before. Despite our marriage being functionally over, I was happy to go back. I had grown tired of the cold northern winters, and still had friends in DeLand and fond memories of the time I had lived there.

While we were preparing to move, I remember reading in a newspaper that Nina had died in California. I was thankful that Clara had passed on four years earlier because, despite their troubled relationship, the loss of her girl would have killed her anyway.

There was one more important reason I wanted to return to Stetson. I still didn't have my B.A. degree.

I had taken what classes I could squeeze in everywhere we went, but transferring credits from one university to another was not an easy task. At that point I had been attending college for at least four years and had only two years credit to show for it.

I wanted to get that degree! John had promised to help pay for classes and by God I was going to hold him to it!

So in 1966 we moved back to Florida. During the nine years we were gone I had only seen Drucilla a few times and Eileen not at all. My entire family consisted of John and my children. And since John was an emotionally absent husband, I really only had my children. That is probably one of the reasons I kept so busy with the theater whenever I could. They were my family!

We found a nice house on University Avenue near the campus. John settled into teaching and I settled into being a full-time student again.

That was also the beginning of my next four year acting career, with both a local group called The Shoestring Theatre in DeLand as well as with the Stover Theater at Stetson and the Daytona Beach Little Theater.

There was a small group of about five women that got the lead in most of the shows. I was one of them and probably got more than my share.

Besides being an actress and a full-time student, I was the mother of two small children. To my husband's chagrin I was also a student activist, writing letters to the editor and marching against the Vietnam War.

My activities marching up to the president's house, not to mention the satirical plays I helped write about the Stetson president and faculty, almost got him fired. Dr. O. Lafayette Walker, head of the Department of Religion, did not appreciate being renamed by me, Dr. O. Lopalong Runner!

In 1968, tragedy struck again when my brother, Robert ("Bobby") Bailey, was killed in a car crash in Georgia. Of all the losses and pain I had suffered in my life up to that point, Bobby's death was the worst blow. I simply could not believe that my brilliant, loving brother, who had just finished his Ph.D. in physics the week before and landed a job with the Defense Department, was gone.

Karen and Greg were also hit hard by the loss of their beloved Uncle Bobby. Unable to cope with my grief, I asked John to go to Georgia to identify Bobby's body and to bring back his things.

I was the administrator of my brother's estate. In that capacity, I was to learn once and for all, the utterly cold nature of the man I had chosen to marry.

Several weeks after Bobby's death, still reeling from my loss, I received a bill in the mail at the house where John and I lived. I stared in utter disbelief. There in black and white was a bill from John for the expenses of his trip to Georgia to identify his brother-in-law's body.

It was for $68.23 and included a receipt from Burger King for a hamburger and Coke.

I still had one year left before I could graduate. I wrote out a check to John for this amount, posted it by U.S. mail to our address, and vowed once more that the minute I had that degree in hand, I would be forever free of him.

In June of 1969, I received a B.A. from Stetson University. I was unable to keep my promise to myself to leave the minute I graduated because Karen got a nosebleed at my graduation ceremony.

But the next day I left with my two children and as we drove out of DeLand I thought, "You did it Susan, you got that degree. Nothing's going to stop you now!

CHAPTER 35

DEB

A LONG CONVERSATION: NINA (1928 -1929)

NINA'S DIARY FOR 1928 contained only two entries, both in December. The second entry, undated but clearly written on New Year's Eve said, "meet you in H___ 1928!"

Missing diaries seemed to consistently signal events that Nina wanted to forget or did not want to risk having anyone read.

Several sources make allusions to a marriage Nina made at age eighteen that Clara then had annulled. While no records were found in the City of Detroit or Wayne County, Michigan records, it is possible that such a marriage could have taken place elsewhere. She was eighteen in 1928, so the absent diary entries might signal truth to this rumor.

There are also hints in 1929 entries that Nina had been previously expelled from the Liggett School for a period of time. Knowing her later mental health issues, it is also possible that she had her first breakdown at this time and was absent for that reason.

In early January, Nina described having a cleaning frenzy in which she cleaned out old letters, heaping several wastebaskets full of papers. While no mention is made of tossing any diaries, it seems conceivable that her grand cleaning-out included pitching the 1928 diary as well.

Increasingly, Nina's teacher-crush seemed to be moving from Mrs. Wiest to an instructor named Eleanor Bogan who Nina called "Liny." Bogan was less tolerant of Nina's inappropriate behavior than Wiest. When Nina grabbed Bogan's wrist and wouldn't let go, Bogan said:

Nina, I want you to let go my wrist, do you hear me? I mean it. I am really very angry. Let me go instantly—do you understand.

Nina let her go but recorded that she would love to see how cross that she could make Bogan.

At this time, the diary occasionally began to include stage directions such as ["Cut!"]. These asides reinforced our belief that Nina intended these diaries to be seen some day and to form the basis for a movie or play about her life. She limited her sharing of information accordingly.

On January 13, 1929, Nina engaged in a lengthy conversation with Clara's best friend Elsa Strauss whom Nina referred to as "Zetty." The importance of this conversation is underscored by the fact that she repeated the gist of the conversation twice, first at the tail end of one diary and again at the beginning of another.

The entire conversation in both entries are written with stage directions, so it is unclear if this event really happened to the degree Nina narrated or whether she inflated in her mind what she wished she had said.

In either case, Nina seems to have had implicit trust in Zetty and, for the first time, poured out her heart about the resentment against her parents that lay beneath the surface.

Clara and Ossip had apparently begun pushing for Nina to attend the University of Michigan in Ann Arbor. Nina vehemently declared that she hated drudgery, which was how she viewed attending the University of Michigan, and that two subjects were the maximum she could concentrate on at one time.

Zetty went on to explain to Nina that "drudgery" was the foundation of learning, that to get to the advanced courses in any subject, all students have to first work their way through the basic general knowledge unique to that field.

When Nina continued to protest, Strauss told her she believed that Nina would never work hard on anything of her own accord. Nina insisted that she would work for acting and for dancing.

Nina expressed her dislike of small towns, lumping both Detroit and Ann Arbor in that category. She said that either Europe or California would be fine.

The previous summer, Nina had apparently chosen to go to Camp Wanalda Woods in northern Michigan over going with Ossip and Clara to

California. Zetty challenged Nina, inquiring why she made that choice if she loved California so much.

Nina's reply revealed the resentment she had bottled up for being ignored by her parents and spending her vacations doing lessons:

> *Let me tell you. When we were out there three years ago, I did nothing but sit in the house most of the day. I did get used to it but I didn't enjoy it. Father was always at rehearsals and Mother didn't feel like going sight seeing.... Well the next summer I had type-writing lessons in the morning and cooking lessons in the afternoon, but that kind of life doesn't suit me.*

Whatever Zetty questioned her about, Nina countered. She declared that "atmosphere" was everything to her. Strauss said that Nina was a "perfect example of the person who is always thinking he would love the thing he hasn't got."

Practical Strauss pointed out that an actor's life was far from easy or glamorous, with grueling rehearsal schedules and no time that they could call their own. Nina swore that the longer rehearsals lasted, the better.

Strauss, sadly, was right. When given a small part in a Liggett School play shortly thereafter, Nina often skipped rehearsals, stating, "I won't waste ½ the afternoon for 4 dam lines."

Strauss encouraged her to "thrash this thing out with your Mother and Father." Nina admitted that her need to please became counterproductive. When Clara had given her the opportunity to say she did not want to go to college in Michigan, she froze and said it was fine:

> *In October when we were discussing it one day, she asked me if I'd rather go to Europe instead. Like an idiot I said. "Oh no I'll go here." I don't know why I did it.... I thought that if I pretended long enough I wanted to go that maybe I'd get to believe it.*

Nina had assumed that Strauss herself had been promoting the University of Michigan where her husband was a professor, but to Nina's surprise, Zetty indicated that it had been Clara and Ossip's idea:

> They said you were getting too set and old maidish in your ways and needed broadening and it would do you good to mix in with all sorts of girls and boys.

Sticking to her guns about Europe, Nina said:

> I can remember long ago Father threatened to stick me in a French school because I was so slow learning—and I was scared stiff. I was only ten and I didn't know anything but "Oui" and "Non." I thought I'd die in a place where I couldn't speak the language. Now I know it enough to get along. I want to get a decent accent and I'm dying to go over.

Strauss insisted that Nina would get homesick. Nina replied:

> Well Mother said before that she'd come over for awhile and the rest of the time my aunt could live near me and I'm crazy about her....It may sound heartless, but Mother and Father have always gone away and often for so long that it's much easier for me. I miss them, but I get accustomed to it.

Strauss jumped on Nina immediately, saying that proved she would spend all her time with her Aunt Pock instead of hanging out with young people: "You'll get to be an old maid like her—or else you won't be happy unless you marry some old codger."

Nina initially replied that it wouldn't kill her to be an old maid, but then admitted she would rather not have that happen. She also confessed to preferring older people because that was who she had been brought up around, referring to most girls her own age as "bridge fiends and boy addicts."

Strauss threw up her hands, saying that no one could change Nina's mind once she made it up, that she could not see anyone else's point of view to which Nina telling countered, "Oh yes I can, but I haven't a chance if I admit it."

After arguing strenuously for hours with Strauss in favor of attending college in California or Europe, Nina suddenly switched gears and said that she had always assumed she would go to university at Sarah Lawrence or some other East Coast school.

Strauss insisted that Nina would hate the "snobs" in such a "stylish" school and asked why on earth she would want to make such a choice. Nina replied:

> *I don't, but there must be some schools out there that aren't just stylish. But what I mean was when Mother spoke of Mich., she spoke so long as usual I said 'Yes, I suppose you're right—and that ended. That's why I won't give in.*

Nina had no real hope of achieving her own goal to attend a university in California or Europe: she simply wanted to thwart Clara in *her* choice.

Nina prevailed by attending Barnard College.

Ossip, Clara, and Nina
With family cat Gavotte

Photo from Nina's personal effects
Courtesy of The Mark Twain House & Museum
Hartford, CT

CHAPTER 36

SUSAN

2013

THANKFUL FOR A HELPING HAND

R EADING ABOUT NINA'S CONVERSATION with Elsa "Zetty" Strauss brought vividly to mind another educated, thoughtful woman and her husband who played an important role in my life.

Just three years after Nina's conversation with her, Strauss passed away of heart failure, Nina's first loss of a beloved adult. I have been fortunate that my "Zetty" lives on. It is not only mothers who shape us, but all the wonderful adults who guide us.

The first week I arrived back at Stetson University when my husband John took a position there, we were invited to a party for new faculty members. There I met Fred Messersmith who was head of the Art Department. I asked him if he knew about any theaters in town and his eyes lit up.

He was a member of the Shoestring Theater on the outskirts of DeLand and they were in the process of casting *Inherit the Wind*, a play about the Scopes monkey trial, that very week. He gave me all the information about the audition and I made sure I was there for it.

I was cast as Susie Brown, the daughter of the town's minister. The minister himself was played by a man named Richard Morland who, at the time, was head of the Education Department at Stetson and later became Dean of the University. The director and many of the cast members were Stetson faculty so I met many new friends much more quickly than I otherwise would have.

Shortly thereafter, I met Jessie Morland, Richard's wife. Jessie wore many hats in DeLand. She was a well known artist, teacher in the junior high school, and a reporter for the newspaper. It was in that capacity that I met her. We got off to a rocky start.

Jessie appeared at rehearsal one night and just walked right up on the stage and started interviewing the actors, interfering with the flow of the rehearsal. Thinking of myself as a 'professional' actress from New York, I objected to this and suggested she make an appointment.

I had no idea who she was or that no one in Jessie's life had *ever* told her to make an appointment. She left in a huff and Dr. John Hodges, the director, was very displeased with me. So I didn't get off to a good start at the Shoestring Theater and learned very quickly that when in DeLand…

Jessie Morland and I were destined to be lifelong friends though. She finally came back out and did that interview for the newspaper and while she was interviewing me she asked if I had ever modeled. I told her I was modeling for the Art Department and she asked me to come model for her.

With some hesitation I accepted. After our first encounter I was a bit afraid of her but I loved her husband Dick and wanted to get to know her better.

Modeling for Jessie though was no piece of cake. She had a small art studio in the back of her beautiful home. She sat me in a chair and put my head in some kind of vice so I couldn't move it. She began by taking pictures of me and then started painting on canvas. She asked me a lot of questions but when I tried to answer she told me to be still.

Finally, during a short break, I did manage to ask her what she thought of the new faculty. She said, "Besides you, I haven't met any of them."

I asked her why and she told me that she and Dick had the same friends for years and they were very content to just socialize with them. She told me she didn't need any new friends. Then she said, "What do you think of that!"

For a moment I hesitated, then I said just one word, "Boring!"

She had a stunned look on her face and then she started laughing. She said, "You're right, it is boring. I'm going to have a party and invite all of the new faculty and you're going to help me."

Well I did help her and the night was quite wonderful. That was the beginning of many more parties and a lifelong friendship with Jessie and Dick. They have been everything to me: first and foremost, friends;

surrogate parents; marriage counselors (Dick once locked me up overnight so I wouldn't go to Atlanta and marry a man he disapproved of!); financial backups when one of my children needed expensive medical treatment; and family in lieu of the one I didn't have.

Once, after surgery, Jessie literally saved my life! She insisted on staying in the room overnight with me. During the night I woke up and my face felt hot and swollen. I woke Jessie up and she went into action immediately, calling the doctor and nurses and within five minutes I was back in the operating room.

I had blood clots and they had to immediately, with no anesthesia, open up the original surgical site and put a shunt in my head to drain the clots. I could very easily have died.

The doctor tried to remove her but Jessie stayed in the operating room with me while all this was going on. I was wide awake! After being released from the hospital several days later, she took me back to her house and cared for me until I was well enough to return to home. How can you ever repay a friend like that? Certainly you can never forget that kind of friendship.

After graduating from Stetson, I managed to see them every year come rain or come shine. They visited me in many of the far-flung places I've lived.

Several years ago Richard died and I was honored to be asked to speak at his memorial. He was much beloved and there were many erudite speakers there expounding on what a great man he was and what he had done for the students and the University. All this was true and necessary.

But all I could speak of was what he meant to me. How, when I drove up to his house after a six month's absence he would meet me in the driveway and with his soft, Alabama accent ask me, "Susie Q, Where have you *been*!!"

Wherever I had been, when I got to Richard and Jessie Morland's house I was back home!

I found myself fervently wishing that Zetty had lived on or that some other adult could have filled the hole in Nina's life that the Morlands filled for me.

As I read Nina's diaries over and over again I realized there were many points in her life that, had she just been given a chance, I believe she could have made it.

But perhaps she was destined to choose friends that would ultimately fail her. Maybe that was her big lesson in life—that she ultimately had no one to depend on but herself. Unfortunately, in the long run, she failed herself!

CHAPTER 37

DEB

LIFE IN NEW YORK: NINA (1929-1932)

"I had taken a couple of pain pills & was in a most amusing daze."
NINA CLEMENS GABRILOWITSCH, JUNE 22, 1932

AFTER MANY YEARS AT THE LIGGETT SCHOOL, Nina's diary entry for June 7, 1929, contained a single word: "Graduation!" Commencement did not, however, signal an immediate end to Nina's studies. Her admittance to Barnard College still hinged upon successful placement on exams in German and algebra as well as a successful score on a general entrance test. The study sessions, particularly in German, were intensive. Nina remarked:

> I got so tired sitting during 3 hrs. German that by one, I had moved around and occupied every place except the ceiling.

With such a knack for turning a phrase, what a shame that Nina did not pursue writing!

Nina's boredom also extended to taking her general entrance exams which she found so boring that "I all but took a nap."

After a summer spent on Mackinac Island and at Camp Wanalda Woods, Nina's life as a schoolgirl drew to a close, bringing with it a fundamental change—with her services no longer required, Mademoiselle Pruischutz's seven year stint as Nina's governess and companion drew to a close.

To Nina's delight, however, Mademoiselle landed a position as governess to the neighboring Walter Briggs family. Nina took comfort in the knowledge that when she came home from breaks at college, Mademoiselle would still be around.

On September 18, 1929, Clara and Nina headed east to New York City to enroll Nina at Barnard. The two had lunch at New York's Plaza Hotel with Clara's cousin, Julia Langdon Loomis. Nina found it "so nice to see someone that's really a relation." From there, Nina headed to campus where she connected with Liggett friend Rolie Paterson.

While Nina's grades and exam scores had been sufficient to gain her entrance, upon registering, she was informed that she would have to tutor in math throughout the year and take an exam the following June in order to be allowed back for her sophomore year.

After a brief bout of freshman homesickness, Nina took to college life with pleasure. Out from under the ever-watchful eyes of parents and Mademoiselle, for the first time in her life, Nina could shape her own days.

She thoroughly enjoyed the cultural bounty which the city had to offer and renewed a closer acquaintance with her mother's relatives. A touch of home was provided by Clara's dear friend Zetty Strauss who was in the city for an extended period following the illness and death of her mother.

Nina also had the pleasure of meeting Twain biographer Albert Bigelow Paine who regaled her with stories about her grandfather and issued a standing invitation for Nina to lunch with him every Saturday that she could. When Paine remarked how much Nina looked like her mother, Nina took it as a compliment to her and a slam to Clara.

Entries from the balance of Nina's 1929 entries show an exuberant freshman, still following her usual patterns of behavior. New Year's Eve found her home for Christmas break, happily surrounded by friends and family.

From December 31, 1929, to November 15, 1931, no diary entries exist. What transpired in that silent period is largely unknown, but the Nina who remerged was a harder young woman.

A January 8, 1931, letter from Clara to Nina cautioned her against throwing away her good health with bad habits, so it appears that her lifelong pattern of drinking began at least that early. The surviving entries for late 1931 make no mention of Nina's first serious love, Carl Roters, who had obtained a divorce from his first wife on December 15th of that year.

She certainly had begun to date him, possibly even to live with him, by mid July of 1932, but his name is not mentioned at all in Nina's 1931-1932 diaries. The 1932 entries cease on June 28, just a few days before Clara wrote a letter cautioning Nina about Carl. True to form, Nina appears to have destroyed her diaries for yet another painful period in her life.

The extant diary entries for 1931-1932 show that Nina's new best friend, Ethel Hollander, was a hard-drinking party girl who was involved with a woman named Sally.

On one occasion Ethel, deathly sick with a hangover, pleaded, "Nina, please save me, please."

Nina also attended a party where the men were all in drag and reported the same evening that Ethel got hit in the face by a policewoman for being in men's clothing.

Nina's relationship with Hollander was passive-aggressive with Nina often avoiding Ethel just to rile her. She was, however, comfortable enough with Ethel's parents to visit them at their home in Weehawken, New Jersey, where Mrs. Hollander told Nina how she hated Sally.

Ethel eventually became a member of the bar in 1939 and worked in her father's law firm. She died in 1950 at age thirty-nine. No cause is mentioned in the obituary.

Nina's habits of hard-drinking and staying out late bothered some of her more conservative friends. Nina roomed with two women named Rhoda and Helen but for awhile Nina maintained a second apartment downstairs. The two insisted that Nina must "give it up; that I have no regard for my reputation & can't live where such things are going on."

They threatened to report this to a Miss Weeks so Nina had to let the room go. It is possible that the objection was to Nina's lesbian friends whom Nina referred to as "spriggins." Rhoda also had to take Nina to task for not paying her share of bills.

Nina continued to see Ossip and Clara with regularity when they were in New York as well as at home in Detroit on holidays. Jaded, she began to chafe at spending time on Mackinac Island, longing to be back in New York with her friends. Looking around the Island, she observed that the Depression had hit Mackinac hard.

Between June 28, 1932 and January 1, 1936, Nina's diaries again went silent.

Nina Gabrilowitsch
Graduation from Liggett School
From Nina's Personal Effects
Photo Courtesy of The Mark Twain House & Museum
Hartford, CT

CHAPTER 38

SUSAN

1969 TO 2009

IT'S A CLASS ACT

R EADING ABOUT NINA'S COLLEGE YEARS brought me back to my own struggles to obtain a degree. I wondered if, like me, Nina felt triumph at being the first person in her family to ever obtain a degree.

I thought that obtaining a college degree would mean smooth sailing ahead for life. I had also gotten out of a bad marriage and was determined to steer my children through safe, happy, undisrupted childhoods.

The day after my long-sought college graduation at Stetson University, I put my children and dog in the car and headed for Tampa and a new life. How many times had I headed for Tampa, or Chicago, or New York, or Canada for a new life only to be disappointed?

But this time there was one major difference: I was in charge! I had that degree. I had a teaching job lined up. I had money left to me by my brother Bobby when he died the previous year. I had bought a new car and paid cash for it. What could stop me now from succeeding?

I had not taken into account that, like Nina, I possessed a heart driven by a bone-deep desire to be special to someone, a desire that could cause me to make decisions that I knew intellectually were not likely to be in my own best interest.

The very first weekend we were in Tampa I met a man at a pool party right outside our back door. He worked for an engineering firm in Cleveland and was just there temporarily. He came over to me and we talked for hours. Soon we were both hungry but I couldn't leave my children alone so I invited him back to my apartment right next to the pool.

As soon as we walked in the door, my eight-year-old daughter Karen came down the stairs. When she spotted Tom, she pointed her finger at him and said, "Mom, where did you find *him?*" Everyone laughed, but that was the beginning of the love affair between my children and the man who was to become my second husband.

Not long after we met, Tom was down on one knee with a ring in his hand, asking me to marry him. I couldn't help but think back to John's moonlit proposal twelve years before. That certainly hadn't turned out as I had dreamed it would. A man down on one knee was not exactly a good omen for me!

This man was so different from John though, so full of love and enthusiasm for life. I gave Tom a conditional "yes" but told him that we would have to wait a while. I really didn't want to jump into a new marriage before I caught my breath and recovered as well as I could from the old one.

I was also concerned about bringing a stepfather into my children's lives after my own disastrous experience with Drucilla's second husband Carlson.

Tom agreed to wait until I was ready. We courted over the summer and Tom, an accomplished pilot, flew me to Cleveland to meet his large family. I fell in love with them. Growing up as I did, basically an only child, I was enthralled with a family that included two parents who were still together after decades, not to mention all those sisters and a brother who clearly loved each other.

The children and I had barely settled into Tampa after a summer stay with some friends in Maryland when Tom called to say he needed us there with him. He wanted me to quit my brand new teaching job and apply for one up there.

I knew that after all my struggles to get where I was, that would be a crazy thing to do. But the triple lure of a man crazy about me, adored by my children, and a member of a large happy family, was more than I could resist.

I accepted.

Tom was wonderful and loving to the children and me throughout the fall, and my children and I had the most beautiful Christmas we had ever had in our lives.

On January 24, 1970, his family came from Cleveland, and we all drove down to West Virginia where we were married in a little chapel.

Afterwards, his father and mother hosted a fabulous wedding dinner for us in a nice restaurant. With this big, happy family around me who were so accepting of us, I thought I had finally found the family that I had longed for all my life. I was the happiest I had ever been. Karen and Greg were ecstatic to have a lot of new cousins to play with.

I was so in love with him. I thought that my life was finally complete since I had found this incredible man. Tom was so gregarious and made friends so easily that there was always someone around. After growing up lonely and then spending twelve years of marriage to John as an outsider to his university life, I loved my life with Tom and the children.

I believed with all my heart that I would grow old with this man, that he would help me raise my children and be their father forever.

In 1971, my youngest child, Jennifer Susan was born, one month early, but perfectly healthy. We brought her home from the hospital on my son Greg's seventh birthday and walked right into a party that Tom's mother had organized for him. I thought again how lucky I was to have this wonderful supportive family and loving husband.

But my happy ending was not to be. After being involved in a horrific auto accident, Tom endured a long hospital stay and returned home a changed man.

To cope with the pain, he began to drink heavily and also turned for relief to smoking marijuana with a brother who had served in Vietnam and was suffering from post-traumatic stress syndrome.

It broke my heart to watch this wonderful man spiral downward. Eventually, he lost his job. When he began to bring strangers into our home at all hours of the day and night, I knew I had to get my children out of the situation.

I had come to Cleveland with two children, a household of furniture, a new car, and about $25,000. I left Cleveland on Easter Sunday, 1972, with three children, $300 borrowed from my mother-in-law (who told me I was doing the right thing), and a car that was registered in Tom's name only. My second marriage was over.

I didn't know where we would go, but I was again running away from what my life had become—again, putting my children through the experience of losing their home and all their friends.

I was depressed beyond belief. I felt that every good decision I had ever made seemed to turn to dust in my hands.

For the next eight years, I worked as a home economist, then a property manager, and eventually returned to teaching. I also started buying real estate, first condos and then a large beautiful house. I would buy them from a bank in a run-down condition, fix them up, and sell them for a profit.

Today people make a living "flipping" houses, but this was an unusual practice for the time. It enabled me to provide my children with a better lifestyle than my teacher's salary alone could ever have afforded. I sometimes worked three jobs and relied heavily on Karen, especially to help take care of Jennifer. I dated, but backed away from any close involvement with a man.

Most of all I was in charge of my own life and it didn't go unnoticed that I did much better by myself than when I turned my life over to a man.

If only Nina had ever learned, as I did, to first love and trust herself before seeking love from a man, she might have gotten to the place of happiness that I reached with my third and final marriage.

My happy ending had an odd beginning, rooted in a memorable childhood incident.

I was staying in Tampa with Drucilla while Eileen and Russ took a vacation. Of course this meant I would be required to attend church every time the doors to Spencer Memorial Baptist were open.

I tried to get out of this by scheduling sleepovers with friends and that night I got my friend Shirley to take me in. They weren't regular churchgoers so I thought I was safe.

However, her father had just bought a new car that day and wanted to go to church to show it off. Everyone, including Shirley's sixteen-year-old brother Haywood, piled into the new vehicle. Her dad parked in a conspicuous place by the door so everyone would see his pride and joy when they exited the building.

After a long prayer meeting, Shirley's dad was the first one out the door. Everyone was there, but the car was not! Someone went back inside and called the police, who arrived on the scene in just a few minutes.

I had been forced by Drucilla to attend this church off and on since I was about four years old, and in all honesty, I can say that was the only excitement I had ever witnessed there, even surpassing the episode when an old lady slipped and fell in the baptismal font and almost drowned before the preacher realized she was not just exhibiting enthusiasm over her salvation.

As the police were asking questions, we saw a car come down the alley between the church and the playground and stop abruptly. All four doors opened simultaneously, and four teenage boys ran like hell in every direction—except that of the church.

Drucilla was standing by a friend of hers, Jessie. Drucilla asked Jessie if that wasn't her son Andrew running away. Jessie answered that she was afraid that it was, but that he had to come home sometime.

Drucilla said to me, "Susie, don't you have anything to do with that Calliham boy when you grow up, because he is up to no good stealing cars."

Thirty years later, I married him!

When I met Andrew again decades later at a party, we realized that we had similar backgrounds and that we had been forced to go to the same church as children. We soon started talking about the night of the grand theft auto, and I found out for the first time that it was Haywood, the son of the owner, who had taken the car.

I learned that Andrew was a retired Air Force pilot who had been heavily decorated in Vietnam and was the senior vice president of a bank. We soon started dating and this time, I did not run away when I became attracted to him.

He had more integrity than anyone I had ever met and I soon came to realize that I could count on what he said to me. We were married one year after we met for that second time. It was the best and most stable partnership I ever had, lasting nearly 30 years.

Andrew helped me raise my three children and put them through college. He was especially close to my youngest child, Jennifer, acting as the only father figure she had ever had. Together we raised our wonderful adopted child, Rory, who died in 2001.

The same year that Andrew and I reconnected, I returned to the world of theatre, this time not as a refuge but as a passion. I wanted to create for the children of Tampa a place where they could foster their love of the theatre and learn to be proud of their accomplishments.

I started a children's musical theater that would become Class Act Productions. It was a school for children ages five through eighteen that offered lesson in drama, dance, voice, piano, violin and other string instruments, as well as academics. We operated only after school, on weekends if we were in production, and in the summers.

The children were picked up after school in our buses and we had tutors that helped them with their homework and projects. We did four shows a year, three during the school year and one major production during the summer.

The second year we were in operation, the company was accepted by Hillsborough County Public Schools for their Arts in the Schools program. This meant financial backing as they paid for each child in Hillsborough County schools to come see our shows and bused them in.

At last I could stop worrying about the substantial bills that come with putting on a major production and concentrate more on the productions.

Our production company grew to 100 students and we had to double cast each show. During the nearly 10 years of its existence, Class Act staged such major productions as *Oliver, The Sound of Music, Bye Bye Birdie* (the kids' favorite), *Annie, Cats, Peter Pan,* and *A Chorus Line,* as well as smaller musical reviews for small audiences.

Once, during a rehearsal for *The Sound of Music,* Porter Anderson, a theatrical reviewer for the Tampa Tribune came to watch. At the same time we were producing *The Sound of Music* with children ages five to 18, a professional dinner theater was producing the same show across the bay in St. Petersburg. He had attended their rehearsal as well.

Several days later his story came out in the newspaper and part of what he said was, "The professionals over in St. Petersburg would be doing themselves a favor if they came over and watched Ms. Bailey's rehearsals before opening. Or perhaps they could just borrow her nuns!"

The night we opened with *The Sound of Music,* I received a private handwritten letter from Maria Von Trapp congratulating me on producing the show with only children. I read it to the audience on opening night and there was thunderous applause. To this day I don't know how she knew unless somehow someone sent her the review in the paper.

There were such talented children in this company that many of them went on to become professional actors, dancers, and singers. Many received college scholarships in the arts. One landed the part of Cosette in *Les Miz* in the Broadway touring company when she was just seven years old. Many of them are now professional actors and theater directors, and one is a Hollywood script writer.

My daughter, Jennifer, spent a large part of her growing up years in this theater company and she was the best dancer I ever had. When she was thirteen years old, her dance teacher told me that I needed to take her to New York for further training, that there was no more she could teach her.

Liz Vassey, a Hollywood actress, scriptwriter, and Class Act alumnae said:

> *Class Act meant the world to me when I was a teenager. Simply put: I didn't fit in at school. Enter Class Act! I found my people there. Kids who cared very deeply about the same things I cared about! Kids who knew every word to Les Miserables before it even came to the United States, kids who dreaded the thought of being diagnosed with vocal nodules from singing incorrectly, kids who not only knew what a tour jete was but could actually do one! Kids who were tiny theatrical misfits. Just like me. So, yes: Class Act taught me a lot about acting. And singing. And dancing. And the list goes on and on. But mostly what I remember was that I felt like I'd finally come home.*

In 1990, after Rory sustained a brain injury at the age of two months, I had to sell Class Act. It broke my heart but Rory simply had to come first. Running Class Act remains one of the proudest accomplishments of my life.

Liz's kind words confirmed that I had accomplished exactly what I had set out to do: teach theatrical skills while utilizing love of the stage to lend the little Susans and Ninas and Lizs of the world a place where they could fit in. I am gratified that Class Act brought pleasure to so many people and changed so many children's lives.

Andrew, my very own "class act," had long known of my supposed Mark Twain connection via Ira Lucia. He was a great admirer of Mark Twain and had read all of his books. Andrew supported me in all the research I had done over the years.

He died in 2009, but was alive long enough to witness the opening stages of my journey of discovery about Nina. I only wish he could have lived long enough to learn about Nina's diaries and all the other surprises that were to come.

I miss him still and will always be grateful for his presence in our lives. I can't help but wonder how different Nina's life might have turned out had she ever found such a stable, loving influence in her life as both Clara and I were fortunate enough to have found.

Andrew was always so proud of me and told me so. It was almost like living with Eileen and Russ again. In his eyes I could do no wrong. If only I hadn't been so young when he and his high school friends stole that car I would have gone after him immediately—if for no other reason than just to spite Drucilla!

I'm more than grateful for the thirty years that I had with him. None of us can go back and change even one thing but, if I could, it would be that Andrew and I had married when we were young and had our entire lives together.

But then again, had that happened, my three wonderful children would not exist. Like Clara, I have never been a classically religious person but have spent a lot of my life seeking spiritual guidance. I still could not tell you exactly what I believe except for this: "It's all in Divine Order."

CHAPTER 39

SUSAN

A FATHER'S DEATH: NINA (1936)

I BRACED MYSELF FOR THE "DIVINE ORDER" that Nina was about to face. I knew already that Ossip's death had a life-altering effect on Clara and Nina, but as I began to read Nina's diary entries from 1936, I found myself feeling tense, wondering how Nina's own words would describe this traumatic upheaval.

As we had learned in our earlier research, Ossip's failing health had drawn Nina back to Detroit and to her childhood home before Christmas of 1935. A brief remission in Ossip's cancer made the family's time together more precious. Her dairies, written over the next several months, chronicle the slow, progressive decline of her once vigorous and talented father.

With her acting career in New York on hold, Nina got involved in Detroit's active local theatre scene, both performing and raising funds. Besides a busy acting schedule, she maintained an active social life, dating frequently, while still spending time reading to her father on a regular basis and trying to keep her mother's spirits up.

Early in January, she had met a man named Jim Humberstone who played a managerial role in the theater group and grew to take on an ever-increasing role in Nina's affections. She continued, however, to socialize with other men as well for the next several months, attending theatres and bars in their company.

My father, Elwood Bailey, visited Detroit frequently in this time period as travelling companion to his brother-in-law, my uncle Charles Lucia. Charlie's father was a purported cousin to Clara Clemens and his mother Harriet, who also lived in Detroit, was experiencing deteriorating health as well.

The photo of Nina and Elwood together that I had been so shocked to find in The Mark Twain House & Museum collection, while undated, when compared to dated press photos of Nina from this period seems to be from this same time in her life.

Between March 7, 1936, and late June, Nina's diaries go strangely silent. By now, I had realized that whenever something significant was happening in Nina's life, something she wanted hidden from the world, she either failed to write about it or, as she strongly hinted, secreted it in a companion diary that she didn't think would ever be found.

Based on my belief that I was born in mid-January of 1937, I had looked forward eagerly to reading Nina's entries from April of 1936 as that is the month in which I would have been conceived.

It is hard to describe my level of frustration that Nina had, deliberately I believe, failed to record any entries in the weeks surrounding my conception.

Sunday, June 21, 1936, found many members of the Detroit Theater Guild moving for the summer to Ironton, a small community on the western shore of Lake Charlevoix in a popular northern Michigan tourist area. Nina and Jim were among this troupe and their relationship appears to have blossomed. Nina wrote the following day:

> I got up feeling a happiness I haven't felt in years. Free! Free! Free! Blue sky, sun shining, lake sparkling, lovely trees all around. Was it really true he loved me! That just made the picture perfect!

She neglected to mention that Humberstone was not only a married man but also the father of a six-year-old boy.

For the rest of the summer, Nina's busy life revolved around performing and socializing with the rest of the troupe members. It may have been her last happy summer. On September 3, 1936, Nina received a wire from Clara telling her to ignore a letter that was on its way. Nina shrugged it off, wondering in passing what the contents might be. The next day, when the letter arrived, Nina recorded in shock:

> Letter from Clara said she thot Vati was dying, & perhaps she should have asked me to come home sooner.

Nina phoned home and Clara admitted that Ossip was feeling "wretch-ed" and that she thought it would cheer him immensely if Nina were to come home immediately. While Nina said she had a foreboding of "some-thing terrible," her movements that day did not display a sense of urgency. With the troupe in the process of pulling up stakes to move to its next venue, Nina still took the time to have lunch, drive to the nearby village of East Jordan, come back and finish packing, and then wait for Jim Humberstone to be ready to leave.

At four o'clock in the afternoon, the pair set off for Detroit. Nina's con-versations with Humberstone revolved not around her father's condition, but her angst that the summer and "a glorious chapter" in her life were over. The pair even stopped for dinner at 8:45 p.m., thus delaying arrival at her Detroit home until 11 p.m.

Mother and daughter then talked for the next two hours, with Nina fi-nally beginning to comprehend the gravity of her father's illness. What a re-lief it must have been for Clara to finally have someone to whom she could pour out her own fears. The days of protecting Nina from the inevitable were over.

For the next ten days, Ossip's condition vacillated. On a day with very little pain, he expressed the hope that a miracle might still happen and lead to his recovery. But with return of pain, came utterances of horror at the thought of having to go on living in unspeakable agony.

At times delirious, Ossip lost touch with reality and asked whether they were in Germany or Switzerland or in a hotel.

Whenever Ossip worsened, Clara called in Mrs. Smith, a Christian Sci-entist healer. Clara's faith in Smith and sympathy for her religious views did not, it appears, extend to Ossip. Presumably, based on the tenets of her faith, Clara withheld pain medication, and Nina mentions that her mother had to reassure Ossip about Smith.

In a telling passage, Nina recorded Ossip, just three days before his death, saying to Clara:

I know why you're afraid to be in room alone with me—you're afraid of what I'll say to you.

Nina and Clara continued to try to distract Ossip by reading to him, but it grew daily more obvious to both mother and daughter that his condition was rapidly deteriorating.

Nina, who had kept a diary at least since the age of ten and wrote almost daily about the most minute details of her life, made no entries at all from three days before her father's death on September 14, 1936, until four days after his demise.

Movements of mother and daughter over the next few days make it nearly certain that not only had they skipped Ossip's Detroit funeral (as we had already learned), but they failed to attend his September 17, 1936, funeral in Elmira as well.

While the Christian Science faith holds that death is an illusion, funeral services are often held at the family's wishes, and led by a Practitioner or Reader. Absent faith-based objections to a funeral, Clara and Nina's failure to honor their beloved husband and father still spoke to me of a need to, or desire to, avoid the public eye.

On September 18, 1936, Nina wrote of a dream in which her father crawled to his death and then sprang back to life again, exclaiming, "I'm healed! I'm free!" while the overwhelmed watching crowd shouted, "That was real Faith!"

Perhaps Nina, who appears to have accepted her mother's Christian Science belief, in some unconscious way blamed her father for lacking sufficient faith to assure his recovery. Clara, however, upon hearing Nina's dream, considered it a message from Ossip, and took great comfort in what she perceived as a sign of his peace and freedom from pain.

Nina, focused on her mother's grief, described Clara as "broken." While Clara dutifully answered condolence wires and letters, Nina sublimated her own grief by continued contact with Jim Humberstone.

On September 18, 1936, Nina received a phone call from Jim who was attending a dance with a woman named Adeline. Nina described her as "feeling better than ever before." While reporting on the woman's health, Nina failed to mention that Adeline was Jim's wife.

Something in Nina drove her to fall for charming married men. In her relationship with Humberstone, and with my father Elwood Bailey, as well as other married men later in her life, she showed no animosity towards the spouse—and no apparent remorse for seeking such attention from their husbands.

It struck me that that the small legal paper that joins two people in matrimony apparently meant little to Nina. Knowing that she later claimed to have been married at age eighteen, but that her parents had it annulled, perhaps that was the genesis of her attitude that marriage was not a serious matter.

Or perhaps she developed that view based on her parents' own marriage. As the diaries were revealing, although Clara and Ossip had a strong bond and great affection for each other, they often led separate lives.

With Ossip dead, the two women now had to navigate their way through life without him. Without his steady eye on the horizon, this navigation was about to go completely off course.

CHAPTER 40
SUSAN

A SEA CHANGE: NINA (1936 - 1937)

A S I CONTINUED TO READ THE 1936 DIARIES, my sense of tension grew. By now, I had learned that Nina was far from straightforward, even in what should have been her most private writing.

I knew it was probably far too much to hope that she would simply say, "I found out I am going to have a baby." Well over seven hundred pages deep in her words, and her maddeningly cryptic style of writing, I knew I would have to search for clues in her actions and words to see if anything would provide evidence to support my belief that Nina was now carrying me.

On September 19, 1936, just five days after Ossip's death, Clara and Nina boarded a train for Chicago, logging the first leg of a frenetic, months-long round of traveling. It was as if they sought to outrun the demons of grief and fear that tore at them.

These two seasoned world travelers, who had always counted on Ossip or servants to handle all arrangements, struggled on their own. Edgar Glanzer was dragged along in their orbit, scurrying across the country to bring them the car at each stop.

After checking into the Drake Hotel, mother and daughter took a stroll along a Lake Michigan boardwalk. They poignantly discussed whether Ossip would really have committed suicide had Clara died before him, a sentiment he had apparently expressed many times.

For the pair, the next twelve days involved nearly non-stop activity. They embarked on a sightseeing whirlwind, attending plays, driving to nearby attractions, and shopping. On one such visit to Chicago's flagship Marshall Field's store, Clara purchased three black dresses. Eschewing her husband's funeral services did not, it seems, mean that the socially conscious Clara would forego this traditional symbol of mourning.

Nina continued to exchange letters with Jim Humberstone and, on September 28, sent seven books to him via the ever-loyal Edgar, who was headed to Detroit for a brief visit with his own family. Nina remarked, "I felt as if I were losing 2 friends—those books and Edgar."

A list of the book titles, contained at the end of Nina's 1936 diary, revealed that all dealt with issues of sex, love and marriage. Among the titles were *Sex, Marriage, and Divorce Problems*, *The Homosexual Neurosis*, *Sex Knowledge For Men*, *Sex Technique in Marriage*, and *The Well of Loneliness*.

Whether Nina was trying to convince Jim to obtain a divorce or to stay married is unclear, but the subject matter of the books clearly implies that the two shared frank communications of the subject of sex and marital status.

I tried to imagine Nina having, as I assume, slept with two married men that spring, finding herself pregnant with me, and knowing that neither man was in a position to marry her. Bookish by nature, perhaps she sought advice in those works on how to proceed with the dilemma she faced.

Due to the subject matter of the books she was reading, there is a good possibility that her mind was on marriage as a way out of her predicament. Even Nina, who eschewed propriety when it came to sexual matters or dating married men, knew that the morality of the time she lived in, and her mother's great desire to protect the reputation of the Mark Twain name at any cost, would not let her keep a baby if she were unwed.

On October 1, 1936, the two women left Chicago by train en route for Mexico City, Mexico, a distance of 2800 miles. On board, Nina, wrote,

I had an inkling then of something wrong—but no conception of what really lay ahead.

As I read those portentous words, it struck me powerfully that her phrasing, "no conception of what lay ahead," was significant no matter how I interpreted those words.

One possible meaning, I thought, was that she *already knew* what heartache lay ahead (my birth and her having to surrender me) and was once again recording the events in her diary after the fact, carefully couched to reveal only as much as she wanted the world to see in the event her diaries ever came to light.

The second way to view those words touched me even more deeply. As a pregnant unwed mother, Nina might simply be expressing her fear that she had no idea what impact becoming a mother would have on her life. The fear was in the not knowing.

I could find no other reasonable explanation for her expressed sense of foreboding.

Five days later, strolling down the Paseo de la Reforma in Mexico City, Nina and Clara returned to the topic of suicide. Nina asked her mother, "if it weren't for me, would you have committed suicide after Vadi's death?"

Clara replied that she would been sorely tempted, but that, even without Nina, "it would be against the Law of things—against what was meant to be, so she wouldn't have done it."

On October 8, 1936, still in Mexico City, Nina read "pathetic letters" from her Uncle Arthur and Tante Pock in Switzerland. These letters were the first mention in the 1936 diary of correspondence from Ossip's brother and sister but were to be far from the last.

Clara fired back a cable to her in-laws and received a return wire expressing the hope that Nina and Clara would come to Italy. To the mother and daughter, looking to elude their grief, and perhaps to escape from a larger problem, this invitation dangled like a lifeline.

Sadly, it was a rescue device that was to remain maddeningly and tantalizing out of reach for many months to come.

On October 16, 1936, Nina and Clara spent time at a train station in San Antonio, Texas, en route for St. Louis. During the layover, Clara sent a cable to Arthur and Pock saying,

> it was difficult to delay our coming at this point; they should select a place for us to meet them, when Pock feels better.

This cable provided the first bit of evidence that Clara felt it imperative that she and Nina move on to Europe without further delay.

I found myself doing math again. At this point, I believe Nina would have been about six months pregnant. Deb had asked me how on earth a woman that far along could possibly still be hiding a pregnancy. To me, though, it was completely comprehensible.

Like my own body, Nina's was slender. While some small women show their pregnancies immediately, I barely showed until almost the very end of my pregnancies. If Nina carried in the same way, Clara may have begun to panic, thinking that their luck at concealment must surely be running out. Her actions in the next few days certainly speak to an ever growing sense of urgency to leave.

Back in Chicago by Saturday, October 17, 1936, Clara became frantic about securing passports for the upcoming European trip. She called her secretary, Phyllis Harrington, who was still in Detroit, asking her assistance in obtaining "emergency" passports. After spending a month trekking 4,458 miles from Detroit to Chicago to St. Louis to Mexico City to San Antonio and back to Chicago again, something precipitated this sudden urgent hurry to get to Europe.

Clara then tried to persuade Nina that they should head to New York City the next day because she was certain they could get their passports more easily there. Nina, displaying a cooler head, persuaded her mother to wait until Monday and continue with the original plan to get them in Chicago.

Nina might, however, have had an ulterior motive for delaying. Boyfriend Humberstone was in town on business and she may have been angling for an opportunity to connect with him. If so, her wish was fulfilled. Nina went to Jim's hotel and spent the following evening with him.

Monday morning found Clara and Nina at the Chicago Post Office at 9:30 a.m. Clara's passport renewal took only ten minutes. However, two additional days passed before Nina was able to secure hers.

After picking the passport up in person on Wednesday, Nina had dinner with a friend named George who expressed what a marvelous person he felt Jim was "for his age" and asked "if I loved him." Nina's diary is silent as to her reply.

Despite having passports in hand, Nina and Clara still spent most of the next day in Chicago. Nina again met friend George, this time at his office, where he tried to talk Nina out of going to Europe.

He said, "he was afraid this trip of ours was going to be an ordeal, and it was all wrong." His parting words to Nina were, "Take care of yourself and keep your soul."

Nina and Clara were about to travel to a Europe already at war which could, perhaps, explain why George was so worried. But the remark about keeping her soul struck me as far more personal in nature.

By 4:45 p.m. that day, Nina and Clara were headed for New York City. Ensconced in her compartment on the train, Nina inscribed a book to be given to Jim:

"To One Half with love from the Other Half. Question: Tempo-rary or eternal? Answer: _____?" He will answer that someday before long.

On arrival in New York City on October 23, 1936, the two proceeded to the Biltmore Hotel where Phyllis Harrington awaited. She had, at Clara's request, scheduled an appointment for Clara to meet with Albert Bigelow Paine (Twain's biographer) and also screenwriter Harold Sherman to dis-cuss the latter's planned screenplay, *The Life of Mark Twain.*

Clara had stipulated that this meeting, which she wanted to get out of the way before embarking for Europe, was to be held upon condition that no one talk to her about Ossip's still too fresh and painful death.

Nina, however, and not Clara, attended the meeting. While this screen-play later became a source of acrimony resulting in Clara filing a lawsuit, there is no indication that this half-hour meeting was anything but amicable.

This encounter signaled a reversal of roles, evidenced for the remainder of the trip, whereby Clara came to rely upon Nina rather than vice versa.

To Nina's delight, she met Humberstone in the lobby of the nearby Commodore Hotel at lunchtime. He went all over the city with her that afternoon as Nina ran errands and did last minute shopping.

The couple then went to dinner and talked and drank until 1:15 a.m. be-fore saying goodbye at nearly 2 a.m. with a final parting: "We drank a toast to my seeing him before the new year!"

The next morning, October 24, 1936, Nina woke with a hangover. At breakfast, she and Clara talked about the planned duration of their trip to Europe and made a bet. Nina said:

> I'll bet we'll be back in this country before the first of the year; she bets it will be after. god, I hope I'm right!

I wanted to be cautious about reading too much into Nina's words, but the thought that popped into my mind was that they were making this bet based on when each guessed Nina was due.

I tried without success to envision other reasons why Nina and Clara would be treating their return date as unpredictable and out of their control.

The two were on the dock at 11:30 a.m., and set sail on the ship *Rex* for Italy. By 12:40 p.m. they were passing the Statue of Liberty and on their way to a very different adventure than either had so far experienced on their many sojourns to Europe.

October 27, 1936, found them on the high seas with a pensive Nina recording in her diary that she had just finished a book entitled *Sparkenbroke* in which the phrase, 'The time will pass,' ran like a jingle in the main character's head. Responding to it, Nina wrote:

> And that's what I keep repeating to myself over and over—it has always passed before, and it will pass this time too, and that is a comfort, when I make myself believe it. "That's what courage is—the numbing of fear. generally it's action does the trick. A man's afraid before he goes over the top—not afterwards!" Also true—and I'm afraid of this trip because I don't know what's ahead—once I got the lay of the land, it won't be so bad.

By October 29, 1936, they arrived in Gibraltar. Nina thought the rock looked marvelous with the town all lit up below it. Her statement that they only stayed an hour because of the war provided yet another stark reminder that this precipitous trip, which Clara deemed an emergency, proceeded in the face of a Europe already at war. That the two, who had survived a terrifying escape from Germany during World War I, should willingly enter another country at war spoke to me of the absolute necessity that they felt the trip to be.

While in Gibraltar, they received a letter from Ossip's brother, Arthur, saying that Tante Pock was sick again and could not see them for another three weeks. They suggested that Clara and Nina wait for them in Italy.

Both thought the idea ridiculous and determined to go straight to Montreux, Switzerland.

The following day, they received yet another cable saying that they could now proceed to Switzerland. Nina said, "Thank God for that." The wire also informed that there would be a follow-up explanatory cable waiting for them upon arrival in Naples.

They arrived in Italy at 12:45 pm the following day to a band playing, beautiful blue skies, and sunshine. Upon checking into the Excelsior Hotel, they were disappointed to find dreary rooms. They were further disappointed when, upon retrieving the promised wire from Arthur, it now instructed them NOT to come to Montreux "because of relatives there."

After traveling half way around the world, they were now stranded in Italy, with no place to go, and no family to meet. Why would Arthur not want them in Switzerland just because other relatives were there? Were he and Pock afraid of other family members seeing a pregnant Nina? A disgusted Clara talked briefly of an early return to America.

That evening Nina watched with regret as the *Rex* sailed back to New York just at dusk and "all lit up like a fairy boat."

Never ones to pass up an opportunity to explore, from November 2 through November 10, 1936, Nina and Clara traveled from one Italian city to another seeing the sights not only of Naples, but of Pompeii, Capri, Amalfi, Lido, and Tivoli, settling finally in Rome. They also began to make arrangements for a four week long trip to Egypt, with an original sailing date of December 27, 1936.

A weary Nina commented on November 8, 1936, that doing so much got monotonous.

282 BAILEY | GOSSELIN

On the tenth of November, they arranged to spend two weeks in Sicily because Ossip's relatives had again agreed to meet them there. However, this invitation, like the earlier ones, was apparently rescinded because there is no mention of such a trip actually materializing.

On November 15, 1936, Nina wrote:

> *Hurrah! Half the month is gone! A month from to-day I'll be even happier—with only 8 weeks to go!*

I reread the odd, contrived construction of that passage several times. It seemed to me that Nina had chosen the phrase "8 weeks to go" deliberately.

Discussion about the trip to Egypt continued as did a whirlwind of sight-seeing. Clara and Nina even managed a visit to the palace where Olivia Clemens had died.

On November 22, 1936, an express letter arrived from Tante Pock. An irritated Nina wrote:

> *She's having a perfect fit at our going to Egypt so soon, so Clara wired her we'd postpone the trip. I knew that would happen! Another added month before I see Jim!*

Clara then changed the date of the Egyptian trip to January 24, 1937, and rebooked their passage back to the US, shifting the return date from February 10 to March 11 (as Nina had feared!).

If Nina were indeed referring to the impending birth when she said "8 weeks to go," then there's a good possibility that she had seen an Italian doctor who had revised her due date to the middle of February, thus prompting Clara to revise their traveling plans.

By that time, Ossip had been dead for well over two months. Clara and Nina had been living in hotels and traveling from one city and continent to another. They had been in Italy, where they had originally been invited by Arthur and Pock, for nearly a month. They still had not seen them!

One invitation after another for Clara and Nina to visit Ossip's siblings (at their home in Switzerland or somewhere in Italy) had been proffered and withdrawn. While Tante Pock expressed outrage at the timing of the trip to Egypt, she still offered no specific plans to meet up with her late brother's family. For a woman who had claimed to be shattered by her brother's death, she seemed to be making no real effort to make connections.

Perhaps she and her brother Arthur were dodging a request for help that, as a spinster and bachelor, they were not certain they were prepared to answer.

On November 27, 1936, yet another letter arrived from Arthur relaying that Pock was insisting that no one could help her with her packing (for what is unknown) and that Pock wanted to know why Clara and Nina could not stay beyond March 11. A thoroughly exasperated Clara said that there was no pleasing Pock:

> So she wrote Uncle Arthur asking him to tell her there was certain reasons why we wanted to and must sail by then & for her not to spoil the allotted time by complaining. Clara says we'll sail March 11 unless a volcano blows us up!

To further add to Nina's unhappiness and frustration, she had heard nothing at all from Jim Humberstone. On November 29, 1936, however, she received a letter from her friend Dot Glenz. The letter said that Dot had shared an evening with Jim, and that she liked him immensely, "but thinks we're not suited to each other unless we both compromise in certain ways."

The next day, Nina cooked up a scheme to get some solitary time and to have a base from which, unbeknownst to Clara, she could send and receive costly cables to try to track down and communicate with Jim.

To do so, she made arrangements for a room at the nearby Pension Hannover, telling the proprietor that she would take the room as of the following Monday. She fired off a cable to Phyllis Harrington, asking her to locate Jim.

When Clara developed a bad cough and became very ill, Nina lovingly took care of her mother for the next several days, putting her plans to move to the Pension on hold. On December 2, 1936, she was thrilled to receive a wire from Phyllis stating that Jim was not in Detroit and that she would cable Nina upon his return. Nina was "relieved beyond words to know he is still alive!"

Nina sent a reply to Phyllis saying that she was eager for more information, but asked her not to mention the Pension or the cables in any letters to Clara. Money had become an issue. Ossip's will had not yet been probated, and the pair, who had never needed to be self-reliant in fiscal matters, were facing the exigencies of being in a foreign country with no source of ready funds.

While Nina was learning to navigate the complexities of wire transfers of money from the Guaranty Trust in Paris, and probably knew how tight money had become, Clara remained blissfully ignorant.

On December 7, 1936, Nina mentioned sending a note to Tante Pock, but gave no indication of the contents. Three days later Clara, feeling somewhat better, also sent a letter to her errant sister-in-law.

Clara vowed to leave by train on December 14, although her intended destination was never mentioned. After weeks of living in each other's pocket, a rarity in the familial lifestyle of these two women, the two were about to split up.

A few days later found Nina living alone in the cold, dreary pension where she composed a letter to friend Dot Glenz, complaining about the bad food and mentioning her long-time rival for Jim's affection, fellow actress Fields:

> *Wrote long letter to Dot glenz telling her about Jim's cable...and quoted the parts from child's letters about Fields.*

Another oddly constructed sentence, I thought. I finally concluded that this was a letter Nina herself had written to "the child," and was quoting from what she had already written.

Another tantalizing reference to a child appeared in a December 21, 1936, dairy entry when Nina, who had just moved to the Grand Hotel, said:

> *Wrote letter to child with swell quotes from Jim's letter.*

I broke out in a cold sweat. There it was. Two mentions of a child. My mind raced, trying to sort through any possibilities for the meaning of those entries other than what I wanted them to mean.

To my knowledge, none of Nina's close female friends had children at this point. Lists of people that she had written letters to that appear at the end of the 1936 diary make no mention of any child. Jim Humberstone had a son, but he was only six years old, certainly not old enough to be writing letters to Nina.

And besides, the subject matter of Nina's affections for Jim, and rivalry with Fields, would not seem appropriate content for communications between an adult and child, even for one so unconventional as Nina.

But if a pregnant Nina was, like many an unwed mother, composing letters to her unborn child in the hope of someday sharing them, then the references make sense. It would also imply that friend Dot was aware of Nina's pregnancy. It also made me sad that Nina's main confidante in those trying days for her seemed to be her unborn child.

I wanted to cry and sing at the same time. If what I was reading into those words was correct, then Nina *did* intend for me to someday know about her. She meant for me to someday read about what was happening in her life at the time she got pregnant with me. And, damn it, like every other adult in my life, she did not deliver on the truth. She did not see to it that I got those letters.

Almost from the beginning of reading her diaries, I felt like our roles were reversed, that I was the mother and she the child.

There are no further entries in Nina's 1936 diary. It concludes with a list of twenty-four "Letters to Cat" (her affectionate nickname for Jim), all of which Nina had mailed between October 1 and December 28.

In return, she received perhaps a half-dozen letters. The lopsided nature of the emotional commitment to their relationship is poignantly summarized in Nina's description of the final letter from Jim.

Dec. 28. (Answer to 2 Xmas letter. Feel put in my place).

As for the college years during which she was involved with first boyfriend Carl Roters, and virtually every period in her life that involved emotional upheaval, it came as no surprise to me that the collection of Nina's diaries contained nothing for the critical next few weeks.

I believe that in that time period, she gave birth to me and wrenchingly left me behind with someone she trusted, probably her Uncle Arthur and Aunt Pock. I suspect the diaries were deliberately destroyed by Nina.

What little else I knew about the next few weeks of Nina's life, I could glean only by inference. The January 10, 1937, letter, addressed to friend Dot (previously shared by her daughter Miggie) had revealed that Nina moved on from Rome to Florence, and thence to a hotel in Bordighera, Italy.

Nina's (and Clara's) whereabouts in the days following January 10, 1937, are unknown. What is clear is that something occurred that caused them to forgo the planned trip to Egypt and change their plans for a March 11 return passage to the US.

A passenger list, as I already knew, showed that the two set sail for home on January 27, 1937, departing from Villefranche, France, once again on the ship *Rex*.

Nina's words, spoken to me as a child in Tampa on the occasion of our only meeting played over and over in my head:

I named you. You're a little French girl.

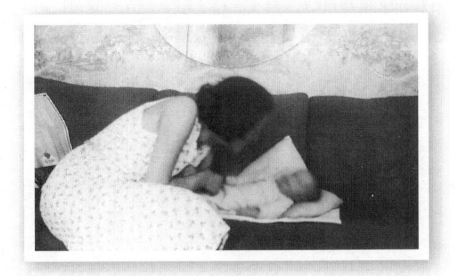

Slender woman (Nina?) with newborn (Susan?)

Only photo with infant found in Nina's personal effects
Courtesy of The Mark Twain House & Museum
Hartford, CT

CHAPTER 41

DEB

2013

THE LAST OF THE DIARIES: NINA (1939-1942)

ATERIALS RELATED TO OSSIP GABRILOWITSCH and held by the Burton Historical Collection in Detroit, Michigan, reveal that prior to leaving for Europe in 1936, Nina sublet her Fifth Avenue apartment for a year.

She clearly had no intention of immediately returning to her life in New York upon her return from Europe.

From the end of 1936 to the end of 1939, no diaries survived. If Nina poured out her heart at the time about a child, her thoughts are lost.

It is also clear that much of the 1940 set is written after the fact as Nina regularly foreshadowed events with phrases such as "if only I had known then."

By the time Nina's personal narrative picked up again in December of 1939, she was in Los Angeles and heavily involved with actor Jack Rhine whom she had met in February of 1939. From a letter discovered earlier in the treasure trove from The Mark Twain House & Museum, the end of this relationship was known: Jack eventually came out of the closet.

The diaries reveal that Nina's relationship with Rhine was of longer duration and intensity than what Susan and I had gleaned from the single letter we had read. Nina was heavily involved with Rhine both emotionally and sexually.

If there had ever been any lingering doubts about the extent of Nina's sexual activity, or her exposure to a very open lifestyle, those doubts were dispelled by the entries for 1939-1942. The possibility of her having given birth to Susan out of wedlock suddenly seemed more than possible.

This was no shy virgin. She spoke with frankness about sexual activity, abortions, homosexuality, and other social topics.

On March 26, 1940, she wrote:

> *My heart was heavy tonight because of Jack. Little did I guess how much heavier it would be a month from tonite, because of him.*

Later that same evening, Nina had a hemorrhage and confided in Jack that she had been having such trouble for the last few weeks. The following day the hemorrhage worsened.

On April 26, Nina learned that Rhine had accepted an offer from a Mrs. May Lowe to fund his efforts to get started in an acting career in New York. Learning this was the event that stunned Nina—perhaps because she had been carrying his child.

A few days later, Nina made one of the most honest entries in all of her diaries:

> *It was such a relief to tell Jack everything last night. It was a curious purge. I felt so much better and so comforted. It was so good to have it all over, & have him close to me again!...*
>
> *Jack said he was so sorry "it" couldn't have seen the light of day. I agreed.*

By implication, Nina had either miscarried or perhaps even aborted a child. Whether that child was Rhine's or someone else's initially seemed uncertain, but the conversation that followed made it clear that Jack was the father—or at least that Nina wanted him to think that he was.

Jack asked Nina if he had anything to do with her "not feeling well" for so long to which she hesitantly responded in the affirmative. He replied, "I thought so. Why on earth didn't you tell me? It doesn't seem right."

Nina responded:

> *I explained the whole story,—about not wanting to worry him,*

*Glen and Lu's help, etc.—Dr. Fist, Dr. Wilson etc. He asked if that
was what I'd worried about last March. I assured him it wasn't. I
wonder if I'll ever tell him what it really was.*

With no diaries from March of 1939, the last statement provides a tantalizing mystery. DNA had proven that Jules Schmidt could not be Susan's
father, but this remark of Nina's raises the possibility that she might have
had *another* child somewhere just prior to March of 1939.

Perhaps Jules was telling the truth after all when he claimed that he had
fathered a child with Nina. Nina met Rhine in February of 1939, so was
clearly not pregnant at that point and did not become sexually involved
with him until November of 1939.

As the time for Jack's departure for New York drew closer, Nina said:
"Awful ache in my heart gone—just feel sort of hopeless, tired, & numb
now."

A September 11, 1940, entry further supports the notion that Nina had
either aborted or miscarried a child in March of that year. She indicated that
"a half a year ago" today something was a load off her mind and made her
happy. There are no diary entries between January 13 and the March 26
entry in which she spoke of having a hemorrhage.

By the spring of 1940, Jules Schmidt was also back in Nina's life (if indeed he was ever out of it) and staying at her house. While they were supposedly good friends, Jules told Nina that she was no good. He also teased
her that he was not ever leaving, although clearly she wanted him to go.

He annoyed Nina by writing something in her diary that she found dis-
gusting. She described Schmidt chasing after a number of women, and he
even admitted that he was attracted to Jack.

Schmidt was prone to wild shouting. By the time he left on June 16,
1940, Nina was exhausted and relieved beyond measure at his departure: "I
feel like a person released from a hospital or a prison."

In a wonderful little bit of history, Nina mentioned going to "McDou-
nel's drive-in" on June 23, 1940. The first McDonald's restaurant opened in
San Bernardino that year.

Nina began to speak more and more of not being able to sleep, of being depressed, sad, and deathly tired. Her sleeping patterns become very erratic. Her normal routine was to sleep most of the day, go to the pool at Clara's house or go to the beach, eat and drink, attend rehearsals, stay up most of the night, and then do it all over again.

While she was still heavily involved with acting, her lifestyle began to take its toll on her career. She began to skip rehearsals when she simply felt "too weary to move."

While Nina maintained contact with college friends such as Ethel Hollander, her new crowd of friends included Meta Von Bernuth—the great-granddaughter of Steinway Piano founder Henry Steinway—and Manon Krause, stepdaughter of famed German soprano and Metropolitan Opera star Lotte Lehman.

Other friends included aspiring actors Wilbur Sparrow, Connie Root and her partner Clara, Bunty Cutler, and Bob Skiles.

Nina and her friends spent a great deal of time speculating about the sexual orientation of all of their friends. In July, 1940, Manon told Nina that she suspected Jack of being gay. It was nearly a year before her analysis proved to be correct.

Sparrow also declared that Jack would "never be any more exciting on the stage than in bed." It seems that Nina willfully ignored the signs that all was not well in her relationship. Ironically, Jack eventually returned to an outwardly heterosexual life, marrying and fathering a child.

In September of 1940, Nina developed a crush on friend Carmelita Parma:

Kept thinking of Carmelita. She fascinates me so, I cant get her out of my mind. If only I were a man—I'd marry her tomorrow.

Later that month, when sitting for portrait painter Lillian Dayton, the discussion turned to homosexuality:

We agreed that every person's life is her own;—there's no excuse for being "smug" just because we're born a certain way. I wondered what Lillian would do, tho, if I suddenly said: "I'm in love with Carmelita!"

The question of Nina's own sexual orientation was one that Susan and I debated frequently. From her high school crushes on female teachers and fellow students, to her interest in Carmelita, to her affair with Lova Dolle (as reported by the latter's daughters), there is evidence that Nina at least toyed with bi-sexuality.

Nina chose, however, not to act on her feelings for Carmelita:

> *Explained to her that the vibrations she gives out, tho they invigo-rate me, make me sad, because they remind me too keenly what life could be and is not.*

Nina was clearly not prepared to face the reactions that living an alternative lifestyle would bring. She was, after all, Clara's daughter, and appearances were everything.

In the end, Susan and I concluded that Nina simply desperately wanted to be loved by someone and that she sought affectation wherever she could find it.

At the point that she became infatuated with Carmelita, Jack had been in New York for less than a month and Nina had already fallen "in love" with someone else. She seemed totally incapable of sustaining feelings in the absence of the object of her affection.

Clara, too, at the age of sixty-six, was grappling with her own sexual and romantic issues. Jacques Samossoud had finally declared his love for her, a situation which Nina described as creating a load on Clara's mind.

Clara, who was by this point dabbling quite heavily in spiritualist pursuits, decided to consult a Ouija board to communicate with Ossip. Nina said:

> *If he says it's part of her spiritual growth to give in to Jacques, which isn't pleasant for her, then she'll try to make herself fall in love with him.*

Apparently Ossip "encouraged" Clara, because a few days later, Clara confided to Nina that Jacques thought they should "experiment" before marrying. In a comical reversal of mother-daughter roles, Nina replied: "I told her about motels. Tried to explain certain sexual things."

Nina's sexually free lifestyle was beginning to catch up with her. In September of 1940, she mentioned buying "tricononius" pills referring to trichomoniasis, a sexually transmitted disease. She was treated again for the same condition a few months later.

In October of 1940, Nina's affections turned to Alex Lockwood, the married actor we had previously learned about from Nina's letters held by The Mark Twain House & Museum.

Learning more about this relationship only brought home the point that Nina's emotional growth seemed to have simply stopped. Her interactions with Lockwood were often childish. She hid his pipe in her pocket. He sprinkled pepper on her bed. She stepped on his feet to annoy him. She took his favorite beret.

As with Jim Humberstone's wife, Nina seemed to have no qualms at all about befriending Alex's wife Hester while at the same time making sexual advances to him.

Lockwood both encouraged and discouraged the relationship. Nina's intense feelings for Alex only furthered exacerbated her drinking and bouts of depression.

Alex minced no words about Nina's excessive drinking:

> *You were cute as the dickens Saturday nite—but when you're drunk the way you were when you wouldn't take us home—you're absolutely revolting.*

As the months wore on, the two regularly teased each other sexually. When Nina fell on him on a bed, Alex said: "I suppose someday we'll have to get this over with but I'm afraid it might spoil our friendship."

Immediately thereafter, Alex asked Nina if she had ever become pregnant. She did not reply.

It must have seemed to Nina at this period that everyone's lives were moving forward except her own. Jules Schmidt called from New York on

February 22, 1941 to tell Nina he was marrying girlfriend Mollie. Less than a month later, she received a letter from first love Carl Roters, telling her that he was marrying his secretary, Ramona.

The news of Roters' upcoming marriage prompted a discussion between Nina and Alex:

> *He asked why we separated—if the "diddling" ceased to be fun? I said worse than that—it became repulsive to me & how Carl & I argued over it.*

Nina bonded even more with Alex when she found out he fainted. Apparently her childhood fascination had never abated. Alex said the sight of blood made him light-headed and also confided that he had fainted the first time he found out what sex was all about.

Alex's wife Hester was clearly not oblivious to the attraction between her husband and Nina. When Alex hopped a train for San Diego in April of 1941 to take on an acting assignment, and Nina was later showing off a new heart-shaped bracelet to a crowd of their friends, Hester remarked: "I know where her heart is—it went to San Diego."

Later that evening, Hester told Nina how she first met Alex and confided that if he fell in love with someone else, it would break her heart, but that she would never show it.

Even Hester's not so subtle pleas for Nina to back off had no effect on Nina's pursuit of Lockwood. She would go visit Hester at her place of work and then turn around and go for long drives with Alex or go back to the Lockwood apartment with him.

Her persistent sexual pursuit finally paid off. The interplay between the two had grown more pronounced until one day in May of 1941, with Nina sitting on his lap, Alex announced, "I'm sorry, Monkey but I can't stand this anymore," and carried Nina to the bedroom where, as Nina recorded, "We were happy almost together."

Achieving her sexual goals did not, however, bring Nina the satisfaction and happiness that she had dreamed of. Rather, it only served to increase her loneliness and frustration. Her writing became filled with laments such as

"Very rarely have I been so tired—body & soul" and "Oh god! How much more pain in this life! Does he love me—or doesn't he?"

Nina began to regularly consult fortune tellers. It is clear that one of her major goals was to find out who would become her husband. Every one told her something different.

Nina's relationship with Clara continued to be outwardly loving. Nina, as she had done in Europe in 1936, took care of Clara when she was sick. After one bout of illness, Clara told Nina, "You deserve a wonderful husband—I must do something about it!"

But as Nina's commitment to acting began to fade, and her drinking and bouts of depression to escalate, she began looking for a scapegoat. When she did not want to examine her own actions, Nina threw the blame on Clara:

> *B. worried only about herself & Jacques—their love—the scenario she wrote, & the novel she's writing. She doesn't lift a finger to help me actually, yet she craves to have me there every nite for dinner, or at least to see me daily, & it's a duty that bores the hell out of me;—the regularity of it kills me—& I loathe that big dining room with only 2 people eating in it. I don't know what the hell I'm out here for at all. She's gloating because she doesn't have to go to Washington, & I'd give my soul if they'd both leave tomorrow. All thru dinner I kept wondering how she'd feel if she knew how I felt about her.*

Despite the viciousness of these words, Nina did not actually express these feelings to Clara until many years later, and then only through a letter written while institutionalized.

Clara was, at this juncture, also caught up in the efforts to make a screenplay about the life of her father. Nina and Clara debated the merits of Spencer Tracey versus Claude Rains to play the part of Twain in the movie.

Neither got their wish. When the screenplay finally came out in 1944, the title part went to Frederic March.

When Nina got to hear screenplay writer Harold Sherman read his script, she was far from impressed:

Such a bore. Just a bunch of episodes; & one gets no distinct picture of Twain, Livy, Susy or anyone. A lot of what Blackie had done such as singing while Twain died, he impersonated in the character of Susy. A lot of it just maudlin slush & phantous of Tom & Huck running about. Most interminable evening I've endured in ages.

Despite being born after his death, Nina spoke as if she had actually known her grandfather.

The looming presence of war began to be felt. Friend Manon's siblings, who were half-Jewish, had been spirited out of Austria in late 1938, possibly just a few months before Susan was brought to the US.

As 1940 wore on, Nina attended a lecture about Adolph Hitler. Friend Kay Grant Verney described her sister leaving England with a young baby, bringing tales of air raids.

Nina made political commentary on world events and mentioned friends being drafted. In a testament to how little she identified with her own heritage, she remarked: "guess I just instinctively dislike Russians." She also commented on another friend's "annoying Jewish habits."

Despite these acknowledgements of the world situation, Nina's diary contains absolutely no mention of Pearl Harbor or the beginning of the United State's involvement in World War II. Other than a mention that her Dutch-born doctor was called home to serve his country, Nina blithely continued on with her life.

The diaries stumbled to a halt with a final December 17, 1941 entry.

The bright, sweet young girl of the early diaries had slowly transformed, over the course of more twenty years and nine hundred fifty pages, into a self-centered young woman caught up in a hedonistic lifestyle that brought her no real satisfaction.

I closed the diaries, grateful for the extended look into Nina's life, but somehow weary to the bone from watching her slow decline. I could only imagine how Susan felt.

Jack Rhine with Dog

Photo from Nina's personal effects
Courtesy of The Mark Twain House & Museum
Hartford, CT

CHAPTER 42

SUSAN

2013

GETTING TO KNOW MY MOTHER

WHAT I WAS FEELING WHEN I FINISHED the diaries was heartbroken for this woman who had been given so much and wound up with other people's crumbs. But that was not a feeling I came to quickly.

I have spent a lifetime trying to locate my mother and the desire to find out the truth never left me. I always wanted to *know* my mother: not just her physical identity, but to actually know all about her.

When I began to see mounting evidence that Nina Gabrilowitsch was my mother, I was disheartened to learn that there was a paucity of information about her and who she really was. I just knew the bare bone facts. That was not nearly enough for a girl who had spent a lifetime searching for her mother.

Deb was successful in combing the Internet and contacting some of the children of Nina's friends for additional information and I was glad for every scrap of information that turned up. Then we made that trip to The Mark Twain House & Museum and were able to read some of Nina's letters and see a wealth of pictures but, compared to her entire life, it was still precious little.

Then Deb found Nina's diaries!

I remember how I felt the day they arrived. A large box was delivered by UPS. It weighed several pounds thanks to the hundreds of pages of Nina's own words! I was beyond excited that now I would be able to read about the life of this woman I had grown progressively more certain was my mother and get to know her in a way that had not been possible before.

I just sat holding that box in my lap for a long time. I can't tell you exactly why I didn't tear it open immediately and start reading, but I didn't. After all my years of searching, I just had to "sit with it" for awhile.

I was eager to know the contents, but also afraid of what I might find. Would I like the woman I was about to meet? What if the material proved she was my mother? What if it didn't? Either way, I knew with certainty that my life was about to change.

I put the box on the dining room table where it stayed for the next two days.

Finally I felt in the right frame of mind, opened it, and begin to the read the words Nina had written almost ninety years ago. I wondered, when Nina was writing them, if she ever pictured that her own daughter would be reading those words so many years later!

The first Nina I met was a child of ten with exceptional writing skills and a keen eye. Her descriptive phrases were outstanding, even though her spelling was not of the same caliber. Describing the changing of the guard at Buckingham Palace she wrote:

> *I went out with Margaret and we walked down towards the King's palace and we saw the centries change the centries ware red coats black trousers white blets, black fur helmets, and they have guns. When they change they all marched up to the centry and then the officer would read the orders and take the centry with him and leave another one in his place.*

I was instantly charmed with this precocious little girl. Intellectually, I knew that Nina did not spring to life as the full-blown thirty-something with alcohol and mental health issues that I already knew, but emotionally I was still surprised and touched by this eager little girl out and about London with a maid.

I also soon discovered that she was "way overbooked!" She had a certain number of books to read, French and German lessons to take even on vacation, and swimming and horseback riding lessons.

Clara (Mutti) thought spending quality time with her girl was poring over a history book with her. I grew up adoring the "Aunt Clara" who took me on adventures in Detroit, but I was quickly beginning to see that being raised by her was a far different experience.

As I continued to read Nina's own words, I quickly came to realize that the diary was her alter ego, her best friend. She was telling her diary the things that, as an only child with few friends, she had no one else to tell.

She clearly also chose to hide painful events by leaving them out, or by destroying entire diaries. Later, when I came to her writing about the year leading up to my birth, this habit became very informative and revealing to me.

Except for giving a detailed daily account of her life (breakfast, lessons, outings, school, reading to Mutti, lessons, supper, then bed), reading the first few years of Nina's diaries was frankly rather boring to me. She was a strictly regimented child who had very little say in her day to day activities.

Much of the material in the first few chapters of her diaries was repetitious. No matter how eager I had been to learn about Nina, this was just not gripping material!

As I was reading, I wasn't particularly looking for similarities in our lives growing up, but found a few anyway. I realized that although Nina, like me, was in many school plays, her parents rarely came to see her act. Only her faithful governess or the servants occasionally attended.

I too was in many school plays that no one in my family came to see. I certainly had no governess so, except for the years I lived with Eileen, there were no family members in my audience. I wondered if it hurt Nina's feelings as it did mine that the adults in our lives did not make what was important to us a priority?

Nina went to the Unitarian and Catholic churches as a child (the latter with Mademoiselle). I also attended those two churches on my own as a child. Clearly Nina was looking for something to believe in. For a number of years, Clara read the Bible to her almost every day but didn't attend church and wasn't particularly religious.

By the time Nina was thirteen though, the two had started reading Hawthorne's *The Scarlet Letter* together. I couldn't help but remember when I was thirteen and knew absolutely nothing about sex. Clara was a bit more advanced than Eileen regarding birds and bees education! For all her public persona as an elegant, cultured woman, Clara had a strong earthy streak.

I was startled by a May 29, 1923, entry:

> *I had a French lesson in the morning out of doors, we started to read a French book called "Aline" by Greville. It is very interesting.*

I have often suspected that when Eileen spent her childhood summers in Detroit, she came under the influence of Clara. But reading this, I wondered if Clara, or Nina, also had a hand in naming her. Eileen was born just four months after this entry and the name on her birth certificate is actually given as Aline!

I knew the two families, who believed they were cousins, had known each other in Detroit, but had never really been sure how far back that friendship stretched. With this diary entry, I now realize that the acquaintance probably dated back even before Eileen was born on September 21, 1923. The perceived familiarity between Clara and Eileen that I had noticed as a child was starting to make a lot more sense.

Reading further, I learned that on the day the Gabrilowitsch family moved into their new house in Detroit, Clara got sick. In an entry dated October 12, 1923, Nina wrote:

> *Exactly five years ago today we arrived in Detroit. Mother went to bed, with what she thought was a cold. She didn't know what she was going in for. She has been sick five whole long years that seem to her like ten. But now thank God she is well.*

Could Nina have been mistaken about this or had Clara really taken to her bed from Nina's eighth to thirteenth year? If so, then Nina was fortunate that she had her governess and servants to watch over her since her father was often out of town giving concerts in other cities.

My "mothers" may not have been perfect, but they were always able to care for me, and both Elwood Bailey and Russell Gooley were present and loving father figures to me. It made me sad to think that this physical issue of Clara's might have contributed to Nina's innate sense of loneliness.

As I read on, I was gaining a strong impression that Nina strived not to be a "burden" to her parents. Even though the family had maids and servants, Nina often scurried to run errands, or fluff Clara's pillows, or bring her breakfast. As I read, she sometimes seemed to be more like the mother than the child.

I saw with a sinking heart the first sign of a disconnect in Nina regarding the feelings of others when she was just thirteen years old:

> *I went to Harriet's house to play. We were played hiding schemes in the ally. We teased a little girl that has hysterics till she cried like everything. Anna, Gina Mary, Edith Jane and Mary Margaret were also there.*

I was appalled that she showed no remorse for the six of them teasing this girl until she cried. Her next comment was, "Mlle finished my blue sweater." The incident meant so little to her that she could just blithely change the subject.

I could see the genesis of Nina's demise in that incident. As a woman who worked with children all my life, I know the emotional pain that torment caused the little girl in the alley.

Sadly, this was not the last time in her diaries that Nina showed no remorse for someone else's pain or downfall. And later on, it became a pattern with her where the wives of her boyfriends were concerned. Nina could summon up huge sympathy for characters she read about in a book but not always for living, breathing people.

And yet she was friendly and cheerful most of the time, writing to her aunt and uncles in Germany, and remarking on how wonderful it was to be alive when she was riding her horse.

I saw echoes of my own childhood in some of her activities. We both loved horseback riding and "did not like the horn." In other words, we rode English.

We both loved to swim and took diving lessons. As we approached our teens, we were both still struggling with piano lessons begun when we were eight.

A powerful thought struck me: did I get involved in all of those very activities because Clara, acting from the sidelines, saw to it that I learned the "proper" things for a young girl?

As a child, I heard her directly inquire of Eileen how my piano lessons were coming (and was appalled that they were not classical in nature), so she certainly seemed up to speed on my activities. It just never occurred to me before reading about Nina's youth that Clara might be orchestrating, and perhaps funding, my extracurricular activities. Now it seemed entirely possible.

One remarkable coincidence occurred when Nina and her family took a trip to California in the summer of 1923. She wrote, "We left the hotel at half past 9. We saw the San Carlos Mission of Monterey built in 1707."

There are hundreds of these old monasteries all over California. Yet this was the same Mission that seventy-six years later had a private mass for the health of my little son, Rory! Of all the old monasteries in California, I was very surprised to read that Nina had visited the only one I had ever been to, only years earlier.

She may have gotten the time wrong on when it was built (1770), but she was actually there and so were Rory and I all those years later. Reading this gave me chills. What were the chances!

I became progressively more bothered by Nina's increasing fascination with death and funerals. At age fourteen, when she and her aunt Pock went to an art gallery in Europe, she wrote:

It is about the worst collection you could find anywhere. The only picture I really loved was The Death of Othello. It showed Desdemona lying dead on the bed. On the floor lay her attendant who had fainted. Othello was stabbing himself, two men are standing up looking on very excited, two other are standing quietly near the door; and one is sitting on a chair looking very interested. The colors are wonderful, such bright reds, and greens and purples. I bought a large postcard of it and then we walked home.

This was not the only example of her morbid fascination but it struck me as a particularly graphic one as she described the painting so vividly, and even bought a postcard of it to take home so she could remember it. I certainly do not recall any interest in such dark matters in my own teenage years!

Although Clara was along during this 1925 trip to Italy, Nina did most activities with her aunt. They especially liked to swim in the Adriatic Sea and play and splash each other. I couldn't help but think of all the childhood days Eileen and I spent at Daytona Beach, Florida, doing the very same things in the Atlantic Ocean.

I know Nina enjoyed having this aunt who was an adult yet willing to take her shopping and play with her in the sea like a child. Both Nina and I were raised as only children and we were both lonely a lot growing up. Times like this were rare, thus making them even more of a treat, more memorable.

While returning to America from this trip, Nina took fencing lessons on the ship. I have never known anyone else who took fencing lessons except me. As a freshman at Stetson I elected to take them for my gym credit. Is fencing in ones genes?!

August 18, 1925, was Nina's 15th birthday, an event she celebrated on Mackinac Island with her family. The words she wrote that day now seem prophetic:

> *What a sad day! I have actually reached the grand old age of fif-teen. I wish I could always stay twelve years old because then one is old enough to understand whats going on and yet one doesn't have to act too grown up.*

If ever someone suffered from arrested development, surely Nina did. All I could think was that she wanted to stop time at a point where she could still glean some attention from her parents, and not have to make any decisions about how to shape her own life.

When Nina returned to Detroit that year and the 10th grade at the Liggett School, she complained about her one-piece tan gym suit with the belt.

Thirty-seven years later nothing had changed. When I was in the 10th grade at Chicago's Von Steuben High School I had exactly the same gym suit only mine was a hideous green. I'm sure Nina hated it just as much as I did!

These odd little bits of information made me feel like I was really coming to know Nina.

Perhaps because of her own youthful health woes, Clara was a worry-wart any time she thought Nina showed signs of a little cold. Clara would forbid Nina to do even the simplest activities at those times, like take a short walk with her and Ossip.

I thought back to the time that Eileen and Russ and I went to Detroit to visit Clara not long after I had been in the polio ward for two months. Clara was extremely concerned and questioned Eileen about my health and whether or not she had found a very good doctor for me.

I believe Clara may have been something of a hypochondriac. But while Nina had no buffer between her and Clara, I had Eileen defending me.

Interspersed in the chapters written in Nina's 15th year were repeated telling of the dreams she had about how she wanted her life to be when she grew up. She longed for a home in California, with lots of bedrooms so she could have her friends come to stay. She dreamed of throwing parties and entertaining lots of people all the time.

I found myself growing angry with Clara that she had treated Nina like a mini-adult as she grew up, spreading before her an endless buffet of cultural opportunities, but almost totally denying her the birthday parties and sleepovers and ordinary social life that little girls thrive on.

Clara put her in the Liggett School, an excellent but all-girl school, took her along on outings with adult friends, and basically acted more like Nina were a favored young house guest than a daughter.

I am sure their hearts were in the right place, but I was coming to believe that Clara and Ossip were just not cut out to be parents. In many ways, they were mimicking their own upbringing, but simply did not seem to comprehend that the leavening effect of having several siblings had kept them on an even keel and taught them about getting along with people their own age. Without that, Nina became an inward-looking being and the effects were unhealthy.

Knowing what Nina's life was actually like later in California I now realize that the seeds were planted at a very early age. She did get that dreamed-of a house in California and her friends were there constantly.

However, she was deep into alcoholism by then and many of them just took advantage of her. Nina's childhood dreams did not come true in the way she imagined.

The public clamor for Clara that followed her wherever she went did not help Nina's self-esteem. When I first witnessed Clara's rock-star attraction, I had no reference to explain it. I thought I understood that when I knew her, people and the press were all over her because she had been absent in California for awhile, and it was a rarity to see her.

However, that wasn't the case when she lived in Detroit and was going to the orchestra on a weekly basis, yet Nina's diaries reveal that this attention from the press existed even then. Apparently Clara was simply very popular. She had scads of friends and people liked her.

To a girl like Nina who said about herself that she had yellow teeth, braces, a hooked nose, and huge glasses, and who remarked that her mother had such beautiful arms and shoulders that she should always wear short sleeves, all this adulation must have made her feel even worse about herself.

When I was with Clara, the attention being showered upon her made me proud that she had chosen me to take on an outing. But then I didn't have to live with her full time, and the only comparison ever made between us is that people have said I look so much like her.

I wonder if Clara, who was frankly vain, was embarrassed by having a daughter she considered homely. Would she have treated Nina differently had she been prettier? It seemed to me that Clara's relationship with Nina became closer once Nina had a nose job and developed a sense of style.

Nina also complained about having a governess at the age of fifteen (what teenager wouldn't!) and said her friends made fun of her. But she looked forward to the time when she would be old enough to go places on her own and do what she wanted to do, and remarked that she would "certainly make the most of it!" We know that she certainly did as soon as she got away from her parents and into college.

I remembered back to my own 15th year. That was when my stitched together family finally came apart, when I was asked to choose between having a home with Eileen and becoming part of the Jehovah's Witnesses (which I thought of as a cult) or having no home at all.

I found myself on my own, living with Drucilla's abusive family at times, staying with my alcoholic Aunt Bruce at others, or sleeping over at any friend's house whose parents would allow me to spend the night. I may not like some of the choices that Clara and Ossip made as parents, but Nina could certainly always count on a well-appointed roof over her head, and always knew where her next meal was coming from. There were times when I could count on neither.

When Nina got to Barnard in her 19th year she considered it a haven from the rules and regulations set down by her parents. That's where she started drinking.

When I got to Stetson in my 17th year I considered it a haven from being homeless and welcomed the rules and regulations administered by the school.

As I left the young Nina behind, the rest of the diaries were almost painful to read. I saw emerge the woman I had already glimpsed in the letters we found early in our search.

On the surface, with Nina's talented family and solid financial background, it looked as if her adult life would be wonderfully successful with a college degree, husband and children, or anything she wanted. She was an exceptional writer and could have made a career of that. She was a good enough actress that she could have become professional.

But in truth, she sabotaged almost every good thing put in front of her with her bad choices until she finally wound up alone in that hotel room in California.

There have been times when I've envied Nina and wished that I could have grown up in that family. Now that I know the whole story I can see that even with all of the unorthodox and often unpleasant events that shaped my childhood, I was by far the more fortunate one growing up with my father's family—the Baileys—and then with Eileen.

I took the challenges that life handed me and used them to develop a backbone of steel, while Nina simply withered.

I set out on the quest to find and know my mother more than fifty years ago. I knew that if I ever located her, I might or might not like the woman I found. Now, hundreds of pages later, and each read by me at least four times, I felt a real sense of who Nina Gabrilowitsch, the woman I had come to believe was my mother, really was.

She seemed to me like two different people inhabiting a single body. I loved her bright mind and wit, her unselfish support of her friends, the tender care she gave Clara whenever she was ill, and that she was loving to me on the single day we met.

But her utter disregard for the pain she caused others with her actions and her addictive personality were painful to digest. I found myself rooting, over and over, for her to stop chasing men (or women) that were never going to love her back, to stop seeking love from other people, and to learn to first love herself.

I wanted her to stop setting herself up for failure, and for her mother to see that what Nina needed was simple love and attention, not "opportunities."

I will always ask myself, "Why"? Why did a girl who was raised with stability, and was given so much, turn out to have nothing or no one in the end? Would her life have been different had she been allowed to keep me?

I had to come to terms with the fact that she was simply not programmed to be happy, that she was a self-saboteur.

I had expected, if I ever found my mother, to feel angry for being set aside. But what I felt after reading Nina's diaries was that something essential to my sense of myself and my well-being was altered forever.

If this was my mother, then I had as good an upbringing as I could have, as I do not think I would have become the successful adult I am had I been raised by Nina Gabrilowitsch.

The bonds between mothers and daughters run bone deep, but they can be destructive as well as loving.

Every fiber of my being told me I had found my mother, but I was finally ready to turn again to DNA testing to see what science had to say on the question.

CHAPTER 43
SUSAN

2012

DNA AND GENETIC GENEALOGY: PART 1

IT HAD BEEN ALMOST A YEAR since I had answered Deb's request for further DNA testing with the well thought out words, "Fat chance!"

During that time several things had transpired. Without a doubt, for me, the major event was finding and reading Nina's diaries. I always said that I only wanted to know my mother. After reading almost 1000 pages of Nina's words beginning when she was 10 years old, I felt that this fervent wish had been granted.

Not only did I have a comprehensive understanding of her personality but I also had, in her own words, strong hints about what I believed to be my own genesis and birth in a foreign country. These words coincided with my first memories of French as my first language.

Deb's comprehensive research as to where Nina was in the time period I was born gave even more weight to her words, confirming what we already knew. While Nina's words, coupled with my memories, provided very strong evidence, they still didn't constitute proof that Nina was my mother.

Meanwhile Family Tree DNA, the company that had reviewed the university's lab results the year before and said that I almost certainly was not a half sibling to the children of Jules Schmidt, had started something called Genetic Genealogy. From their website I read the following:

Adoptees discover their heritage
With the power of an autosomal DNA test, confidently match to
male and female cousins from any of your family lines. This can
provide you with the clues you need to learn more about your birth
parents' families.

Every adopted person, or those who know that one of their parents
or grandparents was adopted, will want to order a Family Finder
test to help identify close and distant relatives.

I still had not completely ruled out the possibility that Jules Schmidt was my father and, while I wasn't adopted per se, I still did not know conclusively who either of my parents were.

If Deb could persuade Schmidt's daughter Maria to take yet another DNA test to provide, this time, what I hoped would be *conclusive* evidence whether we were, or were not, half siblings, then I decided I would submit my DNA for further testing.

After reading the information from the Family Tree DNA website I also had hopes that I could find out once and for all if Elwood Bailey and Nina Gabrilowitsch were my parents by matching their known lineage to that of my DNA "cousins."

These DNA-matched cousins would have to have ancestors in their own trees who were also in Elwood's family tree to match him or in Nina's family tree to match her.

Although I was uncertain about *my* family tree, Nina's was well documented. Elwood's was documented enough that, if he was my father, I should be able to find some matches from his tree.

I understood that these cousin matches would be people who had submitted their DNA to the database, and who matched my DNA. These matches could range from "close and immediate" to "5th cousin to distant cousin." I was ready to try once again to find out just who I am!

I submitted my DNA sample in September, 2012, to Family Tree DNA, almost a year after I had submitted it to the University of New Mexico DNA Lab. I hoped their name would be prophetic and I would be able to finally place *myself* on a family tree.

The last time Deb had handled all the DNA submission and results. When the results came back this time I decided that I had to do it myself, that I had to try and find my own father and my own mother.

This decision wasn't because Deb was incompetent in any way. She's a genealogist. On the contrary, it was because she is *so* competent and knows how to research so well that I figured she might have the answer in a few hours, and that if she did, I might never understand it. I explained this to her and she understood my reasoning and offered help if I got stuck.

I told her what I wanted from her was genealogical verification if I found any matches in either Elwood's or Nina's trees. I wanted that professional backup that I had done it correctly. Having already downloaded and read the e-book on how the interactive website worked, I knew I would be on a high learning curve.

On October 23, 2012, the results came back. I really should call this date my birthday as I was about to open many presents!

The first thing I needed to determine was the relationship between Jules Schmidt's daughter Maria and me. If we did indeed have that gene mutation that the University of New Mexico DNA Lab said was a possibility and we matched now as half siblings, that would mean Jules Schmidt was my father and there would be no further reason to spend time looking for my ancestors in Elwood Bailey's tree.

I logged onto the FTDNA website and clicked on 'Family Finder.' The first category that came up was "Close and Immediate." No one was there, not even Maria. I had no close relatives!

I watched fascinated as the page changed to "All Relationships." I had over 400 matches. All of these people share DNA with me to a greater or lesser extent and therefore all are my genetic "cousins."

Maria wasn't there either.

I typed in her name and, had she been a DNA match to me at all, she would have come up. There was a blank space where her name would have been had we been related.

Hallelujah, Jules Schmidt was not my father! I was now free to start on my search for matches to Elwood Bailey.

I like to think I set out to find my father much like the way he set out to find me in France all those many years ago. The methods were vastly different but I knew the desire for family was the same.

The first thing I did was look at the surnames of the cousins I matched. I was looking for such family names that matched those in Elwood's genealogical tree.

This was time consuming and tedious work. I had to find the matching surnames, email the cousin for a link to their tree, and then search for "grandparents" in their ancestral line that were also in Elwood's line, thus providing evidence for the relationship.

After days of looking, I finally found a cousin named Evelyn Stewart who had 'Holland' (one of Elwood's family names) in her list of surnames and she kindly provided me with her family tree.

After some digging, I found in her tree a couple named Daniel Holland and Zilpha Lane. I knew those names sounded familiar, so I went back to the tree I had constructed for Elwood.

Sure enough, I found that same couple in Elwood's family tree. They are his great-great-great grandparents, thus proving that Evelyn and I matched DNA *and* that she had a pair of the same ancestors in her tree that are in Elwood's tree!

I called Deb.

The two of us went backwards comparing the two trees from Zilpha Lane and Daniel Holland going forward to both Evelyn Stewart and Elwood Bailey.

They matched!

I took a deep breath. I didn't want to do anything the rest of the day. I just lay on the couch for hours listening to Pandora with Yo-Yo Ma playing softly in the background.

I was at peace more that I could remember being in my adult life. It was one of life's peak moments for me.

CHAPTER 44

DEB

2012

RULING OUT EILEEN

WHEN SUSAN CALLED TO SAY THAT Maria Schmidt was not among her DNA matches, I felt enormously happy for her—and relieved for myself. I knew how much turmoil she had gone through over the murky nature of the first DNA results.

Even though I believed with all my heart that the Family Tree DNA Family Finder test would give her an absolute answer that Jules Schmidt was not her father, I had still worried that I was pushing her to do something that might only create more anxiety.

So, I thought, hallelujah that the test came through for her! Susan and I could now both say beyond a shadow of a doubt that Jules Schmidt was *not* her father.

Per the Frequently Asked Questions on the test's website, and per further conversation with the company's ever-helpful president, Bennett Greenspan, I knew that Family Finder test results were deemed to have a probability greater than 99% of correctly predicting a relationship between two matching individuals who are second cousins or closer.

In other words, the probability of Maria and Susan actually being half-siblings and the test *failing* to catch it were less than 1%. I thanked the wonders of modern DNA technology with all my heart for giving Susan this assurance.

The same probability chart on the website showed that the chances of the test finding a match between two people who submit their DNA and are actually third cousins are greater than 90%.

The second time I read the probability chart, something new clicked. In the back of my mind, at least, there still lingered the possibility that Eileen Lucia was Susan's mother.

Based on all the circumstantial evidence we had amassed, I now believed it far, far more likely that Nina was Susan's mother, but up until that moment, there had been no way to prove or disprove either woman as her mother.

But I realized suddenly that I had an ace I could now play with regard to determining whether or not Eileen was Susan's mother. That card could provide almost as much certainty to rule Eileen in or out as we had in concluding that Jules Schmidt was not Susan's father.

I needed to submit *my* DNA for testing.

Ira Clemens Lucia, he of the tall tale that started this all, was my great-great-grandfather. Eileen Lucia was his great-granddaughter. Therefore, if Eileen were Susan's mother, Ira would also be *Susan's* great-great grandfather and she and I would be 3rd cousins. The Family Finder probability charts predicted that test results would be able to spot this at least 90% of the time.

A few weeks later, my DNA results came in. Like Susan, I saw right away that I had no matches that were classified as 'Close or Immediate.' Since, to my knowledge, no one who is a second cousin or closer to me had ever been tested using Family Finder, that did not surprise me.

3rd cousins fell outside that range so I typed in 'Susan Bailey' to see if I could find her among my many matches.

The database returned no results. Susan Bailey and I were *not* genetic matches.

It was now 90% certain that she was not Eileen Lucia's daughter. Even for a research fuss-budget like me, I was willing to call that a certainty.

DNA testing had at that point delivered two powerful gifts of knowledge: Jules Schmidt was not Susan's father and Eileen Lucia was not Susan's mother.

That left the field clear for Elwood Bailey and Nina Gabrilowitsch as remaining contenders.

Since Susan's DNA database showed no 'Close or Immediate' matches, and did not contain any names of people we recognized as second cousins of either Elwood or Nina, I knew that the DNA test was not going to be able to tell us who Susan's parents were with the same level of certainty that it had in ruling out Jules and Eileen.

But then, given both Elwood's and Nina's lack of close relatives, we never expected it to do that.

I also knew that this database was what we had to work with. Susan was never again going to go seeking one-on-one matches as we did that first time with the Schmidts. The emotional cost to all was just too high.

But that did not mean the database of her DNA cousins had no more powerful evidence left to deliver. Susan's discovery that DNA match Evelyn Stewart had in her family tree a couple who were Elwood Bailey's great-great-great grandparents was an incredible start.

I could not wait to see what else Susan would unearth as she continued to mine her DNA database and add to the ever-growing pile of evidence that she might well be not only the daughter of Elwood Bailey but also of Nina Gabrilowitsch.

CHAPTER 45

SUSAN

2013–2014

DNA AND GENETIC GENEALOGY: PART 2

A S SOUL-SATISFYING AS FINDING my first connection to Elwood Bailey was, by the next day I realized that the one DNA match to Evelyn was simply not enough for me. It certainly pointed to my relationship with the Bailey family but I wanted to find more of Elwood's relatives.

I wanted more proof. I wanted to feel even more confident about the identity of my father before turning to the equally imperative task of searching for matches among Nina's relatives.

So I rolled up my sleeves and got back to work. The next few months found me working diligently to comb through the surname lists of my DNA cousins. I was still working alone and just asking Deb to help me verify the results if I thought I had found a match.

So many times when I was excited over a possible genealogical match and called Deb, she would go through and find holes in my research. She would explain to me why the genealogical tie to the particular person did not hold up under scrutiny, and I would reluctantly accept her expertise.

Sometimes I would be frustrated because I had spent so much time and done so much work on an individual and it was all for nothing. I found that there were no shortcuts. I just had to keep chipping away, hoping I would find another matching ancestor, and that the match would hold. By that I mean that the genealogical line would turn out to be provable coming forward in time to both me and my DNA match from the couple that were our common ancestors.

All my hard work paid off! I found four more matches to my father,

Elwood Bailey, in the FTDNA database.

Every time I found one, my heart grew a little lighter as technology helped me to say with ever-growing confidence those sweetest of words: "my father."

Besides those definite connections, there were also several more of my DNA cousins whose surname lists contained names that I recognized from my father's ancestry. However, they did not provide their family trees or respond to my emails so it was impossible to check out the connection.

While I wanted to continue to dig for more matches to the Bailey tree, I realized that I had been putting off searching the database for evidence about the other half of my lineage. In many ways, science was simply putting me slowly on firmer and firmer ground in the belief I had always held in my heart about the identity of my father.

But when it came to the question of my mother, that had been an area of quicksand all of my life. Over the past five plus years, as all of the information about Nina that Deb and I dug up came to light, I felt more and more that I had found my mother at last.

I wanted so much for DNA to back up that growing feeling, but what if the evidence wasn't there? What if, after having "mother" dangled in front of me, the DNA database took her back away? What if I found no matches? I had to look.

With a deep breath, I dove into searching for genetic ties to Nina Clemens Gabrilowitsch.

Since finding matches with my father had been so time consuming, I thought that finding matches with Nina might be next to impossible. The excellent records kept in New England since colonial times proved me wrong.

The process of finding genetic ties to Nina was the same as for my father. Assuming Nina was indeed my mother, there should be, among my DNA cousins, people with ties to the ancestors of Samuel L. Clemens (Mark Twain) or his wife, Olivia Langdon.

I found that more of my matches had uploaded their family trees, so I didn't have to work quite so hard to get the information I needed. It also helped that Nina's ancestral tree was—probably thanks to being the grandchild of such a famous man as Mark Twain!— much more complete than Elwood Bailey's.

Nina's tree was traceable going back into the 1600s. I had never realized that while Olivia Langdon was born in Elmira, New York, her family's roots lay deep in Hartford, Connecticut, and the surrounding area.

It was a red letter day when I found my very first match!

Up cropped a gentleman named Edward T. (last name withheld for privacy) who had not just one but *several* connections to the ancestors of Olivia Langdon Clemens.

Then I found three more matches in quick succession with ties to Olivia. The intermarriages in Olivia's ancestry were so numerous that these matches were falling all over each other.

I also discovered something about these matches that I had not found when looking at the people who had connected me genetically to my father's family tree. By now, I had become more sophisticated in my research and had learned how to use a visual tool called a "chromosome browser" that enabled me to see exactly where and on what chromosome my DNA overlapped with that of my matches.

I could see that these Langdon-side matches all clustered together with me on a particular chromosome, number 18. I knew that greatly increased the odds that the connection I was finding between all of us stemmed from our mutual genealogical ties to Olivia.

I also noticed that many of them still lived around Hartford, Connecticut, where Olivia's deep roots lay and where Twain and Olivia spent so many happy years in the house that is now the Mark Twain House & Museum. I started calling this group, "The Hartford Gang."

Having satisfied myself that I was finally capable of finding my own father and mother, I picked up the phone and gave Deb the good news. She was nearly as excited as I was! I gave her my password to the website and asked her to help me find yet more matches.

With a second pair of hands on deck, more matches were unearthed. But the more I found, the more I wanted to find. In some ways, after my first experience with DNA, I think I was afraid to believe too soon.

Eventually the matches began to slow to a trickle in the FTDNA database. I had by that time found 5 matches to Elwood Bailey, 9 to Olivia Langdon, and 4 to Twain himself!

My closest DNA match to my father connected to me just five genera-tions back (my match and I shared great-great-great grandparents) but the ties to Olivia and Twain, while numerous, were further back in time.

I knew what my heart was telling me: I had found both of my parents. But with Deb always talking about probabilities, I knew that to give myself the greatest level of certainty I could have, I wanted to find not only as many matches as I could, but also the closest possible ones.

I realized that someday, someone even closer to me could show up in the FTDNA database, but I had no way of knowing when or if that would happen.

Then it dawned on me that participating in an additional DNA database might yield even more information. So, I submitted my DNA to Ancestry. com's relatively new AncestryDNA project. What a great idea that turned out to be!

When those results came in, I once again dived in solo, and found that Ancestry.com had make my research far easier because almost all of my matches already had family trees posted on the website.

Once again, I began by searching for matches to my father's family tree. I found match after match! Between the two databases, and with Deb's help, I have found 26 DNA matches with my father, Elwood Bailey...so far! I decided to create a chart of the closest matches to help myself keep track of how these matches were related to my father.

The Match shown in the first column of the chart is my DNA cousin. The matches' names are shown by initials only for privacy, but we have the names on file. The next column shows the names of the common grandpar-ents I share with each match.

Finally, the last column shows each set of grandparents' relationship with my father, Elwood Bailey (shown simply as "Bailey"). My relationship would be one down from Elwood's. In other words, Jesse Pollock and Sal-lie Greenwood are Elwood's great-great grandparents and my great-great-great grandparents.

	ELWOOD L. BAILEY'S DIRECT ANCESTORS	
DNA MATCH WITH ME	COMMON GRANDPARENTS	RELATIONSHIP WITH BAILEY
JP	Jesse Pollock and Sallie Greenwood	2nd Great Grandparents
JD	Jesse Pollock and Sallie Greenwood	2nd Great Grandparents
KSM	Jesse Pollock and Sallie Greenwood	2nd Great Grandparents
MW	Jesse Pollock and Sallie Greenwood	2nd Great Grandparents
S21	Stephen Hurst and Nancy James	2nd Great Grandparents
LWN	Stephen and Mary Weathersbee	2nd Great Grandparents
NLM	Stephen and Mary Weathersbee	2nd Great Grandparents
AMJ	Stephen and Mary Weathersbee	2nd Great Grandparents
YS	Daniel Holland and Zilpha Lane	3rd Great Grandparents
PS5	Lewis Burwell and Mary Frances Willis	4th Great Grandparents

After finishing it, I just stared for awhile at the chart. Seeing all those close matches, and especially the confirmation of having multiple matches to some of the same ancestor couples, brought absolute certainty to my heart about the identity of my father.

I am really and truly a Bailey. No one is ever going to take away my father again!

Armed with that success, I turned next to searching for AncestryDNA matches who shared ancestors with Nina's grandmother, Olivia Langdon Clemens.

Again, the database readily yielded many more matches. Most thrilling was the discovery of a DNA cousin who descends from Olivia's great-great grandparents, Ezra King and Silence Rice.

I had gotten my wish. The AncestryDNA database had led me to even closer genetic matches with Olivia—and thus with Nina!

So far, together Deb and I have found 23 matches in the Langdon branch of Nina's tree. Again, I charted some of the closest matches that I found. My relationship is two down from Olivia Langdon's.

DNA MATCH WITH ME	COMMON GRANDPARENTS	RELATIONSHIP WITH LANGDON
	NINA GABRILOWITSCH'S DIRECT ANCESTORS OLIVIA LANGDON'S LINE	
JLC	Ezra King and Silence Rice	2nd Great Grandparents
JHC	Andrew Morehouse and Phebe Hurd	3rd Great Grandparents
JH	Andrew Morehouse and Phebe Hurd	3rd Great Grandparents
EL	Thomas Langdon and Mary Alberti	3rd Great Grandparents
VS62	John Huckins and Hope Chipman	4th Great Grandparents
AM	Richard Carrier and Elizabeth Sessions	4th Great Grandparents
ML	Joseph Barnard and Sarah Strong	4th Great Grandparents
SN	Joseph Barnard and Sarah Strong	4th Great Grandparents
DA	Joseph Barnard and Sarah Strong	4th Great Grandparents
BLS	Joseph Barnard and Sarah Strong	4th Great Grandparents
LCG	Edward Griswold and Abigail Williams	4th Great Grandparents
OR	Ebenezer Hurd and Sarah Pickett Lane	4th Great Grandparents
TE43	Thomas Langdon and Isabelle Wooster	5th Great Grandparents
JKB	William Buell and Mary Post	6th Great Grandparents

It was hard to deny the effect of all those matches.

Finally, I took a deep breath and began to search for more ties to the ancestors of Samuel Langhorne Clemens himself. Genetically, he is no more significant in proving that I am Nina's daughter than Olivia is, but the tug of proving I descend from this man with the giant persona pulled me onward.

I put in the name 'Lampton,' the maiden name of Twain's mother. Doing this in the FTDNA database had yielded no matches so I expected none in AncestryDNA either.

I could not believe my eyes when not one but two matches popped up! More intriguing was the fact that both descended from Twain's great-grand-parents, William Lampton and Martha "Patsy" Schooler.

That felt amazingly close to me! The find moved me two generations closer in time with DNA proof of my ties to Mark Twain than anything I had found previously. And it put me one generation closer in proof to Twain than the close tie I had been excited about with Olivia!

I next decided to input 'Schooler' with truly startling results. Besides the two matches who descended through Twain's great-grandmother Martha "Patsy" Schooler, I found *five* more who descended from other children of Martha's parents, John Schooler and Martha Wharton.

I spoke with a DNA expert at AncestryDNA who said it was particularly significant that I had found matches descending from more than one child of the same ancestors. He said it makes the connection a greater certainty.

I was grinning from ear to ear and set out to chart the closest matches I had found to Twain.

NINA GABRILOWITSCH'S DIRECT ANCESTORS SAMUEL L. CLEMENS' LINE		
DNA MATCH WITH ME	COMMON GRANDPARENTS	REALTIONSHIP WITH CLEMENS
GZB	William Lampton and Martha Patsy Schooler	Great Grandparents
BM	William Lampton and Martha Patsy Schooler	Great Grandparents
MH	John Schooler and Martha Wharton	2nd Great Grandparents

N1D	John Schooler and Martha Wharton	2nd Great Grandparents
KL17	John Schooler and Martha Wharton	2nd Great Grandparents
CF44	John Schooler and Martha Wharton	2nd Great Grandparents
T89	John Schooler and Martha Wharton	2nd Great Grandparents
RB	Samuel Alexander Carson and Janet Patterson	2nd Great Grandparents
MCJ	Charles Moorman and Elizabeth Reynolds	3rd Great Grandparents
CS	Charles Moorman and Elizabeth Reynolds	3rd Great Grandparents
TD1	Abner Brooks Casey and Harriet Green	3rd Great Grandparents
JKB	Abner Brooks Casey and Harriet Green	3rd Great Grandparents
DG	Abner Brooks Casey and Harriet Green	3rd Great Grandparents

Besides these 13 connections to Samuel Clemens, we also found 12 others plus a large group of DNA cousins who all had ties to the Terrell families of Virginia. The name Terrell appears more than once as a middle name in the Moorman branch above. This strongly hints that it is a family name in Twain's lineage further back up the line from Charles Moorman.

Between the Clemens and Langdon ties, I have now found nearly 50 DNA matches to individuals with known genetic ties to Nina's ancestors.

While I will continue to monitor the two DNA databases, I decided to call my research effectively done.

Testing my DNA has been a rocky road for me but I'm glad I finally did it. While the results, despite the sheer number of matches will likely not offer 100% proof of my parentage to everyone, when coupled with my known relationship with Nina and Clara, and those oh so hard to deny look-alike pictures, I now have very little doubt as to who my parents were.

At the end of the day what is a girl's DNA, whose only known family before this was from North Carolina and Georgia, doing right smack dab in the middle of "The Hartford Gang!"

CHAPTER 46

DEB

2014

THE END OF THE SEARCH

WHAT INDEED? As our six-plus year search to determine the identity of Susan's parents unfolded, Susan's level of certainty often outstripped my more cautious belief. As the evidence concerning her origins piled up, Susan asked one day in exasperation, "What on earth will it take for you to feel certain?"

I promptly replied, "Your European birth certificate or a DNA match to someone who descends from Elwood's or Nina's great-grandparents."

"As a dyed-in-the-wool number cruncher and researcher," I told Susan, "without that ultra-conclusive level of proof, there will always be a small part of me that calculates the odds of alternate explanations about the identity of your parents."

But DNA databases, without any direct solicitation of testing of individuals, have now furnished Susan *eight* matches to descendants of three *different* sets of Elwood Bailey's great-great grandparents as well as a plethora of somewhat more distant matches.

Even to a cautious person, those multiple close matches, coupled with a plethora of others just a bit further back, make the proof of her father's identity seem nearly ironclad. The matches to Bailey kin continue to roll in.

Then Susan's DNA matches to descendants of two different children of William Lampton and Martha Schooler, Twain's great-grandparents, surfaced. This was quickly followed by the match to Olivia's great-great grandparents, Ezra King and Silence Rice.

While the Twain and Langdon DNA ties taken individually did not quite reach the magic mark I had joked to Susan about, a question struck me one day:

What are the odds that some woman *other than Nina* could be Susan's mother and enable her to find genetic matches this close to descendants of *both* Mark Twain and his wife Olivia?

And DNA is just one piece of a larger patchwork of evidence. In a moment of contemplation, looking back over all of the previous information, the look-alike pictures, the information shared by the families of Nina's heirs, the late 1936 trip to Europe, the hints about a child in Nina's diary from that year, and the clear evidence that she was a sexually active woman, Susan and I realized something that still seems fantastical.

In the quest to determine the identity of Susan's mother, all of the arrows kept pointing in one direction. Only that direction seemed to explain the many things that had troubled Susan all her life:

Why had Nina shown up in Tampa and taken Susan out of school when she was seven?

If Nina *wasn't* Susan's mother, how did she even know of her existence, much less her middle name and where she lived?

What had she meant when she told Susan, "You're a little French girl"?

Why was Susan moved to Chicago to live with Eileen the day after Nina took her?

Why was "Aunt" Clara so nice to her and interested in her welfare?

Why was she able to attend expensive universities although her family had little money?

The answers to all those questions fell neatly into place once Nina assumed the role of central player in a tale believed to have unfolded as follows:

Nina Clemens Gabrilowitsch met Elwood Bailey while the latter was on one of many road trips from Tampa to Detroit, and they conceived a child. The picture of the two together confirms that they knew each other.

Involved with Jules Schmidt at the same time, she also told him about the baby. Both men believed they were the father.

Pregnant at the time of her father's death, Nina (as well as mother Clara) skipped Ossip's funeral and the two headed to Europe in the late fall of 1936 to hide Nina's pregnancy and with the intent of leaving the child there.

Susan was born there, probably in mid-January of 1937, and named Susan by Clara, with the middle name of Madeline added by Nina. The first name was probably an homage to Clara's beloved sister and Mark Twain's beloved daughter, Susan Olivia.

With Elwood Bailey already married and not of a social stature acceptable to Nina's mother, image conscious Clara talked Nina into an arrangement with a French speaking middle-aged pair (probably Ossip's sister and brother) and an English speaking nanny who would raise the infant Susan in Europe. Nina's "you're a little French girl" comment and Susan's childhood memories of being raised by a French speaking couple stem from this time in her life.

This arrangement was probably intended to be permanent, but the outbreak of war sent shivers of fear down the spines of Clara and Nina, who had witnessed firsthand during World War I the terrors of being an expatriate in a war-torn country.

Ossip had been arrested as a "spy" during World War I partly because he was Russian, but perhaps also because of his Jewish heritage. For Susan, also partly Jewish; there would be no highly placed intervention to count on to save her if the need arose.

Further, Elwood Bailey, a soldier in France during World War I, would have been well aware of the horrors of war and wanted to get his baby daughter out of there at all costs.

Even though there was probably great animosity between Clara and Elwood at the time of the pregnancy, all parties had to come together for the benefit of one little child.

Arrangements were made for Susan to be brought home to the U.S. by caretaker Gladys. Probably with the help of powerful Bailey family friend Bob Joughin, a false birth certificate was created for Susan, and Elwood and Drucilla Bailey became parents to the little girl.

Since Bailey was a man utterly unknown to anyone close to Clara, except for her cousin Ira Clemens Lucia whom she rarely saw, this was a solution that met her need to keep Susan's existence hidden. Nina was told that she was to be allowed no contact with baby Susan.

Drucilla Bailey, unhappy with raising her husband's out of wedlock child, took her anger out on little Susan, but displayed only love to a second child, Bobby, whose biological origins are unknown.

In 1944, something, perhaps the marriage of her mother to second husband Jacques Samossoud, triggered Nina to defy her controlling mother, and show up in Tampa to see Susan.

When the two were brought to the Bailey home in a squad car, Elwood clearly recognized Nina. He assured Susan that she never had to worry about seeing the woman again and that Nina was an alcoholic. He also told Susan to just forget she had ever seen her, which she tried, but was unable to do.

Elwood, with a fierce protective love for Susan, and perhaps with knowledge of the cancer that would shortly take his life, cast about for the most responsible family member to whom he could entrust Susan's care.

It is a sad testament to the combined Bailey and Lucia clans, that with all the older adults available, only twenty-one-year-old newlywed Eileen Lucia Gooley seemed to fit the bill.

Susan was whisked off to Chicago where she and cousin Eileen lived at the swanky Palmer House until Eileen's husband returned from World War II. With the bill for such a stay well beyond the means of the Bailey's finances, Clara presumably footed the bill.

Shortly thereafter, with Eileen's Uncle Ira as the go-between, Clara began making trips from California to Michigan to visit with young Susan.

Perhaps Clara cut a deal with Nina that she would conduct these visits in exchange for Nina's promise to never try to approach Susan again.

Clara's flimsy (or perhaps even fictional) relationship to the Lucia family provided a cover story for her visits with Ira. Just as she had managed to squelch her father's *Letters From The Earth* for half a century out of fear that the work would tarnish his image, covering up the existence of her unwed daughter's child would have been totally in character.

Pretty, bright little Susan probably engendered some familial feelings in Clara, but of the same somewhat detached nature she often displayed in referring to her "darling little daughter" when raising Nina. To a woman who had vowed for decades never to marry, children simply weren't a major priority in Clara's life.

As Clara's health deteriorated and second husband Jacques drained her resources, visits to Susan came to a halt, and all contact between the two ceased.

Early on, perhaps as part of the arrangement for the Baileys to take Susan in, Clara had provided a college fund for her. Susan was told from her earliest memories that monies were waiting for her when she got ready to go to college. Those funds, which it would have been impossible for the Baileys to accumulate, were indeed there for Susan when the time came.

Nina's life continued on its slow downward spiral. Her letters and diaries make frequent references to her "waking dream" of what she had lost or similar expressions of despair.

Boyfriend George Wrentmore's son expressed that he had heard that giving up a child led her to drink. Jules Schmidt told his brother Lawrence that he had fathered a child with Nina although DNA proved that Susan was not that child.

His story does, however, confirm at least one pregnancy for Nina and her diaries strongly suggest more.

Once Clara died, perhaps Nina might have wanted to locate Susan, but all contact had been lost. Absent knowing Susan's married name, it would have been a needle in a haystack search, and Nina, defeated by life, was probably beyond having the will to pursue the answer.

And so the long and intensive search to determine Susan's parentage had led us to this wholly unexpected conclusion. What had started as a journey to prove Eileen Lucia to be Susan's mother had led us to the incredible conclusion that all arrows pointed instead to Mark Twain's only grandchild, Nina Clemens Gabrilowitsch.

Had we unearthed absolutely incontrovertible evidence of the mother-daughter relationship? No. Only locating an authentic birth certificate or finding an even closer DNA match could provide that level of certainty. Neither has so far happened but we are still finding matches on a nearly daily basis.

The fact of Nina's pregnancy as reported by Jules Schmidt to his brother Lawrence, the circumstantial evidence of Susan's relationship with Clara Clemens Gabrilowitsch, the dozens and dozens of DNA matches between

Samuel and Olivia Clemens' ancestors that Susan had already unearthed, and oh those pictures, speak out as if Nina herself were finally trying to tell the world, "Look, this is my daughter."

After wrestling with this information for nearly seven years, and with encouragement from individuals who believed in our conclusion, we decided to proceed with presenting the story of Susan, and of Nina, to the world.

Despite knowing that even in the face of nearly overwhelming circumstantial evidence, many would question our conclusion, the urge to tell the story simply would not go away.

Whether or not people choose to agree with our conclusion that Nina was Susan's mother, both of these complex and intelligent women had stories that deserved to be told.

Nina, the least known member of the Twain family, certainly deserved to be remembered for the witty, fun-loving part of her nature and not just for the sad way that her life ended.

It is our profound hope that this book will cause additional people with knowledge of Nina to step forward and share their memories of her, good or bad.

And, we believe, somewhere out there even more factual information exists to prove what Susan came to accept in her heart—that she is the daughter of Nina Clemens Gabrilowitsch, the granddaughter of Clara Clemens Gabrilowitsch, and the great-granddaughter of America's beloved "Mark Twain."

I leave it to Susan to end the telling of this stranger-than-fiction tale in her own voice.

CHAPTER 47

SUSAN

2014

THE TWAIN SHALL MEET

READING THROUGH THE WORDS Deb had just written, I found myself with tears streaming down my face. Yes I had, at long last, reached a certainty in my heart about the true identity of my mother.

My sense of connectedness to the Clemens and Gabrilowitsch family resonates in me in a way that can only be true. Staring at the faces of Nina, Clara and Ossip, I see my son, my daughters, and my grandchildren, and know that we are one family.

This journey has been long and arduous but at least the seeking has now come to an end. The family connection will go on forever.

It is hard to describe to those who have always known who their parents are what it's like to go through life with such a fundamental piece of knowledge missing. I didn't even have the love and assurance of a set of adoptive parents. What I had was a series of adults who cared for me, some of whom even loved me, but all of them took the knowledge of my true origins to their graves.

I didn't need the multiple DNA connections to both the Clemens and Bailey family to tell me who I am. That knowledge came sooner for me in this journey. But now that I have them I am happy to share them with the world.

Ever since I was a child, I sensed that I never really belonged to the people around me, except with my father. From the time he died one month past my ninth birthday, I felt like I had been set adrift.

Then in my twenties, when I learned for sure that Drucilla Bailey was not my biological mother, I never stopped looking for the woman who was.

There were years at a time where I barely spared a thought for the question and other periods when it consumed me.

Deb and I have talked at length about the irony that it was a tale of relationship to Mark Twain spun by her and Eileen's great-great grandfather—old Ira Clemens Lucia who died well over a century ago—that drew all the players together. Both she and I had devoted time to analyzing that tale. We still don't know whether there was any truth to his story, nor do we particularly care anymore. Maybe someday we'll find out anyway!

But out of that tale came meetings between Ira's descendants and Clara Clemens Gabrilowitsch. Elwood Bailey crossed paths with Nina Gabrilowitsch because his brother-in-law Charlie Lucia took him along on road trips to Detroit where Nina lived. Deb and I met because her inquiry about Ira's great-granddaughter Eileen Lucia Gooley (prompted by his tale of a Twain relationship) coincided with my search for more information about my cousin Eileen who, since she raised me, I thought might possibly be my mother.

So, here's to you, Ira Lucia. I envision you up there somewhere chuckling at the result your story achieved. When your daughter said that you were a humorist and wrote wonderful prose and poetry, I am sure that she had no idea that your tale of being a cousin to Sam Clemens, true or not, would someday help perpetuate his line and help me find my mother.

When we started digging for proof that Eileen was my mother—because that's the point we started from—I truly believed that was the only result that would bring me peace. Despite the rocky way our relationship ended after her religious conversion, I loved her with all my heart. I wanted her to be my mother.

When I began to achieve a growing level of certainty that the answer lay elsewhere, I went through a period of profound mourning that even *this* "mother" might be lost to me. Nina was not even on our radar. She was just some woman who happened to be Clara's daughter and related to Mark Twain, and, to my knowledge, I had met only once.

Now, after seven years of learning more about Clara, Ossip, and Nina Gabrilowitsch, I fully accept them as my family. Yes, that also makes me related to Mark Twain. I am not naïve, and understand that this will likely be the most important revelation to others.

However, thinking all those years that Eileen was my mother, and with her already believing she was related to Twain, that is a relationship which I had always taken for granted. Now, I have come to accept that it is a far closer kinship than I ever imagined.

Not too long ago my granddaughter asked me, "How do you feel being related to *Mark Twain*? Is it not just the very first thing you think of when you get up in the morning?"

I had to laugh because it probably would be a huge revelation if I had not been told when I was eight that he was related to me. I grew up accepting this so it wasn't the big surprise to me that it was to my children and grandchildren.

I never met Mark Twain. He was gone long before I was born. It is not to him but to the Gabrilowitsch family that I feel a profound connection, including to Ossip who unknowingly put me in his will.

I think of my childhood fascination with Clara. I didn't care, in fact didn't even know for the longest time, that she was the daughter of Mark Twain. To me, she was the nice, sophisticated lady with the boring husband who introduced me to fine dining and the joys of music.

As I came to learn, she was also fiercely protective of the Twain legacy. It may have been the desire to protect this legacy that prompted her to bury the fact of my existence as deeply as she could.

With my birth coming so hard on the heels of her beloved husband's death, maybe she was simply too emotionally distraught to do anything but turn me over to someone else. Perhaps believing her daughter Nina to be incapable of properly raising a child, she may have sent me to be raised by family members to protect me.

Right now I don't know, but it's a question I would love to have answered. I do know I would do anything it takes to protect my own grandchildren, so I simply can't fault her for what she did.

Looking at photos of her, I see my own distinctive triangle shaped nostrils and my cheekbones. Accepting Clara as my grandmother makes me proud and happy.

I think of Ossip Gabrilowitsch who, sadly, died just months before I was born. How I wish I could have met my wonderful musical genius of a grandfather. I wish he had lived to continue to exert his responsible, loving influence on Clara and Nina.

I suspect that my life would have been completely different had cancer not taken him just months after I was conceived. What a talented grandfather I had. Music has always come naturally to my children whether playing the guitar, piano, or singing. I like to think it came from this grandfather I never knew.

But then, I think, I *have* met him. I have had a lifetime of seeing his distinctive Eastern European features stamped so clearly on my son Greg's face. I have been blessed with a life filled with the joys of the exceptional musical talents of Greg, my daughters Jennifer and Karen, and my grandson Kyle and granddaughter Ember.

My other two grandsons, Sean and Jordan are mathematically gifted like their other great grandfather, Elwood Bailey. He would have been so proud of all of them!

And then there is my mother, Nina Clemens Gabrilowitsch. Am I sorry that she did not raise me? No. There is no denying the alcohol abuse and mental health issues that dogged her life. Despite the rocky years when I lived with Drucilla Bailey's abuse, overall I had a childhood far more stable under the loving influence of my father and of Eileen than I ever would have had being raised by Nina.

That's my belief—unless, I think with sadness, George Wrentmore, Jr. is right and that giving me up drove her deeper into the bottle.

I thank Nina for her love of theatre and the acting ability that she handed down to me. I love the wit and humor I read in the letters and diaries she left behind, a legacy inherited from her grandfather, I'm sure.

I'm proud of her getting that college degree. I'm proud that she always gave so generously of her affection and financial support to the struggling actors that were her closest friends. I'm touched that she willed her estate to the American Cancer Society in hopes of combating the disease that took both of our fathers' lives.

Most of all, I am profoundly glad that we had that one day together so long ago when she took me out of school as a child. Had she not had the courage to come and see me that day, I would know her only through her letters and diaries and the conversations about her overheard in my childhood when Clara, Eileen, and Russ mentioned her in whispers.

I will never forget her turning to me with the sparkle of tears in her dark brown eyes and saying, with all her heart, "I'm sorry." With the wisdom of a lifetime, I understand now that she was apologizing for far more than taking me out of school.

Nina, there is no need to apologize and nothing to forgive. You did the best you could, as we all do.

When I was looking for my mother all those years I never expected it to be you. But now that I realize the truth, I thank you for my life and for the gifts you handed down to me and your grandchildren. I wish you could have known them.

And lastly, here's to you Mark Twain. I'm sure you could have told this story better than I, but I'm the only one left to tell it.

The Twain have met!

ACKNOWLEDGMENTS

We wish to thank the following individuals and organizations without whose contributions and support this book could not have been written:

First and foremost, our families and friends for putting up with years of hearing about "the book."

Jeffrey Mainville, former Assistant Curator at The Mark Twain House & Museum, Hartford, CT., and presently Program and Events Manager for the Hartford Public Library, who first gave us access to Nina's personal effects and remained a source of encouragement to us throughout the writing of this book. We can never thank you enough, Jeff.

Cindy Lovell, Executive Director of the Mark Twain House and Museum, Hartford, Ct., who is an absolute encyclopedia of knowledge on all things Twain and who helped us to fine-tune any references to Samuel Clemens. Her enthusiastic support and permission to share photographs and letters from Nina's personal effects have added immeasurably to this book.

The L. Tom Perry Special Collections of the Harold B. Lee Library at Brigham Young University, who generously furnished us copies of Nina's diaries and permitted us to quote excerpts for this book, allowing Nina's own voice to be heard.

The Hannibal Chamber of Commerce (Hannibal, Missouri) who contributed the image of Nina found at the end of Chapter 9, and the Hannibal Free Public Library through its publication arm, Hannibal Library Press, who published the image in "The Mark Twain Zephyr" image collection at www.hannibal.lib.mo.us. Permission to use this image is so appreciated. Braxton Pollard is believed to be the probable photographer.

Maren Rectenwald, niece of Nina's long-time friend and sometime boyfriend, Jules Schmidt, who, together with her niece, Mona Vance, kindly shared Schmidt family photographs as well as letters to and from Nina.

The children of Jules Schmidt—Brian, Maria, and Rachel—for sharing their personal memories of Nina. A very special thanks to Brian and Maria for consenting to DNA testing—twice in Maria's case!

Our very special thanks to Michele Chwan Wayland, the artist who inspired us with an original piece of art featuring Mark Twain and Nina.

Visit her website at www.mcwcreations.vpweb.com or contact her at michele.c.wayland@gmail.com.

John Gouin of Graphikitchen for his amazing cover and book design.

Lula, daughter of Bob Joughin, who consented to DNA testing to rule out Bob Joughin as Susan's father.

Bennett Greenspan, President and CEO of Family Tree DNA, for generously sharing his knowledge, and that of his staff, in helping us understand the meaning of Susan's original DNA testing, and also for suggesting the Family Tree DNA Family Finder test.

The AncestryDNA staff at Ancestry.com for help in understanding the results of Susan's DNA testing through their service as it relates to the Langdon and Clemens line.

George Wrentmore, Jr., son of Nina's last companion, who shared his memories of Nina and first provided information about the rumors of Nina giving up a baby.

Miggie Warms, daughter of Nina's friend Dot Glenz, for sharing a letter from Nina as well as passing on stories shared with her by Dot.

Dr. Dianne Greyerbiehl, PhD, psychologist extraordinaire, who helped Susan bring to light some of her early childhood memories.

Mallory Howard, Assistant to the Director, The Mark Twain House & Museum, Hartford, CT., who painstakingly copied images found in Nina's personal effects at the Museum so that we could include them in this book.

Bill Winter, grandson of longtime Gabrilowitsch family chauffeur Edgar Glanzer, for sharing memories and photographs.

Carlene Roters, daughter of Nina's first love, Carl Roters, for sharing her knowledge of the relationship and friendship between Nina and Carl.

The relatives of Nina's governess Sophie Pruischutz ("Mademoiselle"), who shared their knowledge of Sophie and her time with the Gabrilowitsch family.

The Los Angeles County Coroner's Office for unearthing Nina's autopsy from deep storage.

Mrs. Schisler, heir of Jacques Samossoud, for sharing her memories of Jacques and his final hospital stay.

The late Chris Aprato, researcher extraordinaire, for unearthing Nina's probate records. His enthusiasm and dedication will long be missed.

Michelle Aymond of Von Langen, LLC (a top-flight forensic genealogy firm) for the invaluable research skills she taught co-author Deb Gosselin during her time as a genealogy subcontractor to that firm.

Linda Epstein with the Jennifer DiChiari Agency for her help and guidance along the way.

The many other descendants of Nina's friends who also generously shared their knowledge.

REFERENCES

Chapter 12 International Monkey
"a very special kind of school": *My Husband Gabrilowitsch;* Clara Clemens Samossoud.

"Nina in my arms": Ibid.

"gentlest and most musical American accent": London's *Times,* July 31, 1921

Chapter 13 Young Adulthood: Nina(1925-1935)
"You greatly underrate your intelligence": Original letter, Clara to Nina; January 8, 1931.

Chapter 14 The Pivotal Years: Nina (1935-1937)
"but neither of us had the least foreboding": *My Husband Gabrilowitsch;* Clara Clemens Samossoud

"the patient must not suspect": Ibid.

"I am tickled to hear": Ibid.

"Our play is getting along well": Postcard; held by Mark Twain House & Museum (MTHM), July 9, 1936.

"How I have absorbed and assimilated": Original letter, NCG; location unknown.

"On Dec 22 I moved": Original letter, NC:G; held by Miggie Warms, daughter of Dorothy Glenz.

"An old duffer": Ibid.

"Mrs. Clara Gabrilowitsch": *New York Times*, February 5, 1937.

Chapter 18 Nina Takes Center Stage(1937-1941)
"Last Saturday, Jules": Original letter, NCG; held by Mona K Vance.

"She also made a few records": Ibid.

"still desperately trying to get a job": Ibid.

"There was Nina Clemens": *Los Angeles Times*, December 31, 1938

"Nina Clemens is unique in style": *Los Angeles Times*, April 5, 1939.

"Mr. Duffy said": Original letter, NCG, dated February 10, 1953; held by MTHM.

"Then a couple of months ago": Original letter, NCG, dated April 23, 1941; held by MTHM.

"It wasn't my meat at all": Original letter, NCG, dated April 23, 1941; held by MTHM.

"We decided we were wasting our time": Ibid.

"A's type of love-making": Original letter, NCG, dated February 22, 1938; held by MTHM.

"Alex said in a very sour way": Original letter, NCG, dated May, 1941; held MTHM.

"If you think you can walk": Ibid.

"I realized later what a rude": Ibid.

"The strange twilight": Ibid.

"Now I try to avoid his kisses": Ibid.

"So I guess we'll just be very good friends": Ibid.

"And often I wonder": Original letter, NCG, dated May, 1941; held by MTHM.

"a really lovely and courageous": Original letter, NCG, dated April 23, 1941; held by MTHM.

"After talking to Jack": Ibid.

"She described a man I know": Ibid.

"Manon accused him outright": Ibid.

"Samossoud threw back his head": Original letter, NCG, dated June 9, 1941; held by MTHM.

Chapter 19 Nina and Clara (1942-1962)

"I can't tell you how": Original letter, NCG, dated August 21, 1945; held by Mona K Vance.

"There's a world in my heart": Ibid.

"you can check out any time you like": "Hotel California;" The Eagles.

"When I entered [Dr. Warrick's]": Original letter, NCG, dated May 14, 1953; held by MTHM.

"My dislike for her has grown steadily": Ibid.

"When I was at Las Encinas": Ibid.

"I wanted your happiness!": Original letter, NCG, dated February 8, 1953; held by MTHM.

"We cannot with immunity": Ibid.

"Sometimes, the person you want": Original letter, NCG, circa January 1954, held by MTHM.

"She didn't realize how disastrous": Ibid.

"I haven't been feeling well for one thing": Original letter, NCG, circa 1957; held by MTHM.

"Yes, dear heart": Original letter, NCG, undated; held by Mona K Vance.

Chapter 21 Nina's Struggles (1962-1966)

"The appointments were made": *Los Angeles Times*, March 28, 1964.

"I'm bitter now, Jules": Original letter, NCG, undated; held by MTHM.

"The picture of George": Original letter, NCG, dated February 26, 1964; held by Mona K Vance.

"I think he hates G": Ibid.

"I'm sober now": Ibid.

"Jules came out here to marry me": Ibid.

"...she did not want to shock me": Ibid.

"I was getting close": Original letter, NCG, dated September 13, 1965,; held by Mona K Vance.

"At first I thought": Ibid.

"I can't count on Pat Gleason": Ibid.

"Maybe you have changed your plans": Ibid.

"This one's Carl Roters": *Los Angeles Herald-Examiner*, November 29, 1965.

"My mother recently": Original letter, Rochelle Vickey, circa December 1965; held by MTHM.

Chapter 23: No Peace in Death: Nina (1966-1989)

"Up in that garage of my house": Original letter, NCG, undated; held by MTHM.

Chapter 26 The Mystery of Jules Schmidt

"corduroy pants and tailored shirts": Email from Maria nee Schmidt.

"As far as my father and Nina having children": Email from Brian Schmidt.

Chapter 29 Adventures in Europe: Nina (1921)

"After that we went home": MSS 1910; Diaries; 20th Century Western & Mormon Manuscripts; L. Tom Perry Special Collections (LTPSC), Harold B. Lee Library, Brigham Young University, May 24, 1921.

"This morning we had breakfast earlier": MSS 1910, LTPSC, June 23, 1921.

"Father told me that Mother had gone on": MSS 1910, LTPSC, June 30, 1921.

"Mutti, Vatti, and I went together": MSS 1910, LTPSC, June 15, 1921.

"because all the books I had gotten": MSS 1910, LTPSC, May 22, 1921

"fixed Mutti on the balcony": MSS 1910, LTPSC, July 5, 1921.

"Vatti said that he thought we would go": MSS 1910, LTPSC, May 26, 1921.

"because this one was too expensive": MSS 1910, LTPSC, May 24, 1921.

"This morning at breakfast": MSS 1910, LTPSC, June 5, 1921.

"Vatti said he is going to take me to my Aunts": MSS 1910, LTPSC, July 2, 1921.

"Happy birthday": MSS 1910, LTPSC, August 10, 1921.

Chapter 30 Changes: Nina (1923)

"My silver pencil had my initials on it": MSS 1910, LTPSC, Undated entry.

"I think Miss Shover is a very tiresome person": Ibid.

Page "...but just because she is there": Ibid.

"I love to tease her": MSS 1910, LTPSC, January 13, 1923.

"said to me. If I have to listen": MSS 1910, LTPSC, January 15, 1923.

"at lunch is nearly the only time": MSS 1910, LTPSC, January 4, 1923.

"That is one reason why husbands": MSS 1910, LTPSC, December 23, 1923.

"I love these days at Santa Barbara": MSS 1910, LTPSC, August 12 1923.

"more fun than anything I have ever done before": MSS 1910, LTPSC, May 29, 1923.

"We cantered on the sand": MSS 1910, LTPSC, June 5, 1923.

"While we were having our lunch": MSS 1910, LTPSC, September 17, 1923.

"nearly died": MSS 1910, LTPSC, November 5, 1923.

"couldn't stand being sick any longer": MSS 1910, LTPSC, August 22, 1923.

"I don't take the ice bag any more": MSS 1910, LTPSC, September 2, 1923.

"Everyone says we have made": MSS 1910, LTPSC, December 22, 1923.

"I saw my bedroom for the last time": MSS 1910, LTPSC, December 29, 1923.

Chapter 31 A Personality Shift: Nina (1925)

"I lost my trunk key": MSS 1910, LTPSC, June 20, 1925.

"Harriet read in two of my diarys": MSS 1910, LTPSC, December 29, 1925.

"I hopped out and asked her to come in the car": MSS 1910, LTPSC, May 1 1925.

"...all through the wonderful ride": MSS 1910, LTPSC, May 23, 1925.

"some idea of music": MSS 1910, LTPSC, December 29, 1925.

"We talked the while": MSS 1910, LTPSC, June 11, 1925.

"an awful reputation at school": MSS 1910, LTPSC, undated, 1925.

"I had no more idea how to go about": MSS 1910, LTPSC, May 28, 1925.

"Both of them said I don't concentrate": MSS 1910, LTPSC, May 12, 1925.

"makes me so mad I could swear": MSS 1910, LTPSC, May 28, 1925.

"Father said we couldn't go there anymore": MSS 1910, LTPSC, June 15, 1925.

"It is awful to have a cancer": MSS 1910, LTPSC, June 18, 1925.

"I have a perfect horror of any kind of boat": MSS 1910, LTPSC, June 1, 1925.

"Father is just having the worst fit": MSS 1910, LTPSC, July 1, 1925.

"At times like these I wish heartily": MSS 1910, LTPSC, July 4, 1925.

"masked and cloaked": MSS 1910, LTPSC, July 8, 1925.

"I felt very important and grown up": MSS 1910, LTPSC, August 9, 1925.

Chapter 32 A Carefree Visit to Mackinac Island: Nina (1925)

"I wish I could always stay twelve years old": MSS 1910, LTPSC, August 9, 1925.

"We stayed out two hours": MSS 1910, LTPSC, September 7, 1925.

"Mother gave me a lecture": MSS 1910, LTPSC, September 16, 1925.

"If I ever have a house of my own": MSS 1910, LTPSC, September 9, 1925.

"Above us on the steps were two women": MSS 1910, LTPSC, September 12, 1925.

"silly Gump from Gumpdom": MSS 1910, LTPSC, September 11, 1925.

"He told me some things": MSS 1910, LTPSC, September 28, 1925.

Chapter 33 Lessons Learned: Nina (1925-1927)

"Thats why I could never bear": MSS 1910, LTPSC, November 25, 1926.

"I practiced on three pages": MSS 1910, LTPSC, June 13, 1925.

"pumpkin on a match": MSS 1910, LTPSC, July 25, 1927

"for heavens sake, you look just like": MSS 1910, LTPSC, March 22, 1926.

"a Russian monkey is homelier": MSS 1910, LTPSC, April 29, 1927.

"of course she does": Ibid.

" he said that you can't get along in life": MSS 1910, LTPSC, July 10, 1927.

"That remark hurt": MSS 1910, LTPSC, December 22, 1926.

" Mother and Mrs. Strauss": MSS 1910, LTPSC, April 25, 1925.

"babyish": MSS 1910, LTPSC, April 29, 1927.

"Come to think of it": MSS 1910, LTPSC, November 27, 1926

"I was wishing the other night": MSS 1910, LTPSC, November 9, 1925.

"kind of quiet and solemn": MSS 1910, LTPSC, November 11, 1926.

"It's a wonder": MSS 1910, LTPSC, Undated entry, 1926.

"That's probably to keep from": MSS 1910, LTPSC, January 28, 1927.

"Such a pleasant little intermission": MSS 1910, LTPSC, October 6, 1927.

"thought it would be only kind": MSS 1910, LTPSC, March 30, 1927.

"It was very sad to see them go": MSS 1910, LTPSC, April 17, 1927.

"knew grandfather": MSS 1910, LTPSC, July 6, 1927.

"positively these are my ashes": MSS 1910, LTPSC, July 22, 1927.

"it is very hard for me": Ibid.

"Show me a picture": Ibid.

"where grandfather used to stay": MSS 1910, LTPSC, September 6, 1927.

'Father dug up": Ibid.

"saw the log cabin": Ibid.

"That's a lovely way": MSS 1910, LTPSC, March 1, 1927.

"I love any place": MSS 1910, LTPSC, April 28, 1927.

"and have poor Mother ashamed": MSS 1910, LTPSC, June 4, 1927.

"Gee I love the smells": MSS 1910, LTPSC, May 31, 1926.

Chapter 35 A Long Conversation: Nina (1928-1929)

"meet you in H___ 1928!": MSS 1910, LTPSC, December 31, 1928.

"I won't work for music": MSS 1910, LTPSC, January 13, 1929.

"Let me tell you": Ibid.

"perfect example of the person": Ibid.

"thrash this thing out": Ibid.

"I won't waste": Ibid.

"In October when we were discussing": Ibid.

"They said you were getting too set": Ibid.

"I can remember long ago": Ibid.

"Well Mother said before": Ibid.

"You'll get to be an old maid": Ibid.

"Bridge fiends and boy addicts": Ibid.

"Oh yes I can": Ibid.

"I don't, but there must be": Ibid.

Chapter 37 Life in New York: Nina (1929-1932)

"I had taken a couple of pain pills": MSS 1910, LTPSC, June 22, 1932

"Graduation!": MSS 1910, LTPSC, June 7, 1929.

"I got so tired sitting": MSS 1910, LTPSC, June 15, 1929.

"I all but took a nap": MSS 1910, LTPSC, June 19, 1929.

"so nice to see someone": MSS 1910, LTPSC, September 19, 1929.

"Nina, please save me": MSS 1910, LTPSC, December 5, 1931.

"give it up": MSS 1910, LTPSC, November 17, 1931.

Chapter 39 A Father's Death: Nina (1936)

"I got up feeling happiness": MSS 1910, LTSPC, June 22, 1936.

"Letter from Clara said": MSS 1910, LTPSC, September 4, 1936.

"wretched": Ibid.

"something terrible": Ibid.

"a glorious chapter": Ibid.

"I know why you're afraid": MSS 1910, LTPSC, September 1, 1936

"I'm healed! I'm free!": MSS 1910, LTPSC, September 18, 1936

"broken": Ibid.

"feeling better than ever before": Ibid.

Chapter 40 A Sea Change: Nina (1936 - 1937)

"I felt as if I were losing": MSS 1910, LTPSC, September 28, 1936.

"I had an inkling then": MSS 1910, LTPSC, October 1, 1936.

"if it weren't for me": MSS 1910, LTPSC, October 6, 1936.

"it would be against the law of things": Ibid.

"pathetic letters": MSS 1910, LTPSC, October 8, 1936.

" it was difficult to delay": MSS 1910, LTPSC, October 16, 1936.

"for his age": MSS 1910, LTPSC, October 21, 1936.

"if I loved him": Ibid.

"he was afraid this trip of ours": MSS 1910, LTPSC, October 22, 1936.

"Take care of yourself": Ibid.

"To One Half with love": Ibid.

"We drank a toast": MSS 1910, LTPSC, October 23, 1936

"I'll bet we'll be back in this country": October 24, 1936.

"And that's what I keep repeating": MSS 1910, LTPSC, October 27, 1936.

" Thank God for that": MSS 1910, LTPSC, October 30, 1936.

"because of relatives there": MSS 1910, LTPSC, October 31, 1936.

"all lit up like a fairy boat": Ibid.

"Hurrah!": MSS 1910, LTPSC, November 15, 1936.

"She's having a perfect fit": MSS 1910, LTPSC, November 22, 1936.

"So she wrote Uncle Arthur": MSS 1910, LTPSC, November 27, 1936.

"but thinks we're not suited": MSS 1910, LTPSC, November 29, 1936.

"relieved beyond words": MSS 1910, LTPSC, December 2, 1936.

"Wrote long letter to Dot glenz": MSS 1910, LTPSC, December 17, 1936.

"Wrote letter to child": MSS 1910, LTPSC, December 21, 1936.

"Dec. 28. (Answer to 2 Xmas letter)": MSS 1910, LTPSC, undated entry, 1936.

Chapter 41 The Last Of The Diaries: Nina (1939-1942)

"My heart was heavy tonight": MSS 1910, LTPSC, March 26, 1940.

"It was such a relief to tell Jack": MSS 1910, LTPSC, May 4, 1940.

"I explained the whole story": Ibid.

"Awful ache in my heart" : MSS 1910, LTPSC, August 24, 1940.

"I feel like a person released": MSS 1910, LTPSC, June 18, 1940.

"too weary to move": MSS 1910, LTPSC, June 30, 1940.

"never be any more exciting on the stage": MSS 1910, LTPSC, July 24, 1940.

"Kept thinking of Carmelita": MSS 1910, LTPSC, September 11, 1940.

"We agreed that every person's life is her own": MSS 1910, LTPSC, September 18, 1940.

"If he says it's part of her spiritual growth": MSS 1910, LTPSC, October 1, 1940.

"I told her about motels": MSS 1910, LTPSC, October 14, 1940.

"You were cute as the dickens": MSS 1910, LTPSC, October 14, 1940.

"I suppose someday we'll have to get this over with": MSS 1910, LTPSC, March 14, 1941.

"He asked why we separated": MSS 1910, LTPSC, March 21, 1941.

"I know where her heart is": MSS 1910, LTPSC, April 6, 1941.

"I'm sorry, Monkey": MSS 1910, LTPSC, May 17, 1941.

"Very rarely have I been so tired": MSS 1910, LTPSC, May 25, 1941.

"Oh god! How much more pain": MSS 1910, LTPSC, May 27, 1941.

"You deserve a wonderful husband ": MSS 1910, LTPSC, July 12, 1941.

"B. worried only about herself": MSS 1910, LTPSC, September 28, 1941.

"How bitterly grandfather hated": MSS 1910, LTPSC, October 2, 1941.

"Such a bore": MSS 1910, LTPSC, November 24, 1941.

"guess I just instinctively dislike Russians": MSS 1910, LTPSC, November 24, 1941.

"annoying Jewish habits": MSS 1910, LTPSC, April 5, 1941

Chapter 42 Getting To Know My Mother

"I went out with Margaret": MSS 1910, LTPSC, May 22, 1921.

"I had a French lesson in the morning": MSS 1910, LTPSC, May 29, 1923.

" Exactly five years ago today": MSS 1910, LTPSC, October 12, 1923.

"I went to Harriet's house": MSS 1910, LTPSC, October 13, 1923.

"Mlle finished my blue sweater": Ibid.

"We left the hotel at half past 9": MSS 1910, LTPSC, September 19, 1923.

"It is about the worst collection you could find": MSS 1910, LTPSC, July 15, 1925.

"What a sad day!": MSS 1910, LTPSC, August 18, 1925.

"At four we went riding": MSS 1910, LTPSC, August 18, 1925.

"At five o'clock Mother, Father, and I took a walk": MSS 1910, LTPSC, September 4, 1925.

"There was quite a crowd to see mother": MSS 1910, LTPSC, October 31, 1925.

THE AUTHORS

Susan Madeline Bailey

Susan grew up in Europe, Florida, and Illinois. Her history is chronicled in the manuscript of The Twain Shall Meet, but there is more to her background and personality. As a child, she was painfully shy, but her inhibitions vanished when she stepped onto a stage. A widow with three children and several grandchildren, she has written poetry most of her life but this is her first book. She graduated from Stetson University in 1969 with a B.A. in Speech and Education. Susan recently returned to the stage, and continues to promote music for children by serving on the board of a youth orchestra. When she's not seeking a standing ovation, she enjoys spending time with her children, grandchildren, and a wealth of friends. She swims, bikes, and is a voracious traveler.

Deborah Lynn Gosselin

Deb's genealogical research experience spans nearly 40 years and she is happiest when following the threads that unravel a mystery. As owner of Ancestry Helper, Inc., a genealogy consulting firm, she has worked on solving family history mysteries all over the US and Canada. Her professional genealogy background has also included serving as an expert with Ancestry.com's former Hire an Expert service, and consulting with a nationwide firm that traces heirs for probate cases. A self-described Renaissance woman, Deb also holds degrees in psychology, educational counseling, and engineering. She presently lives in her native state of Michigan where she works as an engineer. She enjoys reading, gardening, and spending time with her large, wonderful, rambunctious family.

Made in the USA
Lexington, KY
26 June 2016